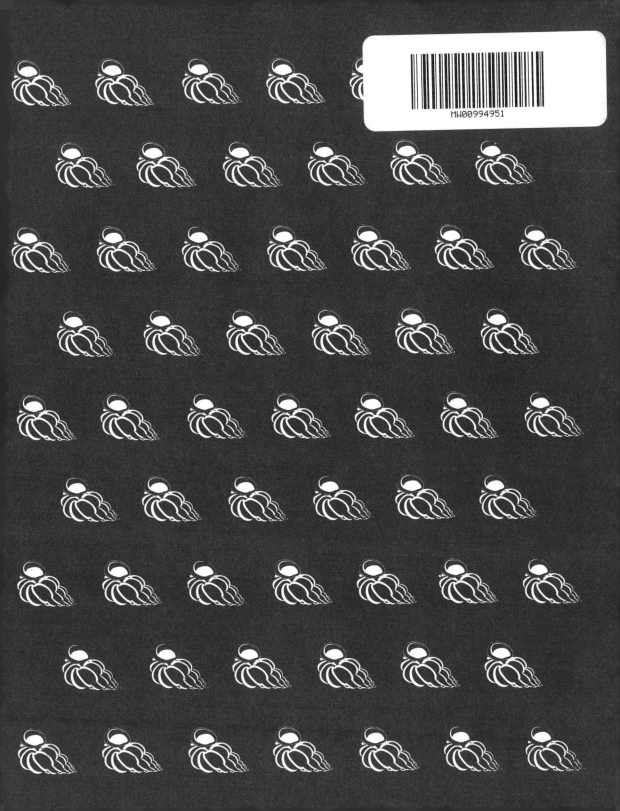

IN

LOVING MEMORY

OF

BETTY ANNE STEPHENSON

May 23, 1951

July 10, 1991

GOURMET BY·THE·BAY

BY
DOLPHIN CIRCLE
OF THE
INTERNATIONAL ORDER OF THE KING'S DAUGHTERS AND SONS

THE VIRGINIA BEACH COOKBOOK

First Printing
May 1989

Books In Print
43,000

Library of Congress Card Catalog No. 88-72311
ISBN 0-9621080-0-6

Title by
Jerry Davis of Davis & Phillips

Graphic Design by
Lynette Crain

Typesetting by
Deadline Typesetting

Printed in the USA by

WIMMER
The Wimmer Companies
Memphis
1-800-548-2537

DOLPHIN CIRCLE
proudly dedicates
GOURMET BY THE BAY
to the fulfillment
of the Circle's purposes

To help those who are unable to help themselves.
To contribute to community needs.
To endeavor to develop the spiritual life of the community and
to stimulate Christian activities.

Foreword

The Dolphin Circle, by its affiliation with the Virginia Beach City Union, is a member of the International Order of The King's Daughters and Sons Incorporated, an international and interdenominational organization dedicated to community service.

Proceeds from *Gourmet By The Bay* help support local charities and have established the HALO Fund at the Children's Hospital of The King's Daughters in Norfolk and the Betty Anne Stephenson Pediatric Fund at Virginia Beach General Hospital.

Dolphin Circle Members

Chris Lindsey Abriss
Penny Besaha Alberico
Cathy Beasley Anderson
Sandra S. Battaglia
Rachel Ellen Winstead Becka
Gigi Harrison Bounds
Kay Breseman
Wanda S. Browning
Debra Chianelli
Kimberly Wiley Corner
Denyce K. Corzatt
LaVerne Redman Crown
Daphne Clark Curtis
Karen Jensen Dickinson
Cheri O'Donnell Downing
Janet Belch Dunn
Joyce Humphreys Fain
Kathleen Stephens Ginnow
Cindy H. Gooch

Linda Poston Hedrick
Catherine Day Holroyd
Mallory Davis Horbal
Julianne E. Inglima
Darlyn C. Janson
Robin McDonald
Patricia Tynch Morris
JoAnn Melchor Peterson
Cheryl Lienhop Price
Sara Pearson Shield
Kay Spindle Shiflett
Cathy Pearse Snyders
Janet Ward Snyders
Jacqy Lewis Soderberg
Susan Halstead Spears
Sherry Ann Szejk
Mary Devine Timberlake
Jena Woodley Virga
Vicki Worley Whited

Table of Contents

OFFSHORE OPENERS

Appetizers

Artichoke Squares

1 medium onion, chopped	1/2 teaspoon salt
2 tablespoons butter	1/4 teaspoon pepper
4 eggs, beaten	2 6 ounce jars marinated
1/4 cup bread crumbs	artichokes, drained and chopped
Dash of Tabasco	1/8 teaspoon garlic powder
1/2 teaspoon oregano	2 cups shredded cheddar cheese

Saute onion in butter. Combine eggs, bread crumbs, Tabasco sauce, oregano, salt, and pepper. Stir in artichokes, onion, garlic, and cheese, mixing well. Bake in greased 9x13 pan for 30 minutes at 325. Cut into squares and serve warm.

Addictive Asparagus

20 slices white bread	1 14 ounce can asparagus
3 ounces bleu cheese	spears, drained
8 ounces cream cheese	1 cup butter, melted
1 egg, beaten	

Remove crusts from bread and flatten with rolling pin. Combine cheeses and egg in a small bowl. Spread evenly on bread. Place 1 spear asparagus on each slice, roll up and secure with 3 toothpicks. Dip into melted butter. Place on baking dish and freeze overnight. Partially thaw and slice each roll in 3 equal pieces before cooking. Bake at 375 for 15 minutes.

"Perfect for pre-party preparation because they must be frozen before cooking!"

Spicy Meatballs

1 pound hot sausage
1 pound mild sausage
2 eggs
1 cup cracker crumbs

1/2 cup milk
2 bottles chili sauce
1/2 box brown sugar
1 cup apple cider vinegar

Mix sausage, eggs, cracker crumbs, and milk in bowl; blend well. Form into bite-size meatballs and place on broiler pan. Bake at 325 for 30 minutes. In saucepan, combine chili sauce, brown sugar, and vinegar. Cook over low heat until sugar is dissolved. Add meatballs and simmer in sauce for 30 minutes. Serve hot.

Oriental Meatballs

1 1/2 pounds ground beef
2 eggs, slightly beaten
1/2 teaspoon salt
1/4 cup seasoned breadcrumbs
1/4 cup soy sauce

1/4 teaspoon garlic powder
1 can water chestnuts, drained
  and finely chopped
1 bottle Teriyaki sauce for dipping

Combine all ingredients, except Teriyaki sauce, and shape into 1 inch balls. Place in foil-lined baking dish and bake at 375 for 18 minutes, or until meatballs are cooked. Drain and serve with sauce.

Chili Munchies

1 pound hot sausage, cooked
  and drained
1 pound sharp cheddar
  cheese, shredded

6 eggs, slightly beaten
1 4 ounce can chopped
  green chilies
1/2 teaspoon chili powder

Sprinkle sausage in a greased 9x13 baking pan. Cover the sausage with cheese. Mix together eggs, chilies, and chili powder; pour over cheese and sausage. Bake at 350 for 30 minutes. Cool slightly and cut into bite-size pieces.

Danish Meatballs

1½ pounds ground beef
1 teaspoon salt
¼ teaspoon pepper
1 egg, slightly beaten
¼ cup onion, minced
¼ cup half and half
½ cup seasoned breadcrumbs

¼ cup butter
¼ cup flour
2 cups chicken broth
¼ teaspoon salt
1 tablespoon dried dill weed
1 cup sour cream

Combine beef, salt, pepper, egg, onion, half and half, and breadcrumbs. Shape into 1 inch balls and place in foil-lined baking dish. Bake at 375 until thoroughly cooked, or about 30 minutes. Drain and place in warming dish. In saucepan, melt butter and stir in flour. Whisk in broth, ¼ teaspoon salt, and dill weed. Cook until thickened, stirring constantly. Remove from heat; stir in sour cream. Pour over meatballs and serve warm.

"An exciting variation to an old favorite."

Broccoli Cheddar Squares

3 tablespoons butter, melted
2 10 ounce packages
   frozen broccoli
3 eggs
1 cup flour
1 cup milk

1 teaspoon salt
1 teaspoon baking powder
1 pound grated cheddar cheese
2 tablespoons minced onion
   Seasoned salt

Pour melted butter into 9x13 baking dish. Partially cook broccoli and transfer to processor. Chop finely with on/off turns. Beat eggs in large bowl. Add flour, milk, salt, baking powder and whisk together. Stir in cheese, broccoli, and onion. Spread evenly in buttered dish and sprinkle lightly with seasoned salt. Bake until set, approximately 45 minutes. Let stand 10 minutes before cutting into bite-size squares.

Carrot Fritters

2¾ cups flour
1½ cups milk
6 tablespoons green
   onions, chopped
2 tablespoons fresh parsley, minced
2 tablespoons baking powder

2 teaspoons salt
2 teaspoons pepper
1½ teaspoons dried thyme, crumbled
6 cups carrots, grated
   Oil for frying

Mix flour, milk, green onions, parsley, baking powder, salt, pepper, and thyme in large bowl. Gently fold in carrots. Cover and let rest at room temperature for 3 hours. Heat oil in deep fryer to 375. Gently lower batter into oil by tablespoons, being careful not to crowd. Fry until golden brown, about 10-12 minutes, turning occasionally. Drain and serve immediately.

Cheese Puffs

7 eggs
6 ounces Parmesan cheese
5 ounces mozzarella cheese, cut
   into ¼ inch cubes
5 ounces Swiss cheese, cut into
   ¼ inch cubes
¼ cup cottage cheese

1 tablespoon parsley, chopped
1 teaspoon garlic salt
2 teaspoons dried
   red pepper flakes
1 teaspoon pepper
1 cup flour
   Oil for deep frying

Heat oil to 375. Combine all ingredients except flour in large bowl, mixing well. Stir in flour. Gently lower mixture into oil by tablespoons in batches, being careful not to crowd. Fry until golden brown, turning frequently. Remove and drain. Serve immediately.

"So-o-o cheesy."

Herb and Cheese Pull-Aparts

1 8 ounce package cream
   cheese, softened
1 teaspoon dried parsley flakes
1 teaspoon dried basil
1 teaspoon chopped chives
1/2 teaspoon dill seeds

1/8 teaspoon garlic powder
1 package refrigerated crescent
   dinner rolls
1 egg, beaten
1/2 teaspoon poppy seeds

Combine cream cheese, parsley flakes, basil, chives, dill seeds, and garlic powder; stir well and set aside. Unroll crescent rolls into 2 rectangles, connecting ends to make one long rectangle; press edges to seal. Spread cream cheese mixture over dough to within 1/2 inch of edge. Roll starting at long side, jelly roll fashion. Pinch edge to seal. Place on a lightly greased baking sheet. Using kitchen shears, cut 1/2 inch slits alternating from right to left side of dough, being careful not to cut roll apart. Pull out alternating sides, exposing jelly roll pattern. Brush with egg; sprinkle with poppy seeds. Bake at 375 for 12 to 15 minutes. Serves 6-8.

Cheese Strips

1/2 pound Cracker Barrel
   cheese, shredded
6 slices bacon, cooked
   and crumbled
1 small package slivered almonds

2 teaspoons Worcestershire sauce
1 small onion, finely chopped
1 cup mayonnaise
   Salt and pepper
1 loaf Arnold's bread

Mix cheese, bacon, almonds, Worcestershire sauce, onion, mayonnaise, salt, and pepper. Remove crusts from bread and spread mixture on slices. Cut each slice into 3-4 strips. Bake at 400 for 10 minutes or until crisp and lightly browned. Yields about 72.

"May be frozen and baked as needed."

Captivating Cheese Delights

4 tablespoons green
    onion, chopped
8 ounces shredded Swiss cheese
2/3 cup bacon bits

1/2 cup mayonnaise
1/2 cup green olives, chopped
    Sliced party rye

Mix ingredients together. Spread on party slice rye bread. Broil until cheese melts.
Serve hot.

Toasted Triangles

1 loaf sliced white bread,
    crusts removed
2 8 ounce packages
    cream cheese, softened
1 cup grated Parmesan cheese

1/4 cup mayonnaise
8 green onions, minced
    Dash Tabasco sauce
1/4 cup bacon bits

Toast all bread on one side only. Combine remaining ingredients and spread
mixture on untoasted side of bread. Cut each slice into 4 triangles, place on tray
and freeze; store in plastic wrap. To serve, bake frozen triangles on cookie sheet at
350 for 4-5 minutes, then broil until bubbly. Serve immediately.

Rapturous Ryes

1 can pitted black olives
2 cups Cheddar cheese, shredded
2 tablespoons onion, minced
1 cup mayonnaise

1 package party rye bread
1/2 pound bacon, cooked
    and crumbled

Drain and squeeze out all excess liquid from black olives. Mince olives and blend
well with cheese, onion, and mayonnaise. Spread on slices of party rye bread; top
with cooked bacon. Bake at 350 for 10 minutes or until bread is browned
on edges.

Parmesan Strips

1 loaf white bread
1/2 pound butter, melted
2 8 ounce packages cream cheese
6 tablespoons mayonnaise

6 green onions with tops, chopped
6 drops Tabasco sauce
  Parmesan cheese

Trim crusts off bread and cut into strips. Spread one side with melted butter. Lightly toast both sides under broiler. Mix cream cheese, mayonnaise, onions, and Tabasco together and spread on buttered side of bread. Dip each strip, spread side down, into a bowl of Parmesan cheese, coating only spread side. Broil until brown and bubbly. Serve hot.

"May be frozen before broiling."

Almond Chicken Puffs

1 1/2 cups cooked chicken, finely chopped
1/3 cup toasted almonds, chopped
1 cup chicken broth
1/2 cup oil
2 teaspoons seasoned salt

1/8 teaspoon cayenne pepper
1 teaspoon celery seed
1 tablespoon parsley flakes
2 teaspoons Worcestershire sauce
1 cup flour
4 eggs

Mix chicken and almonds together. In saucepan, combine chicken broth, oil, seasoned salt, cayenne pepper, celery seed, parsley flakes, and Worcestershire sauce and bring to a boil. Whisk in flour and cook over low heat, beating until mixture leaves sides of pan and forms smooth dough. Remove saucepan from heat; add eggs, one at a time, beating well after each addition. Stir in chicken and almonds. Drop by teaspoonful onto greased baking sheet. Bake at 450 for 10-15 minutes, or until lightly browned. Serve hot. Yields approximately 80 puffs.

Chinese Chicken Wings

3-4 pounds chicken wings
2/3 cup soy sauce
1/2 cup honey

2 tablespoons oil
2 teaspoons five spice powder
1/4 teaspoon garlic powder

Cut each wing at joint into 3 pieces, discarding tip. Place wings into glass or plastic dish. Combine remaining ingredients and pour over wings. Cover and refrigerate 3-4 hours. Place in foil-lined baking dish and brush with marinade. Bake 30 minutes at 325. Turn chicken and again brush with marinade. Bake until tender, about 30 minutes. Yields 30-40 appetizers.

"Five spice powder can be found in the Oriental food section."

Gala Chicken Triangles

2 pounds chicken breasts
1 cup chopped green onion
1 8½ ounce can water chestnuts
2 eggs, beaten
2 teaspoons salt

¼ cup cornstarch
16 slices white bread, crusts
    trimmed and each piece cut into
    8 bite-size triangles
    Oil

Bone and skin chicken. Cut into 1-inch pieces. Combine chicken with onion and water chestnuts in processor and blend into paste. Mix in eggs, salt, and cornstarch. Spread each piece of bread with mixture and refrigerate until ready to fry. In large skillet heat 1 inch oil over medium-high heat. Add triangles face down and fry until golden brown, or about 1-2 minutes. Serve immediately or keep warm, up to one hour, in 250 oven.

"Triangles may be frozen before frying. To cook, fry without thawing, allowing extra time to cook thoroughly."

Olé Souffle

2-3 cans chopped green
    chili peppers, seeded
    Sharp cheddar cheese, grated

8 eggs
  Salt and pepper
  Paprika (optional)

Line bottom of 3 quart oblong baking dish with green chilies. Layer cheddar cheese to 1½ inches high in baking dish. Beat eggs with hand mixer and pour over cheese. Salt and pepper and lightly sprinkle with paprika (optional). Bake at 350 for 35 minutes or until knife blade comes out clean. Let cool 15 minutes. Cut into squares to serve. Serves 12.

Mushroom Magic

9 ounces cream cheese, softened
¼ pound butter or
    margarine, softened
1½ cups flour
1 large onion, minced
½ pound mushrooms, minced

3 tablespoons butter
1 teaspoon salt
¼ teaspoon thyme
2 tablespoons flour
¼ cup sour cream

Combine cream cheese, butter, and flour to form dough; cream together thoroughly and chill 1 hour. Saute onion and mushrooms in butter. Add remaining ingredients, except sour cream, and cook until thickened. Stir in sour cream. Divide dough in half and roll each half thinly. Cut into rounds and place as much of the mixture, approximately 1 teaspoon, on each. Fold over to make half round and seal. (May be frozen at this point.) Preheat oven to 450. Remove desired quantity from freezer and pierce each top with knife point. Brush each with a mixture of one egg yolk, beaten with 1 teaspoon water. Bake 12-15 minutes. Yields approximately 4 dozen.

"Guests will love them."

Chinese Mushrooms

24 large mushrooms
  Lemon juice
 4 tablespoons butter, melted
½ pound ground pork
¼ cup water chestnuts, chopped

¼ cup green onions, chopped
 1 egg, beaten
 1 teaspoon soy sauce
¼ teaspoon garlic powder
¼ cup sesame seeds

Remove stems from mushrooms and chop. Rub caps with lemon juice and brush bottoms with melted butter; place in shallow baking dish. Combine remaining ingredients, except sesame seeds. Spoon mixture into mushroom caps and top with sesame seeds. Bake at 350 for 40 minutes. Serve immediately.

Cheese and Mushroom Morsels

½ pound mushrooms, chopped
 2 tablespoons scallions, chopped
 2 tablespoons butter
 2 eggs, separated
½ pound grated sharp
  cheddar cheese

  Salt & pepper
 1 small party loaf
  pumpernickel bread

Saute mushrooms and scallions in butter. Combine egg yolks, cheese, and seasonings. Stir mixture. Add mushrooms and scallions. Beat egg whites until stiff. Fold in egg yolk mixture. Toast one side of the pumpernickel slices. Heap 1 tablespoon of the cheese mixture on the soft side. Bake at 375 until firm and puffy.

Mozzarella Mushrooms

18-24 large mushrooms
3 ounces grated Mozzarella
6 tablespoons mayonnaise
1½ tablespoons parsley flakes

1 teaspoon Worcestershire sauce
⅛ teaspoon garlic powder
⅛ teaspoon crushed oregano
Salt and pepper

Preheat oven to 350. Lightly grease 9x13 baking dish. Remove stems from mushrooms and arrange caps in dish. Chop stems and add to bowl with remaining ingredients. Spoon mixture into caps and bake 20 minutes, or until tender. Serve hot.

Oysters Marianne

2 dozen unshucked oysters
1 cup herb-seasoned stuffing
mix, crushed
½ cup parsley, minced
¼ teaspoon salt
⅛ teaspoon pepper
⅛ teaspoon Accent
⅛ teaspoon ground mace

1 teaspoon Worcestershire sauce
3-4 drops hot sauce
¼ cup butter or margarine, melted
2-3 tablespoons fresh lemon juice
4 slices bacon, cooked
and crumbled
2 tablespoons chopped pimiento
Rock salt

Wash and rinse oysters thoroughly in cold water. Shuck oysters reserving deep half of shells; drain oysters in colander. Set aside. Combine next 8 ingredients in medium saucepan. Place over medium heat; gradually add melted butter. Stir until moistened. Place oysters in shells. Line a shallow roasting pan with foil and cover with rock salt. Arrange shells in rock salt. Spoon lemon juice over each oyster. Cover with 1 tablespoon stuffing mixture. Sprinkle with bacon and pimiento. Bake at 500 for 3-5 minutes or until edges of oysters begin to curl.

Oysters Bienville

2 dozen unshucked oysters
Dry white wine
2 slices bacon, minced
1 2 ounce can mushrooms,
   drained and minced
4 green onions, minced
1 tablespoon butter or margarine
2½ tablespoons all purpose flour
½ cup milk
¼ pound shrimp, cooked, peeled,
   and minced

1 tablespoon lemon juice
1 tablespoon sherry
1 tablespoon parsley, chopped
½ slice American cheese, diced
   Hot sauce
   Salt
   Yellow food coloring
   Rock salt

Wash and rinse oysters thoroughly under cold water. Shuck oysters, reserving deep halves of shells and 5 tablespoons liquid. Place oysters in saucepan and cover with wine; simmer about 1 minute or until edges curl. Remove from heat. Arrange oysters in shells; set aside. Fry bacon until browned. Add mushrooms and onion. Saute until onion is wilted. Add butter; stir until melted. Blend in flour; cook 5 minutes. Stir constantly. Do not allow flour to brown. Add milk and cook until thick; stir constantly. Stir shrimp, reserved oyster liquid, lemon juice, sherry, and parsley into sauce. Cook 2-3 minutes; stir constantly. Add cheese, hot sauce, salt, and a few drops of yellow food coloring. Cook until thick; stir constantly. Spoon about 1 tablespoon sauce over each oyster. Place shells filled with oysters and sauce on a bed of rock salt. Broil until sauce bubbles and begins to brown. Serve immediately. Serves 4.

French Pizza

1 package frozen puff pastry
1 egg yolk mixed with
   1 teaspoon water
1/3 cup bottled spaghetti sauce
16 slices pepperoni

6 ounces ham
1/4 cup green onion, chopped
1/2 teaspoon oregano
6 ounces Mozzarella cheese

Thaw pastry sheets and roll into a 9x16 inch rectangle. Cut into two rectangles, one 4-inch and one 5-inch width. Brush edges with egg yolk mixture.
   Place larger rectangle on cookie sheet. Pour spaghetti sauce down center of dough to within one inch of edge. Place a layer of pepperoni, cheese, ham, and onions on sauce. Place other crust on top. Crinkle edge with a fork. Brush top with egg yolk and water mixture. Make 3 slits across top. Bake at 425 for 25 minutes. Cut into 18 bite-size pieces.

Spanakopeta

1 small onion, chopped
1 tablespoon butter
2 packages frozen
   chopped spinach
1/2 teaspoon dill (optional)
   Pepper

1 pound feta cheese
1 8 ounce package cream cheese
6 large eggs, beaten
1/2-3/4 pound butter
1 pound filo dough (can be found
   in frozen food section)

Saute onion in butter. Parboil spinach and drain well. Add spinach to onion, gently heating. Add dill and pepper; set aside to cool. In large bowl crumble feta cheese. Add cream cheese and blend well. Stir in spinach mixture. Combine mixture with beaten eggs.
   Butter 11x13 pan well. Using 14 filo sheets for bottom layer, butter every second sheet with pastry brush. Spread spinach mixture evenly over filo. Top with 12 filo sheets, buttering every second sheet. Brush top layer with butter. Score top with very sharp knife into serving size pieces. Bake at 350 approximately 1 hour, or until golden brown.

Party Ham Rolls

1   package Pepperidge Farm
    Party Rolls
¼   pound butter, softened
1½ tablespoons poppy seeds
½   tablespoon Worcestershire sauce

1½ tablespoons mustard
1   small onion, grated
¼   pound sliced Swiss cheese
¼   pound sliced baked ham

Slice rolls in half lengthwise. Mix together butter, poppy seeds, Worcestershire, mustard, and onion. Spread mixture on both sides of rolls. Cover bottom halves of rolls with ham; top halves with cheese. Slice into serving-size pieces and wrap in foil. Bake at 400 for 10 minutes.

Chutney Sausage Balls

2   pounds hot sausage
1   cup sour cream

1   bottle Major Grey chutney
¼   cup sherry

Roll sausage into bite-size balls and bake at 350 for 20 minutes. Drain and place into chafing dish. Combine sour cream, chutney, and sherry in saucepan and cook until heated through. Pour sauce over sausage balls and serve warm.

Spicy Sausage

1   pound hot bulk sausage
1   egg, beaten
⅓   cup seasoned breadcrumbs
2   teaspoons curry powder
¼   teaspoon chili powder

⅓   cup ketchup
1   8 ounce can tomato sauce
1   tablespoon soy sauce
1   tablespoon Worcestershire sauce

Mix sausage, egg, breadcrumbs, curry powder, and chili powder; blend well. Shape into bite-size balls and brown over medium heat until well done. Drain; place in chafing dish. Combine remaining ingredients in saucepan and heat thoroughly. Pour over sausage balls and serve hot.

Chinese Barbecued Ribs

3 pounds spareribs
2 tablespoons sugar
1/4 teaspoon garlic powder
1 tablespoon salt

1/2 cup ketchup
2 tablespoons hoisin sauce
1 tablespoon white wine

Have butcher cut ribs lengthwise to halve bones. Slice to separate each rib piece and place in glass or plastic dish. Combine remaining ingredients. Pour over ribs and marinate covered 3-4 hours in refrigerator.

Preheat oven to 375. Place ribs in single layer in shallow baking dish. Brush with sauce and cover. Bake 45 minutes. Remove cover and brush again with sauce. Bake until tender, approximately 45 minutes.

"Hoisin sauce can be found in the oriental food section of the grocery store."

Clam Stuffed Mushrooms

2 pounds medium-sized
  mushrooms
1/2 cup butter, melted
3/8 teaspoon garlic powder
6 1/2 ounce can minced clams,
  drained (reserve juice)

1/2 cup Italian breadcrumbs
1/4 cup parsley flakes
3/4 teaspoon salt
1/4 teaspoon pepper

Remove stems from mushrooms and mince. Stir garlic powder into warm butter and coat mushroom caps with mixture. Arrange on baking sheet. Combine clam juice, stem pieces, and remaining butter in small saucepan. Heat over medium heat until tender and juices are reduced two-thirds. Add clams, breadcrumbs, parsley, salt, and pepper. Divide evenly among caps. Cook at 350 until tender, or approximately 20 minutes.

Clams Casino

¼ cup green peppers, chopped
¼ cup onion, chopped
⅔ cup butter
4 ounces pimientos, chopped
¼ teaspoon Worcestershire sauce

Salt and pepper
24 clams on the half-shell
3 slices bacon, cooked crisp
   and crumbled

Saute peppers and onion in butter. Add pimientos, Worcestershire, salt, and pepper. Arrange clams on flat pan and cover each with mixture. Top with bacon. Bake at 400 for 6-8 minutes. Yields 24.

Toast of the Town Clams

1 8 ounce package cream
   cheese, softened
¼ teaspoon garlic powder
1 teaspoon Worcestershire sauce

Pinch of salt
1 can minced clams, drained
   Melba toast rounds

Blend cream cheese with garlic powder, Worcestershire sauce, and salt. Beat until creamy; add clams. Chill 2 hours. Spoon mixture on Melba toast rounds and place on foil-lined cookie sheets. Broil quickly, until golden brown. Serve immediately.

Clam Roll Ups

2 6½ ounce cans minced
   clams, drained
8 ounces cream cheese, softened

1 loaf bread, crusts trimmed
½ cup butter, melted
¾ cup Parmesan cheese

Combine clams with cream cheese and blend thoroughly. Spread on bread and roll jelly roll fashion. Cut each into 5 pieces. Dip in melted butter and coat with Parmesan. Arrange closely on baking sheet with edges touching. Bake at 400 for 15 minutes or until lightly browned.

Tipsy Clams

½ cup butter, melted
½ cup breadcrumbs
¼ cup beer
1 small onion, minced
½ teaspoon garlic powder
1½ tablespoons parsley flakes

1½ teaspoons Italian seasoning
½ teaspoon oregano
Salt and pepper
4 6½ ounce cans minced clams, drained, reserving juice
36 toast rounds

Lightly grease baking sheet. Combine first 9 ingredients and blend well. Add clams. If mixture seems too dry, moisten with clam juice. Spread on toast rounds and bake at 375 for 10 minutes. Remove from oven and preheat broiler. Broil until tops are golden brown. Serve immediately.

Clam Puffs

1 8 ounce package cream cheese, softened
1 7½ ounce can minced clams, drained
¼ teaspoon salt

1 tablespoon lemon juice
2 tablespoons onion, grated
1 tablespoon Worcestershire sauce
1 egg white, stiffly beaten
Cocktail loaf bread

Beat cream cheese until smooth. Stir in clams, salt, lemon juice, onion, Worcestershire sauce, and egg white, mixing well. Spoon onto bread slices and bake at 450 for 3-4 minutes.

Puffed Crab

1 6 ounce can crabmeat,
   drained and flaked
1/2 cup shredded sharp
   cheddar cheese
3 green onions, chopped
1 teaspoon dry mustard

1 teaspoon Worcestershire sauce
1 cup water
1/2 cup butter
1/4 teaspoon salt
1 cup all purpose flour
4 eggs

Combine crabmeat, cheese, onions, mustard, and Worcestershire; set aside. Combine water, butter, and salt in medium saucepan. Bring mixture to a boil. Reduce heat to low. Add flour and stir vigorously until mixture leaves sides of pan and forms a smooth ball. Remove saucepan from heat and allow mixture to cool slightly. Add eggs, one at a time, beating with a wooden spoon after each addition. Beat until batter is smooth. Add crab mixture; stir well. Drop batter by heaping teaspoonsful onto ungreased baking sheets. Bake at 400 for 15 minutes. Reduce heat to 350 and bake an additional 10 minutes. Serve puffs warm.

Note: To freeze before baking, cover baking sheets with foil before dropping crab mixture onto them. Freeze until hard. Store in an airtight container until ready to use. Bake frozen at 375 for 35 minutes.

Crab Puffs

1 egg, beaten
1/3 cup water
1 teaspoon Worcestershire sauce
1/4 teaspoon Tabasco
1 1/2 cups Bisquick
1/3 cup grated Parmesan cheese

1/4 cup green onion, chopped
1/2 pound crabmeat
   French's Dip-N-Spread mustard
   Oil for frying

In small bowl blend egg, water, Worcestershire sauce, and Tabasco. Combine Bisquick, cheese, onion, and crab. Gently stir both mixtures together just until blended. Drop a teaspoonful at a time into oil and fry until golden brown, or about 1-2 minutes, turning as needed. Drain and serve immediately with mustard.

Crab Bites

1/8 pound butter
1/4 teaspoon garlic powder
1 tablespoon mayonnaise
1 jar Old English cheese spread
    or 1/2 pound Velveeta

1 can crabmeat
4 English muffins

Melt butter. Add garlic, mayonnaise, and cheese, heating until cheese melts. Gently stir in crabmeat. Spread on split English muffins and broil until bubbly, approximately 3 minutes.

"Cut into small pieces for appetizer or serve whole for luncheon."

Tuna Temptations

1 7 ounce can tuna, drained
11/2 teaspoons mustard
1/4 cup mayonnaise
11/2 teaspoons onion, minced
1/4 teaspoon Worcestershire sauce
2 tablespoons green
    pepper, chopped

1 loaf cocktail bread
1 tomato, sliced
1/2 cup mayonnaise
1/4 cup Monterey Jack cheese,
    shredded

Blend tuna, mustard, mayonnaise, onion, Worcestershire sauce, and green pepper. Spread on slices of bread. Cut tomato slices into wedges and top each piece of bread. Blend cheese with remaining mayonnaise and spread on tomato wedge. Broil until topping puffs and browns.

"Yet another great tuna dish!"

Spinach Cut-Ups

1 10 ounce package frozen chopped spinach, thawed and squeezed dry	1½ cups milk
1 pound mushrooms, chopped	2 tablespoons flour
⅔ cup green onion, chopped	1 teaspoon salt
4 eggs, beaten	¼ teaspoon pepper
	1 clove garlic, minced
	½ teaspoon oregano

In large bowl, combine all but ½ pound mushrooms. Pour into greased 7x11 baking dish. Top with remaining mushrooms and bake at 350 for 50 minutes, or until set. Cut into bite-size squares and serve hot.

Zucchini Squares

3 cups zucchini (about 2 small), very thinly sliced	⅛ teaspoon garlic powder
1 cup Bisquick	½ cup oil
½ cup Parmesan cheese	Dash of pepper
½ teaspoon salt	½ cup onion, minced
½ teaspoon oregano	½ teaspoon seasoned salt
	4 eggs, slightly beaten

Grease 9x13x2 pan. Mix all ingredients, except zucchini, thoroughly. Gently fold in zucchini slices and pour into greased pan. Bake at 350 for approximately 40 minutes. Cut into bite-size squares. Serve warm.

"Do Ahead Tip: Prepare as above, except bake only 30 minutes and freeze. Thaw and reheat at 350 for about 10 minutes."

Zesty Veggies

1 pound mushrooms
1 head cauliflower
1 head broccoli
1 pound carrots
1 tablespoon Accent
1 tablespoon black pepper

½ tablespoon garlic powder
½ tablespoon Aromat
1 tablespoon salt
1 tablespoon dill weed
1 cup vinegar
½ cup oil

Cut vegetables into bite-size pieces and place in large plastic or glass container with lid. Sprinkle Accent, salt, pepper, dill weed, garlic powder, and Aromat over vegetables. Pour oil and vinegar over top, cover and turn container to mix ingredients and coat vegetables. Refrigerate overnight. Serve chilled.

"Knorr Swiss Aromat can be found in the specialty section of the grocery store."

Crispy Egg Rolls

1 pound lean pork, chopped
½ cup shrimp, chopped
3 large cans fancy mixed
chop suey vegetables
1 teaspoon salt
½ teaspoon monosodium
glutamate

2 cups shredded cabbage
1 large can bean sprouts, drained
2 teaspoons cornstarch
2 tablespoons soy sauce
3 packages egg roll wrappers

Heat 3 tablespoons oil in skillet over high heat and cook pork, stirring until meat loses its pink color. Add shrimp; cook 1 minute. Add vegetables and seasonings. Cook 2 minutes, stirring often; sprinkle with cornstarch. Mix well and stir in soy sauce. Cook 1 minute, then drain.

Placing wrapper with a corner towards you, put 2-3 tablespoons cooled filling on dough, slightly below middle. Brush edges with beaten egg. Fold the corner nearest you up and over the filling. Fold the sides into the center; roll towards the top corner to form a cylinder. Repeat with rest of wrappers. Cook rolls 3-4 at a time, in 2 inches of oil, until crisp and golden. Serve with hot mustard or sweet and sour sauce.

Layered Cheese Pate

2 8 ounce packages cream cheese, softened	1/4 cup pecans, finely chopped
1 1/4 teaspoons dried Italian seasoning	3/4 cup fresh parsley, chopped
1/8 teaspoon pepper	1 3 ounce package Roquefort cheese, crumbled
1/2 cup Gruyere cheese, shredded	Fresh spinach leaves

Combine cream cheese, dried Italian seasoning, and pepper in bowl, beating with mixer at medium speed until smooth. Line a lightly oiled 6x4x2 loaf pan with plastic wrap, leaving a 2" overhang on each side. Carefully spread about 1/3 of cream cheese mixture in loaf pan, smoothing to corners of pan. Next, layer the Gruyere and chopped pecans; top with half of remaining cream cheese mixture. Sprinkle 1/2 cup parsley on loaf and crumble Roquefort over top of mixture. Top with remaining cream cheese mixture, firmly pressing layers to seal. Cover with overhanging plastic wrap and chill at least 8 hours.

   To unmold, lift cheese loaf out of pan using plastic wrap and invert onto serving dish lined with spinach leaves. Remove plastic and sprinkle loaf with remaining 1/4 cup parsley. Allow loaf to reach room temperature and serve with crackers.

Sensational Swiss Spread

1/2 pound ham, minced	1 1/2 tablespoons parsley flakes
1/2 pound grated Swiss cheese	1 1/2 tablespoons Dijon mustard
1 cup sour cream	1/2 teaspoon Worcestershire sauce
3 tablespoons onion, minced	1/2 teaspoon pepper

Combine all ingredients and serve on bread rounds or with crackers. Yields 3 cups.

"Cool and light; perfect for a summer party."

Roquefort Grapes

1 10 ounce package almonds, pecans, or walnuts
1 8 ounce package cream cheese
1/8 pound Roquefort cheese

2 tablespoons heavy cream
1 pound seedless grapes, red or green, washed and dried

Preheat oven to 275. Spread nuts on cookie sheet and bake until slightly browned. DO NOT overcook. Chop toasted nuts coarsely in food processor. Combine cream cheese, Roquefort, and cream, beating mixture until smooth. Drop clean, dry grapes into cheese mixture and stir gently to coat grapes evenly. Roll coated grapes in chopped nuts. Place on wax paper and chill until ready to serve.

No Bake Crab

1 8 ounce package cream cheese, softened
1 8 ounce carton sour cream
2 tablespoons lemon juice

1 tablespoon sherry
1 envelope Italian dressing mix
1 pound crabmeat

Mix all ingredients together well. Serve hot or cold with Melba toast.

Fanciful Crab

1½ packets unflavored gelatin
3 tablespoons water
1 can cream of mushroom soup
6 ounces cream cheese

1 cup mayonnaise
1 pound crabmeat
1 cup celery, chopped
1 medium onion, minced

Dissolve gelatin in cold water. Add to saucepan of warmed cream of mushroom soup. Stir in cream cheese and heat until melted. Add mayonnaise, crab, celery, and onion. Pour into a 3 quart mold. Refrigerate for several hours or overnight. Unmold and serve with crackers.

Cucumber Whimsies

1/2 pound crabmeat
  1 scallion, minced
  1 tablespoon chopped dill
  1 teaspoon grated lemon zest
  1 small tomato, chopped
1/4 cup mayonnaise

1/8 teaspoon cayenne pepper
     Salt and pepper
  1 10-12 inch English cucumber
     Lemon pepper
     Dill sprigs or fresh parsley
     for garnish

Drain crabmeat. In mixing bowl, place crabmeat, scallion, chopped dill, lemon ze
tomato, mayonnaise, cayenne, salt, and pepper. Chill for at least one hour to
allow flavors to marry. Score cucumber with tines of a fork, being careful to sco
evenly for pretty slices. Cut cucumber into 1/4 inch slices and sprinkle with lemo
pepper. Mound 1-1/2 teaspoons of crabmeat on each cucumber slice and garnis
with sprig of dill or parsley.

"Light, refreshing, and very elegant."

Scallop Seviche

1/4 cup fresh lime juice, strained
  2 teaspoons capers
  2 dashes Tabasco sauce
1/2 teaspoon salt
1/4 teaspoon freshly ground pepper
1/2 pound scallops, cut into
     1/2 -inch cubes

2-3 green onions, chopped
     (include green tops)
1-2 ripe tomatoes, chopped
1/2 pound cooked shrimp, peeled
     (optional)
     Green curly lettuce for garnish

Thoroughly mix lime juice, capers, Tabasco sauce, salt, and pepper in a glass or
plastic bowl. Add scallops and toss them until evenly covered with mixture.
Cover and stir occasionally. Marinate scallops in the refrigerator for at least 2
hours, or until they are white and opaque. Just before serving, combine scallops
with the green onions, tomatoes, and shrimp, tossing lightly. Spoon over a few
leaves of lettuce or serve in shell bowls for individual appetizers.

Shrimp Mousse

1 can condensed cream
  of shrimp soup
2 envelopes Knox gelatin
1/2 cup cold water
1/4 teaspoon pepper
1 cup cottage cheese
1 cup mayonnaise

1/2 cup plain yogurt
1 tablespoon lemon juice
1 6 ounce package frozen,
  cooked shrimp, thawed
4 eggs, hard boiled and quartered
3 green onions, sliced

In saucepan, combine soup, gelatin, water, and pepper. Allow to stand 10 minutes, then cook over low heat, stirring until gelatin is dissolved. Remove from heat and cool slightly. In food processor, combine gelatin mixture, cottage cheese, mayonnaise, yogurt, and lemon juice. Add shrimp, eggs, and onions; process with on-off switch. Lightly oil a 6-cup mold and pour mixture into mold. Cover and chill until firm. Serve with cocktail loaf bread.

"Beautiful and delicious."

Spiced Nuts

1/2 cup sugar
1/2 teaspoon salt
1 teaspoon cinnamon
1/4 teaspoon nutmeg

1/4 teaspoon cloves
2 tablespoons water
1 1/2 cups walnut halves

Heat sugar, salt, cinnamon, nutmeg, cloves, and water, stirring constantly, to 230 degrees, or soft ball stage on candy thermometer. Gently stir in walnuts. Remove from heat and stir to coat. Spread on buttered cookie sheet and cool. When cool enough to handle, break apart. Store in airtight container.

"Try not to eat them all in one sitting!"

Boursin Cheese

8 ounces whipped butter, softened
16 ounces cream cheese, softened
1/2 teaspoon garlic salt
1/2 teaspoon garlic powder
1/4 teaspoon marjoram leaves

1/4 teaspoon basil
1/4 teaspoon dill seed
1/4 teaspoon oregano
1/4 teaspoon celery salt
1/4 teaspoon Beau Monde seasoning

Mix all ingredients well. Do NOT use beater, mixer, or food processor. Chill. May be shaped into a ball, placed in a crock, or shaped like a pine cone with tips of almonds pressed into it. Remove from refrigerator at least 15 minutes before serving.

Cheese Easy

8 ounces Cheez Whiz
8 ounces mayonnaise

1 large onion, minced

Blend all ingredients. Serve on crackers.

Holiday Cheese Ball

2 8 ounce packages cream cheese
1 8 1/2 ounce can
   crushed pineapple, drained
2 cups chopped pecans
1/4 cup green pepper, chopped

2 tablespoons onion, chopped
1 tablespoon seasoned salt
   Pecans, chopped
   Red cherries and parsley
   for garnish

Soften cream cheese and carefully stir in pineapple, pecans, green pepper, onion, and seasoned salt. Chill well. Form into ball and roll in pecans. Garnish with red cherries and parsley. Serve with crackers.

Pungent Peppery Pie

2 tablespoons milk
8 ounces cream cheese, softened
1/2 cup sour cream
2 1/2 ounces shredded dried
beef (glass jar)

2 tablespoons onion, minced
2 tablespoons coarse
ground pepper
1/4 cup ground walnuts
Crackers

Blend milk and cream cheese together. Add sour cream. Mix in dried beef, onion, and ground pepper. Pour into 8 or 9 inch pie plate and top with walnuts. Bake at 350 for 15 minutes. Serve hot with crackers.

"So surprisingly spicy and so very different."

Sherried Edam

1 whole 2 pound Edam or Gouda
cheese, room temperature
1/4 cup butter or
margarine, softened
1/2 teaspoon dry mustard
Dash of Worcestershire sauce

1/2 cup pimiento-stuffed olives,
finely chopped
1/4 cup onions, finely chopped
2 tablespoons dry sherry
Fresh parsley

Carefully cut off top quarter of cheese. Cut or scoop out cheese from bottom section, reserving a half inch shell of cheese in wax. Discard top shell of wax after removing cheese. Cut cheese into small pieces. Position knife in food processor and add cheese. Process until cheese is smooth and forms a ball. Add butter, mustard and Worcestershire sauce. Process until mixture is blended. Knead in olives, onions, and sherry until blended. Pack cheese into cavity of whole cheese. Garnish with parsley. Serve with crackers.

Horseradish Cheese

1 2 pound package
   Velveeta cheese
2 5 ounce jars
   prepared horseradish

1 8 ounce jar mayonnaise

Heat all ingredients in double boiler until thoroughly melted and mixed. Cool and serve with crackers.

"This recipe can easily be halved. Try garnishing with chopped parsley or pecans, or as an option, add cooked crumbled bacon to mixture."

Pepper Jelly

3-4 large bell peppers (enough to
     fill blender)
  6 hot peppers, chopped
1½ cups white vinegar

6½ cups sugar
    Green food coloring
 1 bottle liquid fruit pectin

Wash, core, and seed bell peppers (leave seeds in the hot peppers). Chop peppers and put in blender with 1/2 cup vinegar. Liquify in blender until mixed. Put in saucepan with sugar and remaining vinegar and boil 3 minutes. Remove and add green coloring. Wait 5 minutes. Add pectin. Stir. Wait 10 minutes and stir again. Skim and place in jars, sealing tightly. Serve on cream cheese with crackers.

Cream Cheese Crab

1 pound backfin crabmeat
8 ounce package cream cheese
½ cup mayonnaise
1 medium onion, grated

1 tablespoon Worcestershire sauce
1 tablespoon lemon juice
   Salt

Mix all ingredients and refrigerate overnight. Spread on crackers or Melba toast.

Crab Eleanor

1/2 cup chili sauce
1 clove garlic, chopped
1 tablespoon horseradish
1/8 teaspoon Tabasco
    Dash Accent, optional
1 cup crabmeat

1/2 cup mayonnaise
1/2 teaspoon dry mustard
1 tablespoon Worcestershire sauce
1/2 teaspoon salt
1 egg, hard boiled and chopped

Combine all ingredients. Chill 4 hours, or overnight, before serving.

Kuralt Crab

1 pound crabmeat
16 ounces cream cheese, softened
2/3 cup prepared horseradish

1/4 cup mayonnaise
1 teaspoon hot pepper sauce
2 teaspoons Worcestershire sauce

Mix all ingredients together well with fork. Place in mold and chill until set. Sprinkle with paprika after unmolding.

"Wonderful combination of crabmeat and horseradish."

Sensational Salmon

1 16 ounce can red sockeye
    salmon, drained and flaked
8 ounces cream cheese, softened
1/4 cup green onion, finely chopped
1 tablespoon lemon juice

2 teaspoons prepared horseradish
1/4 teaspoon salt
1/2 cup chopped parsley
1/2 cup chopped walnuts

In a medium bowl, blend salmon, cream cheese, onion, lemon juice, horseradish, and salt. Wrap in wax paper to form ball. Chill one hour or until firm. Roll in parsley and nuts; chill until ready to use. Serve with crackers.

Sumptuous Shrimp Spread

1   pound cooked shrimp, deveined, shelled, and chopped
1/2 cup celery, minced
1/2 cup scallions, minced

1 1/4 cup mayonnaise
3   tablespoons prepared horseradish
1   tablespoon Worcestershire sauce
    Salt and pepper to taste

Mix shrimp, celery, and scallions well. Blend together mayonnaise, horseradish, Worcestershire sauce, salt, and pepper. Combine all ingredients together, mixing well. Serve with crackers or as a dip.

Shrimp Sublime

2   8 ounce packages cream cheese
4   tablespoons ketchup
1   small onion, grated
    Juice of 1 lemon
    Dash hot sauce

3/4 cup mayonnaise
1   teaspoon seasoning salt
1   pound frozen cooked shrimp, cut into small pieces

Soften cream cheese. Beat all ingredients except shrimp. Thaw and cut up shrimp. Fold shrimp into mixture. Serve with chips or crackers.

Shrimp Spread

2   8 ounce packages cream cheese, softened
1/2 cup mayonnaise
1/4 teaspoon garlic powder
2   teaspoons sugar

2   teaspoons mustard
2   teaspoons onion, minced
1   pound cooked shrimp, chopped
1/4 cup fresh parsley, chopped
4   tablespoons white wine

In saucepan, heat cream cheese over low heat. Blend in mayonnaise, garlic powder, sugar, mustard, and onion. Stir in shrimp and parsley; add wine. May be served hot or chilled with crackers.

Shrimp Butter

2 5 ounce cans small
   shrimp, cleaned
1 tablespoon onion, minced
   Juice of 1 lemon
4 tablespoons mayonnaise

1 stick butter (at
   room temperature)
1 large package cream cheese
   Salt to taste
   Parsley or watercress as garnish

Put all ingredients in a bowl and mix with electric beater or whip well by hand. Turn into a mold or small bowl which has been rinsed out in cold water or lightly buttered. Chill. Unmold and surround with crackers or Melba toast. Garnish with parsley or watercress, if desired.

Hot Artichoke Dip

1 frozen package artichoke hearts,
   thawed and chopped
1 cup mayonnaise

1 cup grated Parmesan cheese
¼ teaspoon garlic powder

Mix all ingredients and put into baking dish. Bake at 350 for 20 minutes or until bubbly. Serve with crackers or bagel chips.

"A classic."

Cheddar Perfection

10 ounces sharp Cracker Barrel
    cheese, grated
10 ounces mayonnaise

1 tablespoon dried onions
   Breadcrumbs for topping

Mix grated cheddar cheese, mayonnaise, and onions; mix well. Spoon into casserole dish and sprinkle breadcrumbs on top. Bake at 350 for 25 minutes. Serve with Triscuits.

Crowd Pleasing Chili Cheese

1 pound ground beef
1 pound American or
  Velveeta cheese
1 can green chilies and
  tomatoes, drained

2 tablespoons Worcestershire sauce
1/2 teaspoon chili powder or
  1/2-3/4 cup chili sauce

Brown ground beef and drain. Mix together all ingredients in crock pot. Cook at high for 1 hour, stirring often. Turn to low and serve up to 6 hours later. Serve with nacho chips.

Firecracker Dip

1 pound hot sausage
1 pound ground beef
2 pounds Velveeta, melted
1 can cream of mushroom soup
1 8 ounce can El Paso jalapeño
  and tomato relish or hot
  picante sauce

1/2 small can green chilies or
  2 fresh green chilies, chopped
  Garlic powder

Brown sausage and ground beef; drain. Mix all ingredients and heat. Serve warm with taco chips.

Jalapeño Cheese Dip

32 ounces processed
  American cheese
1/2 stick margarine
1 small can jalapeño peppers
  (7 1/2 ounces)

1 fresh tomato, cut up
3 1/2 ounce can chili peppers or
  1 green pepper
1 onion, diced

Melt one-half amount cheese and all of margarine in double boiler. Add other ingredients. (Can add more cheese if need full amount). Makes 1 1/2 quart.

Layered Nacho Dip

1 16 ounce can refried beans
1/2 package taco seasoning mix
1 6 ounce carton Marie's Bacon
   and Chive Salad Dressing
1 8 ounce carton sour cream
1 4 1/2 ounce can chopped
   olives, drained

2 large tomatoes, chopped
1 small onion, minced
1 4 ounce can chopped
   green chilies
1/2 cup Monterey Jack
   cheese, shredded

Combine beans and seasoning mix; spread evenly in 8x12x2 baking dish. Layer remaining ingredients in order listed. Refrigerate at least 2 hours. Serve with tortilla chips.

"Always a hit."

Fiesta Sizzler

1 pound lean ground beef
1/2 cup onions, chopped
1/2 cup extra hot ketchup
1 tablespoon chili powder
1 teaspoon salt

1 16 ounce can kidney beans,
   with liquid
1/2-1 cup sharp cheddar
   cheese, shredded

Brown ground beef and onions in large pot. Add ketchup, chili powder, and salt. Mix thoroughly. In small bowl, pour kidney beans, a small amount at a time, and mash thoroughly. Add to meat mixture. Heat 10 minutes. Pour in a fondue dish to keep warm. Top mixture with cheese. Serve with tortilla chips.

Hot Cheesy Crab

16 ounces cream cheese, softened
1/2 pint sour cream
4 tablespoons mayonnaise
1/2 teaspoon lemon juice
1 teaspoon dry mustard

1 cup shredded cheddar cheese
Dash onion salt
Dash paprika
1 pound backfin crabmeat

Preheat oven to 325. Blend all ingredients except crabmeat and 1/3 cup cheddar cheese, in blender. Fold in crabmeat. Bake for 30-45 minutes. Top with remaining cheese and serve hot with crackers.

Hot Crabmeat Dip

8 ounces cream cheese
1 tablespoon milk
1 cup crabmeat
2 tablespoons chopped onion

1/2 teaspoon horseradish
1/4 teaspoon salt
Pepper to taste

Soften cream cheese with the milk and beat well. Add remaining ingredients to the cream cheese and blend well. Put in oven-proof shallow dish. Bake in oven at 375 for 15 minutes. Toasted almonds may be sprinkled on top. Canned clams may be substituted for crabmeat.

Creamy Crab Dip

8 ounces cream cheese, softened
1 tablespoon milk
6 1/2 ounces fresh or canned crabmeat
2 tablespoons onion, chopped

1/4 teaspoon salt
Dash of pepper
1/2 cup toasted, sliced almonds
Melba toast or toast rounds

Combine cream cheese with milk. Add crabmeat, chopped onion, salt, and pepper. Blend well. Spoon into baking dish and sprinkle with almonds. Bake at 375 for 15 minutes. Serve hot on Melba toast or toast rounds.

Crabmeat Mornay

2 cloves garlic, diced
1 stick butter
1 small bunch green onions, chopped
1/2 cup parsley, finely chopped
2 tablespoons flour

1 pint half and half
1/2 pound grated Swiss cheese
1 tablespoon sherry
1 pound backfin crabmeat
Cayenne pepper to taste
Salt

Melt butter in heavy pot and saute onions, garlic, and parsley. Blend in flour, cream, and cheese, heating until cheese is melted. Add other ingredients, gently folding in crabmeat. Keep warm in 300 oven or chafing dish. Serve with Triscuits, Melba toast, or in pastry shells.

Clam Loaf Dip

1 large, round loaf of bread, unsliced
2 8 ounce packages cream cheese
3 cans clams, drained
1/4 cup clam liquid
2 tablespoons onion, grated

2 tablespoons beer (optional)
2 teaspoons Worcestershire sauce
2 tablespoons lemon juice
1 teaspoon Tabasco
1/2 teaspoon salt
1 small loaf of bread

Cut hole in top of large loaf of bread and hollow out, leaving a 1 1/2 inch shell of crust. Reserve remaining bread. Mix together cream cheese, clams, clam liquid, onion, beer, Worcestershire sauce, lemon juice, Tabasco, and salt. Pour into shell and replace top. Place bread in center of two large pieces of foil which have been crossed over each other to form an X. Fold foil over to completely enclose. Bake at 250 for 3 hours. To serve, cube reserved bread and smaller loaf for dipping.

"Combining a loaf of dark bread with a loaf of white makes a very attractive combination."

Shrimp and Cheese Dip

1 pound cream cheese, softened
2/3 cup cottage cheese
8 ounces frozen tiny shrimp,
  thawed and drained
3 tablespoons red pepper, minced

1 teaspoon garlic, minced
1 teaspoon Dijon mustard
1/4 teaspoon salt
1/8 teaspoon pepper
1/4 teaspoon Hungarian paprika

In large bowl, beat cream cheese and cottage cheese with electric mixer until light and fluffy. Fold in remaining ingredients and transfer to serving bowl. Cover and chill at least 2 hours. Makes 4 cups.

Cool-As-A-Cucumber Dip

1/2 cup plain yogurt
1/2 cup sour cream
1/4 teaspoon salt
1/4 teaspoon dried dill weed

Dash Tabasco sauce
1 small cucumber, seeded and
  cut into chunks

In food processor, combine all ingredients. Process with on-off switch until blended. Cover and chill overnight. Serve with fresh vegetable pieces.

Tangy Vegetable Dip

2 cups mayonnaise
1 cup cottage cheese
3/4 cup green onions, chopped
1 1/2 tablespoons prepared mustard
1 1/2 tablespoons Worcestershire
1 1/2 teaspoons caraway seed

1 1/2 teaspoons celery seed
1 teaspoon garlic salt
1 teaspoon salt
1 teaspoon Tabasco
1/2 teaspoon seasoned salt
  Sliced green onions for garnish

Combine all ingredients, beating until smooth. Garnish with green onion slices. Serve chilled with fresh vegetable dippers. Yields 3 cups.

"Quick and easy; great for unexpected company!"

STORMY
WEATHER
FARE

Soups and Sandwiches

Cantaloupe Soup

1 3 pound cantaloupe
4½ cups unsweetened orange
    juice, divided
3 tablespoons lemon juice

¼ teaspoon ground ginger
¼ teaspoon ground allspice
    Fresh mint leaves (optional)

Cut cantaloupe in half and remove seeds. Peel each, and cut fruit into 1 inch cubes. Combine half of cantaloupe and ½ cup orange juice in blender; process until smooth. Repeat processing with remaining cantaloupe cubes and an additional ½ cup orange juice. Combine cantaloupe mixture, remaining 3½ cups orange juice, lemon juice, ginger, and allspice; blend well. Cover and chill thoroughly. Garnish with mint leaves, if desired. Yields 6 cups.

Cold Cucumber Soup

2 tablespoons butter
½ onion, finely chopped
1 clove garlic, finely chopped
3 large cucumbers, peeled, halved
    lengthwise, seeded, and chopped
3 tablespoons unbleached
    white flour

2 cups chicken broth
½ teaspoon salt
¾ cup sour cream or yogurt
1 tablespoon fresh dill
    weed, snipped
1 tablespoon lemon rind, grated
⅛ teaspoon mace

Heat butter in a heavy skillet. Saute the onion, garlic, and cucumbers in butter until onion is tender, about 10 minutes. Sprinkle with flour and stir well. Gradually stir in chicken broth. Add salt and bring to a boil. Cover and simmer until cucumber is tender. Cook. Puree the mixture gradually in blender or food processor. Stir in sour cream or yogurt, dill, lemon rind, and mace. Chill several hours.

Cold Curry Soup Curzon

1 cup rice, uncooked	6 cups beef broth
1/2 tablespoon curry powder	1 cup whipping cream
Butter or margarine	Juice of 1/2 lemon
1 tablespoon ketchup	1/2 tablespoon Dijon mustard

The day before serving, saute rice with curry powder in some butter; stir often so it will become curry color. Add ketchup. Mix the rice mixture with the beef broth and bring to a boil. Cook for 15-18 minutes; then let soup cool down. Put in refrigerator. When ready to serve, skim the fat from the soup and add the whipping cream and lemon juice mixed with the mustard. Serve ice cold.

Iced Tomato and Watercress Soup

2 tablespoons butter	1 cup watercress leaves, firmly packed
1 medium leek, white part only, chopped	1 tablespoon fresh parsley, minced
1/4 cup onion, chopped	Pinch of sugar
1 garlic clove, minced	2 tablespoons red wine vinegar
1 1/2 cups chicken broth	1/2 cup whipping cream
1 cup potato, peeled and cubed	Salt
2 large ripe tomatoes, peeled, seeded, and chopped	Fresh ground pepper
	Watercress sprigs for garnish

Melt butter in a heavy, medium sized saucepan over low heat. Add leek, onion, and garlic. Cover and cook until vegetables are tender, about 10 minutes. Add broth, potatoes, and tomatoes. Increase heat and bring to a boil. Reduce heat and simmer until potato is tender, 10-15 minutes. Add watercress leaves, parsley, sugar, and vinegar; simmer 10 minutes. Cool to room temperature. Puree soup in processor or blender until smooth. Blend in cream. Season generously with salt and pepper. Refrigerate until chilled. Ladle into bowls and garnish with watercress sprigs and serve.

Shrimp Gazpacho Soup

1 46 ounce can V-8 juice	2 tablespoons chives
1/2 cucumber, diced	2 tablespoons parsley
1 stalk celery, diced	1 tablespoon basil
1 carrot, diced	1 tablespoon tarragon
1 medium onion, diced	1 tablespoon chervil
1 green pepper, diced	1 tablespoon paprika
1 teaspoon salt	1 tablespoon sugar
1 teaspoon pepper	1/8 cup lemon juice
Tabasco	1 pound boiled shrimp, shelled
Worcestershire sauce	

Combine all vegetables with V-8 juice. Add spices and shrimp. Chill for 3-4 hours.

"This is a cold soup, but is also delicious served hot with melted cheddar cheese on top."

Chicken Chowder

4 chicken breasts, skinned	1 17 ounce can cream-style corn
4 cups water	1 15 ounce can tomato sauce
1/2 teaspoon salt	with tomato bits
2 medium potatoes, peeled and cubed	1/4 teaspoon pepper
2 medium carrots, coarsely chopped	

Combine chicken, water, and salt in a Dutch oven; bring to a boil. Cover, reduce heat, and simmer 30-40 minutes or until chicken is tender. Remove chicken from broth, reserving 3 cups broth in Dutch oven. Remove meat from bones and cut into bite-size pieces; set aside. Add potatoes and carrots to broth; bring to a boil. Cover, reduce heat, and simmer 10-12 minutes. Add chicken, corn, tomato sauce, and pepper; cover and simmer 15 minutes or until vegetables are tender, stirring occasionally. Makes 2 quarts.

Cream of Broccoli and Potato Soup

3 cups chicken stock
2 cups broccoli, chopped
1 cup potatoes, diced
1/2 cup onions, chopped
1/4 teaspoon ground nutmeg
4 tablespoons butter

4 tablespoons flour
1/2 teaspoon salt
1/8 teaspoon white pepper
1 cup evaporated milk
1 cup milk

In a large saucepan, combine the first 5 ingredients and bring to a boil. Lower heat, cover and simmer for 10 minutes or until the vegetables are tender. Remove 1 cup of vegetables with a slotted spoon and set aside. Puree remaining mixture in blender or food processor and set aside. Melt butter in saucepan. Stir in flour, salt, and pepper. Cook; stir constantly for 1 minute. Add milk all at once. Cook and stir until thick and bubbly. Stir in reserved vegetables and pureed mixture. Cook and stir until soup is heated thoroughly.

Vegetable and Cheese Chowder

1/2 cup onion, chopped
1 clove garlic, minced
1 cup celery, sliced
3/4 cup carrots, sliced
1 cup potatoes, cubed
3 1/2 cups chicken broth
1 17 ounce can corn
1 17 ounce can baby lima beans
1 16 ounce can tomatoes

1/4 cup butter
1/4 cup flour
2 cups milk
1 teaspoon prepared mustard
1/4 teaspoon white pepper
1/8 teaspoon paprika
2 teaspoons diced pimientos
2 cups cheddar cheese, shredded

Combine onion, garlic, celery, carrots, potatoes, and chicken broth in a dutch oven and bring to a boil. Cover and reduce heat; cook for 15-20 minutes, or until the vegetables are tender. Stir in corn, lima beans, and tomatoes, including their liquids, and remove from heat. In a separate saucepan, melt butter; add flour, stirring until smooth and cook for 1 minute. Slowly add milk, continuing to stir until smooth. Add mustard, pepper, paprika, and pimientos to the cream sauce. Gradually stir in shredded cheddar cheese until it has completely melted. Combine cheesy sauce with soup in the dutch oven, mixing thoroughly. Serve hot.

Red Pepper Soup

8 red peppers
3 carrots, peeled and thinly sliced
3 shallots, peeled and thinly sliced
1 clove garlic, peeled and
thinly sliced
1 pear, peeled and quartered
1 tablespoon olive oil
4 tablespoons unsalted butter

1 quart chicken stock
1 tablespoon crushed red pepper
Cayenne pepper
Salt
Black pepper
Paper bag
Sprigs of fresh tarragon for garnish

Slice thinly 6 of the peppers, carrots, shallots, garlic, and pear. Heat oil and butter in large skillet and saute the sliced vegetables and pear over medium low heat until tender. Add the stock, diced red pepper, cayenne pepper, salt, and black pepper. Bring to a boil and simmer for 25-30 minutes.

While soup is cooking, roast remaining red peppers, rotating them until completely charred. Put in paper bag for 5 minutes to sweat. Wash off blackened skin under cold running water and remove seeds. Drain on paper towel.

Puree soup in a food processor or blender adding one of the roasted red peppers. Pour soup back into the pan and reheat on low. Julienne the remaining red pepper and add to soup. Serve with French bread. Serves 4-6.

French Onion Soup

3 tablespoons butter
4-5 onions, minced
1/4 teaspoon peppercorns, crushed
1 tablespoon flour
3 cans condensed beef broth

3 cups water
1 bay leaf
French bread, sliced and toasted
Swiss cheese

Heat butter in heavy saucepan over medium heat. Add onions and peppercorns. Cook, stirring frequently until onions are light brown. Sprinkle onions with flour. Cook 1 minute. Add beef broth, water, and bay leaf. Bring to a boil, then simmer on low heat for 30 minutes. Place toast slices on top. Sprinkle with cheese. Place under broiler until cheese melts.

Cream of Lettuce Soup

2 small heads of iceberg lettuce
1/2 cup shallots (or green onion),
  finely chopped
4 tablespoons butter
2 garlic cloves, minced
5 tablespoons parsley, chopped

2 teaspoons salt
1/2 teaspoon freshly ground pepper
1 1/2 cups water
6 cups chicken stock
3 egg yolks, slightly beaten
3/4 cup heavy cream

Wash, core, and tear lettuce into chunks; set aside. Saute shallots in butter until transparent, but do not brown. Combine garlic and parsley; add to shallots along with salt, pepper, lettuce, and water. Cover pan and cook long enough to wilt lettuce, about 15-20 minutes. Cool slightly and then puree in blender. Return to saucepan, add chicken stock and bring to a boil. Mix egg yolks and cream; gradually add to hot mixture.

   May be served hot or cold. If cold, add a spoon of sour cream to float on top. If hot, spoon slightly salted whipped cream on top and place under the broiler to lightly brown. Can be frozen! Serves 16.

"If you don't tell your guests this is lettuce soup, they would never guess the main ingredient!"

Fresh Mushroom Soup

3/4 cup scallions, chopped,
  including tops
4 tablespoons butter
2 cups mushrooms, sliced
2 tablespoons flour

1 cup milk
1 cup chicken stock
1 teaspoon sugar
  Salt and pepper

Cook scallions in butter over low heat for 5 minutes. Add mushrooms and cook 2 more minutes. Add flour; stir and cook 3 additional minutes. Remove from heat. Combine milk and chicken stock; heat until hot, but not boiling. Add to mushroom mixture. Cook over medium heat for 5 minutes, stirring occasionally. Add sugar, salt, and pepper. Serves 4.

Magnificent Minestrone

1 cup navy beans, dried
2 14½ ounce cans chicken broth
2 teaspoons salt
1 small head cabbage, cored and shredded
4 carrots, peeled and sliced
2 medium potatoes, peeled and diced
1 28 ounce can Italian plum tomatoes, chopped

2 medium onions, chopped
1 stalk celery, chopped
1 large fresh tomato, peeled and chopped
1 clove garlic, minced
¼ cup olive oil
¼ cup parsley, chopped
¼ teaspoon pepper
1 cup vermicelli, broken into pieces

Pesto Sauce

¼ cup butter, softened (no substitutions)
¼ cup Parmesan cheese, grated
½ cup parsley, chopped
1 clove garlic, minced

1 teaspoon basil
½ teaspoon marjoram
¼ cup olive oil
¼ cup walnuts, chopped (or pine nuts)

Cover beans with water and soak overnight. Drain. Measure chicken broth and add water to measure 3 quarts. Add salt. Cook beans in broth mixture until almost tender. Add cabbage, carrots, potatoes, and canned tomatoes. Saute onions, celery, fresh tomato, and garlic in olive oil; add to soup. Stir in parsley and pepper. Add vermicelli to soup 15 minutes before serving. Serve hot in bowls with a spoonful of pesto sauce in each bowl.

Do not omit pesto sauce as it contains ALL the seasonings!!! Serves 10-12.

Garden Tomato Soup

4 small spring onions, thinly sliced
1 small cucumber, sliced
1/2 cup green pepper, diced
4 large tomatoes, peeled and
  cut into small pieces
1 cup canned chicken broth

1 cup canned tomato juice
  Juice from 1 lemon
2 teaspoons sugar
1 teaspoon seasoned salt
1/4 teaspoon seasoned pepper

In large saucepan bring to boil onion, cucumber, green pepper, and tomatoes in chicken broth. Simmer for 5 minutes. Add tomato juice, lemon juice, sugar, salt, and pepper. Simmer 10 minutes more. Transfer to a bowl and refrigerate.

Cream of Tomato and Parmesan Soup

2 14 ounce cans Italian plum
  tomatoes, undrained
1 cup whipping cream
1/4 cup fresh basil, chopped
1/4 cup fresh parsley, chopped

1 teaspoon freshly ground pepper
1/4 teaspoon salt
1/2 cup Parmesan cheese,
  freshly grated

Place all ingredients, except cheese, in food processor. Pulse until mixture is smooth. Pour into saucepan. Cook over medium heat until hot and thoroughly blended. Stir in cheese and heat until cheese melts.

Crab Bisque

1 can cream of mushroom soup
1 can cream of asparagus soup
1 1/2 soup cans of milk
1 cup light cream

1 pound crab meat
1/4 cup dry white wine
  Butter

Blend soups and stir in milk and cream. Heat just to boiling. Add crab; heat through. Stir in wine just before serving. Float butter atop. Serves 6.

Crab Asparagus Soup

2 quarts chicken stock
1 15 ounce can white asparagus,
   cut into 1/2 inch pieces or
   1 pound fresh green asparagus,
   steamed until tender crisp
1/2 pound crab meat

Salt
White pepper
1 tablespoon cornstarch
1 egg white, lightly beaten
  Parsley, minced

Combine chicken stock and asparagus in saucepan and bring to a boil over high heat. Cut heat back to medium once soup boils. Add crab meat. Season with salt and pepper. Dissolve cornstarch with small amount of chicken stock. Add this mixture and beaten egg white to saucepan; stir until soup thickens slightly and egg white congeals. Sprinkle individual servings with parsley. Serve hot.

Bay Scallop Chowder

3 medium potatoes, diced
1 small carrot, chopped
1 stalk celery, chopped
1 medium onion, chopped
2 cups chicken stock
1/2 teaspoon salt
1/4 teaspoon freshly ground pepper
1/2 bay leaf
1/2 teaspoon thyme, crumbled

1/2 pound fresh mushrooms, sliced
1 1/2 teaspoons butter
1 pound fresh bay scallops
1/2 cup dry white wine
1 cup heavy cream
1 egg yolk, lightly beaten
2 tablespoons parsley, chopped
  Paprika

Place potatoes, carrots, celery, and onion in a large pot; cover with chicken stock. Bring to a boil. Add salt, pepper, bay leaf, and thyme. Simmer covered until vegetables are tender. Remove bay leaf and transfer mixture to blender or food processor. Blend until smooth. Meanwhile, saute mushrooms in butter. Add scallops and wine. Cook for 1 minute. Stir in cream mixed with egg yolk. Combine this mixture with the pureed vegetables and broth. Heat through and serve with a sprinkling of parsley and paprika.

Crab Meat Bisque

6 tablespoons butter	1 cup milk
4 tablespoons green pepper, finely chopped	1 teaspoon salt
4 tablespoons onion, finely chopped	1/8 teaspoon white pepper
	Dash Tabasco
2 scallions, chopped	1 1/2 cups half and half
2 tablespoons parsley	1 1/2 cups crab meat, cooked
2 tablespoons flour	3 tablespoons dry sherry

Heat 3 tablespoons butter in skillet. Add green pepper, onion, scallions, and parsley. Saute until soft, about 5 minutes. In a separate saucepan, heat remaining 3 table-spoons butter. Gradually stir in flour. Add milk a little at a time. Cook, stirring until thickened and smooth. Stir in salt, pepper, and Tabasco. Add sauteed vegetables and half and half. Bring to a boil, stirring constantly; reduce heat. Add crab meat. Simmer uncovered for 5 minutes. Just before serving, stir in sherry.

Note: Canned or frozen crab meat can be used. If desired, you may substitute shrimp for the crab meat.

Plantation Peanut Soup

3 cups chicken broth	1/2 teaspoon sugar
1 cup peanut butter	1 1/3 cups cream
1/8 teaspoon celery salt	Peanuts, chopped
1/8 teaspoon onion salt	

Heat chicken broth to boiling. Add peanut butter, stirring until smooth. Add celery and onion salts. Add sugar; stir in cream. Heat, do not boil. Top with chopped peanuts.

Spiced Beef and Vegetable Soup

2 pounds boneless beef chuck,
  cut in 1 inch cubes
1/2 cup flour
1 tablespoon salt
1/2 teaspoon pepper
1/2 teaspoon paprika
2 tablespoons shortening or oil
1 cup onions, chopped
6 cups water
  Garni—1 clove and 1 teaspoon
  pickling spice in cloth

3 cups tomatoes, peeled
  and chopped
3 cups potatoes, diced
2 cups carrots, diced
1 cup celery, sliced
1 cup green peas
1 teaspoon sugar
2 teaspoons salt
1/4 teaspoon pepper
3 tablespoons cornstarch, blended
  with 1/4 cup cold water

Dredge beef cubes in mixture of flour, salt, pepper, and paprika. Brown in fat on all sides in large heavy kettle. Add onions and brown lightly. Add water and garni. Simmer, covered, for 30 minutes. Add vegetables and seasonings. Simmer, uncovered, for 30 minutes. Discard garni. Blend a little of the hot gravy into cornstarch mixture and stir into stew until thick. Serves 8 to 10.

Dutch Pea Soup

1 bag split green peas
8 cups water
1 package pork ribs
  or barbecue ribs
2 beef broth cubes

2 medium potatoes, cubed
1 bunch leeks, thinly sliced
1 bunch celery, chopped
1 large onion, chopped
  Salt and pepper

Soak split peas 24 hours in 6 cups of water. Add 2 cups of water and meat; bring to a boil. Let simmer for 1 1/2 hours; stir often. Remove meat, trim fat, and debone. Return meat to pot with the beef broth, potatoes, leeks, celery, and onion. Add salt and pepper. Simmer for 1 1/2 hours; stir often and add water if necessary. Serves 8.

"Great with brown bread and cheese."

Mexican Bean Soup

8 slices bacon, chopped
1 cup onion, chopped
1 cup celery, chopped
1 clove garlic, minced
1 4 ounce can chopped
   green chilies
2 16 ounce cans refried beans

1/2 teaspoon pepper
2 tablespoons taco seasoning
2 10 1/2 ounce cans chicken broth
2 cups water
1 cup cheddar cheese, grated
   Tortilla chips

In a 4 quart saucepan, cook bacon until crisp. DO NOT DRAIN FAT. Add onion, celery, and garlic; cook covered over low heat for 10 minutes. Add green chilies, beans, pepper, and taco seasoning. Stir in chicken broth and water. Bring to a boil; then lower heat. Simmer 10 minutes, stirring occasionally. Serve in bowls and garnish with cheddar cheese and broken tortilla chips. Serves 8.

Pane Italiano

1 loaf Italian bread
   Olive oil
1/2 cup tomato sauce
2 cups Italian plum
   tomatoes, drained
1/2 teaspoon sweet basil
1/2 teaspoon oregano
3/4 teaspoon salt

1/4 teaspoon pepper
1 clove garlic, minced
1/4 pound pepperoni, sliced
1/4 pound Italian salami, sliced
1/4 pound mozzarella cheese, diced
1/4 cup Romano cheese
   (or Parmesan), grated

Cut a 1/2 inch slice off top of bread. Hollow out inside of loaf, leaving a 1/2 inch shell. Brush inside and outside of loaf with olive oil. Place loaf on baking sheet and heat at 400 for 5-10 minutes. (Inside should be dry, not brown.) In saucepan, combine tomato sauce, plum tomatoes, the seasonings, and meats. Heat until bubbly; lower heat and simmer for 10 minutes. Remove from heat; stir in mozzarella cheese. Spoon into loaf and top with grated Romano cheese. Bake at 400 for 15 minutes. Cut into thick slices and serve hot. Serves 4-6.

Marinated Beef Pitas

½ pound extra-lean sliced roast
  beef, cut into strips
1 cup red onion, finely chopped
2 tablespoons parsley, chopped
⅓ cup vegetable oil
4 tablespoons red wine vinegar

1 teaspoon dry mustard
  Garlic salt
  Ground pepper
3 pita breads, cut in half
  Leaf lettuce
1 large tomato, thinly sliced

In large bowl, combine beef, onion, and parsley. In small bowl, mix well oil, vinegar, and mustard; stir into meat mixture. Season with garlic salt and pepper. Cover and refrigerate 1 hour. Stuff pita bread with meat mixture, lettuce, and tomato.

Roast Lamb Gyros

Sliced lamb shoulder roast
Vinaigrette dressing
Pita bread rounds
Lettuce, shredded

1 small onion, chopped
2 tomatoes, peeled, seeded,
  and diced

Slice leftover lamb roast and marinate in vinaigrette dressing for 2 hours or more in refrigerator. Cut pita rounds across in half and open halves. Stuff with lamb, lettuce, onions, and diced tomatoes. Pass vinaigrette dressing for individuals to pour on sandwiches.

Vinaigrette Dressing

¼ cup red wine vinegar
1 teaspoon dry mustard
  Salt and freshly ground pepper
2 cloves garlic, minced

2 teaspoons fresh or dried oregano
10 tablespoons vegetable oil
3 tablespoons olive oil

Mix vinegar, mustard, salt and pepper, garlic, and oregano in small bowl. Slowly whisk in oils.

Hot Ham Sandwiches

¼ cup butter, softened	2 tablespoons Dijon mustard
1 tablespoon onion, finely chopped	1-2 tablespoons Worcestershire sauce
2 tablespoons mustard	6 hamburger buns
with horseradish	6 slices cooked ham
2 tablespoons poppy seeds	6 slices Swiss cheese

Combine butter, onion, mustards, poppy seeds, and Worcestershire sauce; mix well. Spread on both sides of buns. Place 1 slice ham and 1 slice cheese on bottom of each bun. Cover with top bun. Wrap each sandwich in foil. Bake at 350 for 25 minutes.
    Note: These may be served on small rolls for appetizers.

Italian-Style Hero Sandwiches

1 6 inch whole wheat or regular French bread	3 thin slices tomato
⅛ teaspoon dried Italian seasoning	1 ounce semi-soft cheese, such as Havarti, sliced
Dash garlic powder	2 ounces extra lean ham, sliced
4 thin slices green pepper	2 ounces extra lean Italian beef, sliced
4 thin slices red pepper	Cherry tomatoes, optional
1 medium onion, thinly sliced	

Sprinkle cut surfaces of bread with Italian seasoning and garlic powder. On one bread half, arrange green pepper, red pepper, onion, tomato, cheese, ham, and Italian beef. Cover with top portion of bread. Grill just before serving. Cut sandwich in half and garnish with cherry tomatoes, if desired.

ENDLESS SUMMER SALADS

Salads

Cauliflower Salad

1 head cauliflower, broken
  into flowerettes
1/2 cup green onions, sliced

5 ounces water chestnuts, sliced
1 cup radishes, sliced
Dressing

Mix cauliflower, onion, water chestnuts, and radishes.

Dressing

3/4 cup mayonnaise
3/4 cup sour cream
1 package Hidden Valley
  ranch dressing

Salt and pepper
Dillweed

Blend mayonnaise, sour cream, and ranch dressing. Pour over vegetables. Season
with salt, pepper, and dillweed. Chill.

Broccoli Crunch

1 bunch broccoli, chopped fine
8 slices bacon, cooked
  and crumbled
1/4 cup onion, chopped

1/4 cup raisins
1 cup Cheddar cheese, grated
  Sunflower seeds
  Dressing

Combine broccoli, bacon, onion, raisins, cheese, and sunflower nuts.

Dressing

1 cup mayonnaise
1/4 cup sugar

2 tablespoons white vinegar

Blend mayonnaise, sugar, and vinegar. Refrigerate. Add dressing to salad
immediately before serving.

Broccoli and Almond Salad

3 10 ounce packages frozen
broccoli flowerettes, thawed
4 ounces slivered almonds

1 cup pimiento olives, chopped
1 cup onions, chopped
1/2 cup mayonnaise

Combine broccoli, almonds, olives, and onions. Chill. Stir in mayonnaise and serve.

"A great dish for summer dining."

Sweet Broccoli Salad

1 bunch fresh broccoli
1 head lettuce, torn into
bite size pieces

1 red onion

Wash and drain broccoli. Cut off flowerettes. Peel and slice stems. Peel, wash, and slice onion. Separate onion into rings. Combine broccoli, lettuce, and onion rings.

Dressing

14 ounces sweetened
condensed milk
2 eggs
1/2 cup white vinegar

3 tablespoons prepared mustard
Salt
1/2 pound bacon, cooked
and crumbled

Combine condensed milk, eggs, vinegar, mustard, and salt in blender or processor. Mix well. Pour over salad and toss to coat vegetables. Garnish with bacon just before serving.

Taco Salad

1 head lettuce, torn
16 ounces barbecued beans,
   rinsed and drained
1 medium onion, chopped
2 tomatoes, chopped

1 cup sharp cheddar
   cheese, shredded
1 pint bottle of Catalina dressing
4 cups corn chips, crushed

Mix lettuce, barbecued beans, onion, tomatoes, cheese, and Catalina dressing 1/2 hour before serving. Add corn chips when ready to serve.

Corned Beef Salad

3 ounces lemon gelatin
1 cup boiling water
3/4 cup cold water
1 cup mayonnaise or salad dressing
12 ounces corned beef, shredded
1 cup celery, chopped

3 eggs, hard-boiled and chopped
1 small onion, chopped fine
12 ounces pimiento, chopped
   and drained
   Lettuce leaves
   Egg slices

Dissolve gelatin in boiling water. Add cold water and chill until slightly thickened. Combine mayonnaise, corned beef, celery, eggs, onion, and pimiento. Stir well. Pour in lightly oiled 8 inch square pan and chill overnight. Cut into rectangles and serve on lettuce leaves. Garnish with egg slices. Serves 6.

Fantastic Cole Slaw

3/4 cup sugar
1 cup vinegar
1 tablespoon salt
1 teaspoon dry mustard
1 teaspoon celery seed

1 large head of cabbage,
   finely chopped
2 onions, finely chopped
1 green pepper, finely chopped

Mix together sugar, vinegar, salt, dry mustard, and celery seed. Heat to boiling. Pour over cabbage, onions, and green peppers. Toss and refrigerate overnight.

Paella Salad

1½ cups water
 ½ pound fresh medium shrimp
 5 ounce package yellow rice mix
 ¼ cup tarragon vinegar
 2 tablespoons vegetable oil
 ¼ teaspoon curry powder
 ⅛ teaspoon dry mustard
 ⅛ teaspoon white pepper

2 cups cooked and diced
   chicken breast
1 medium tomato,
   peeled and chopped
 ½ cup frozen peas, thawed
 ⅓ cup celery, thinly sliced
 ¼ cup onion, minced
2 ounces pimiento, drained

Cook shrimp in boiling water until shrimp is bright pink, 3-5 minutes. Chill, peel, and devein. Prepare rice according to package directions, omitting the butter.

Combine vinegar, oil, curry, dry mustard, and white pepper. Add to rice and stir well. Add shrimp and chicken, tomatoes, peas, celery, onion, and pimiento. Toss gently. Cover and chill. Serve on lettuce leaves and garnish with lemon slices.

Chicken Salad Pie

2 cups cooked chicken or
   turkey, diced
 ¾ cup cheese, shredded
 ½ cup celery, diced
4½ ounces crushed
   pineapple, drained
 ⅓ cup slivered almonds

½ teaspoon paprika
½ cup mayonnaise
½ teaspoon salt
1 9 inch pie shell, baked
½ cup whipped topping
½ cup mayonnaise

Mix lightly chicken, cheese, celery, pineapple, almonds, paprika, salt, and ½ cup mayonnaise. Put in cooled pie shell. Mix whipped topping and ½ cup mayonnaise. Top pie with mixture. Garnish with carrot curls. Serves 6 to 8.

Fried Chicken Salad

2 heads bibb or Boston lettuce
8 cherry tomatoes
1/2 cup peanut oil
1/2 cup all purpose flour
1/2 teaspoon salt
1/4 teaspoon coarse black pepper
1/3 cup milk
2 whole fryer chicken breasts
(4 halves), boned and cut into
1/2 inch strips

2 tablespooons white vinegar
2 teaspoons Dijon mustard
1/2 cup mushrooms, sliced
1 shallot, minced
1 tablespoon fresh tarragon,
chopped, or 1 teaspoon
dried tarragon
1 tablespoon capers
1 sweet Vidalia onion
Tarragon leaves for garnish

Arrange lettuce and tomatoes on 4 salad plates. Heat oil in frying pan on medium high heat. In a shallow mixing bowl, mix flour with salt and pepper. Put milk into another bowl. Dip chicken strips into milk, then into flour to coat. Fry chicken on both sides until golden brown, about 5 minutes. Drain on paper towels. Reserve oil in pan. Add vinegar to oil in pan, stirring and scraping sides of pan to deglaze. Pour oil and vinegar into mixing bowl, add mustard, and mix. Add mushrooms, shallots, and tarragon. Season to taste with salt and pepper.

To serve, put chicken strips on lettuce leaves. Scatter capers and sliced onion on top of salads. Pour just enough vinaigrette to moisten leaves. Serve remaining vinaigrette on side. Serves 4.

Fiesta Corn Salad

4 1/2 cups fresh or frozen corn
3 cloves garlic, minced
4 tablespoons butter
1 medium fresh tomato,
peeled, seeded, and chopped
1 green pepper, finely chopped
1 red bell pepper, finely chopped
1/2 cup Spanish onion,
finely chopped

4 tablespoons fresh
parsley, chopped
2 tablespoons chili powder
1/2 teaspoon Worcestershire sauce
Tabasco to taste
Salt to taste
Pepper to taste

In a skillet on range top saute corn and minced garlic in melted butter until just warmed. Combine remaining ingredients. Refrigerate until chilled.

Chicken Super Salad

1 head iceberg lettuce, torn into
   bite-size pieces
2½ cups chicken, cooked and diced
5 ounces water chestnuts, sliced
10 ounces frozen green peas
½ cup celery, chopped
½ cup green pepper, chopped

½ cup red onion, sliced
6 ounces cheddar
   cheese, shredded
10 slices bacon, cooked
   and crumbled
3-4 eggs, hard-boiled and sliced
   Topping

Assemble ingredients in large salad bowl in order listed above. Lightly season each layer with salt and pepper as desired.

Topping

1 cup mayonnaise
1 cup sour cream

2 tablespoons sugar

Mix mayonnaise with sour cream and sugar. Spread mixture evenly over top of salad, sealing the edges of the bowl. Cover and refrigerate overnight.

Cheesy Egg Salad

6 eggs, hard-cooked and chopped
1½ cups shredded Swiss or
   medium cheddar cheese
1 cup mayonnaise
2 tablespoons chopped fresh chives
   or 2 teaspoons dried chives

1 teaspoon prepared mustard
½ teaspoon salt
4-5 medium tomatoes, chilled
   Dill weed (optional)

Combine all ingredients, except tomatoes. Stir gently. Cover and chill for 2-3 hours. To serve, cut each tomato into sixths, cutting through to within 1 inch of stem end. Fill with ½-⅔ cup of cheesy egg salad. Sprinkle with dill weed, if desired. Serves 4-5.

Ham and Cheese Salad

1½ pounds red potatoes, skinned
2 cups cooked ham, julienned
½ pound Swiss cheese, julienned

2½ cups red cabbage, shredded
½ cup walnuts, halved
Dressing

Boil potatoes and drain in colander. Cool potatoes.

Dressing

3 tablespoons white wine
2 tablespoons white wine vinegar
2 tablespoons minced shallots
1½ teaspoon Dijon mustard

¾ teaspoon salt
¼ teaspoon pepper
¼ cup minced parsley
½ cup olive oil

Combine white wine, white wine vinegar, shallots, mustard, salt, and pepper in jar with lid. Shake well. Add parsley and olive oil. Shake well.
Pour ⅔ of dressing over potatoes. Add ham, cheese, and ½ remaining dressing. Blend well. Toss cabbage and remaining dressing. Cover dish with cabbage. Mound potatoes, cheese, and ham mixture in center. Sprinkle with walnuts.

Spring Salad Souffle

3 ounces lime gelatin
½ cup boiling water
10½ ounces condensed
    asparagus soup
½ cup mayonnaise

1 tablespoon vinegar
½ cup cucumber, shredded
½ cup celery, chopped
1 teaspoon onion, grated
Dash of pepper

Dissolve gelatin in water. Add soup, mayonnaise, vinegar, cucumber, celery, onion, and pepper. Beat well and chill. Garnish with parsley.

Board of Directors Shrimp Salad

2 pounds medium size shrimp, cooked and peeled	¼ tablespoon salt
10 ounces water chestnuts, sliced	¼ tablespoon pepper
¼ cup imported capers	½ tablespoon celery salt
1 tablespoon Old Bay seasoning	Homemade mayonnaise

Cut shrimp into halves. Mix shrimp, water chestnuts, capers, Old Bay, salt, pepper, and celery salt.

Homemade Mayonnaise

2 eggs	2 teaspoons dry mustard
2 teaspoons salt	2 cups oil
4½ tablespoons cider vinegar	

Place eggs, salt, cider vinegar, dry mustard, and approximately ¼ cup oil in blender. Mix at medium speed until thoroughly mixed. Slowly add oil until all ingredients are well coated. Makes about 2½ cups. Store unused mayonnaise in refrigerator. Add enough mayonnaise to coat salad ingredients. Serve on bed of Romaine lettuce or in an avocado.

Layered Crab and Cheddar Salad

1 head lettuce	16 ounces cheddar cheese
1 bunch green onions	4 cups mayonnaise
5 eggs, hard-boiled and chopped	1 cup sour cream
1 pound fresh crabmeat	2 tablespoons Dijon mustard
10 ounces frozen tiny green peas, thawed	

Using a clear glass bowl, layer ingredients in order of recipe. Combine mayonnaise, sour cream, and mustard. Spread over cheese layer. Refrigerate overnight.

Red and White Layered Salad

1 envelope unflavored gelatin	2 eggs, hard-boiled and chopped
1/4 cup cold water	2-3 sweet pickles, chopped
1/4 cup boiling water	1 cup celery, chopped
1 cup whipping cream	6 1/2 ounces tuna
1 cup salad dressing	Topping

Soak gelatin in cold water. Add boiling water and stir. Whip whipping cream and mix with salad dressing. Add gelatin, eggs, pickles, celery, and tuna to salad dressing mixture. Pour into 9x9 or 7x10 dish and chill.

Topping

2 cups tomato juice Salt
3 ounces raspberry gelatin

Dissolve gelatin in 1 cup hot tomato juice. Stir in 1 cup cold tomato juice and dash of salt. Cool to room temperature. Pour over tuna mixture and chill. Serves 10.

Spicy Shrimp Mold

5 ounces small shrimp, cooked and deveined	1 envelope unflavored gelatin
1/2 cup chili sauce	1/2 teaspoon Worcestershire sauce
1/4 cup ketchup	1/2 teaspoon horseradish
1/2 teaspoon sugar	1 1/2 tablespoon lemon juice
1 tablespoon onion, grated	Dash Tabasco sauce

Combine all ingredients except shrimp and heat until gelatin is dissolved. Add shrimp and stir. Pour into mold and chill until set. Serve on plate or tray with greens as garnish.

"Tastes like shrimp cocktail."

Wild Rice and Crabmeat Salad

  1 box wild rice, cooked
 12 ounces fresh crabmeat, flaked
  2 eggs, hard-boiled and chopped
  1 cup celery, chopped
 1/4 cup plus 2 tablespoons
    onion, chopped

 1/4 cup plus 2 tablespoons
    red sweet pepper, chopped
 1/4 cup sweet pickle relish
 1/2 cup plain low-fat yogurt
 1/4 cup reduced-calorie mayonnaise
  1 teaspoon lemon juice

Combine rice, crab, eggs, celery, onion, pepper, and relish. Stir well. Combine yogurt, mayonnaise, and lemon juice in small bowl. Stir well. Pour over crab mixture, toss gently. Cover and chill. Serves 6.

"Low in calories."

Korean Spinach Salad

 1/2 cup brown sugar, packed
  1 cup salad oil
  1 tablespoon Worcestershire sauce
  1 medium onion, quartered
 1/4 cup vinegar
 1/3 cup ketchup
  1 pound fresh spinach,
    washed and torn

  2 eggs, hard-boiled and chopped
  8 strips bacon, fried crisp
    and crumbled
  8 ounces water chestnuts
  1 cup fresh bean sprouts
 1/2 pound fresh mushrooms,
    cleaned and sliced

Puree brown sugar, salad oil, Worcestershire sauce, onion, vinegar, and ketchup in blender. Store in refrigerator. Just before serving, toss remaining ingredients. Pour refrigerated mixture over salad, toss, and serve immediately.

Spinach and Mushroom Salad

1½ pounds fresh spinach
½ pound fresh mushrooms
½ cup salad oil
3 tablespoons white wine vinegar
1 tablespoon onion, grated
2 teaspoons Dijon mustard

1 teaspoon salt
1 teaspoon sugar
Freshly ground pepper
4 slices bacon, cooked
and crumbled

Remove stems from spinach, wash leaves, and pat dry. Tear into bite-size pieces. Rinse mushrooms and slice thin. Combine oil, vinegar, onion, mustard, salt, sugar, and pepper in a jar. Shake well. Combine spinach, mushrooms, and dressing in a salad bowl. Toss until well coated. Sprinkle with bacon.

Spinach Fruit Salad

½ pound spinach leaves
11 ounces Mandarin oranges
1 banana, sliced

½ cup pecans, crushed
Bacon bits
Dressing

Layer all ingredients in above order on 8 individual salad plates.

Dressing

12 ounces whipped topping
2 tablespoons honey

1 teaspoon prepared mustard
¼ cup orange juice

Combine whipped topping, honey, mustard, and orange juice. Pour over layered salads. Serves 8.

Gazpacho Salad Mold

1   cucumber, peeled
1   stalk celery
1   green onion
1/3 of a green pepper
1   pound stewed tomatoes
1½ cups V-8 juice
1-2 tablespoons wine vinegar

1-2 tablespoons olive oil
1   teaspoon Tabasco
2   packages gelatin
¼   cup cold water
    Mayonnaise
    Sour cream
    Chives or dill

Cut cucumber, celery, onion, and green pepper into chunks. Combine with tomatoes in container of food processor. Use metal blade pulse approximately 6 times. Heat V-8 juice, vinegar, oil, and Tabasco. Combine gelatin with cold water. Add to V-8 mixture. Stir until well blended and gelatin is dissolved. Add vegetable mixture. Grease ring mold with Pam. Pour mixture into ring mold. Chill until firm.

Make dressing by combining equal parts of mayonnaise and sour cream. Add chives or dill to taste. Chill.

To serve, unmold on plate. Serve dressing on the side or in small bowl in center of mold.

Artichoke and Rice Salad

1   box Chicken Rice-A-Roni,
    cooked and cooled
6   ounces marinated artichokes,
    drained reserving the liquid
1/3 cup mayonnaise

1½ teaspoons curry powder
½   cup green olives, chopped
½   cup green peppers, chopped
½   cup green onions, chopped

Toss Chicken Rice-A-Roni, drained artichokes, mayonnaise, curry powder, olives, peppers, and green onions. Add artichoke liquid and toss again. Serve on a bed of salad greens.

Italian Vegetable Salad

1 head cauliflower
1 bunch broccoli
1 pound carrots, sliced
1 pound fresh mushrooms

Seasoned salt
Accent
Dressing

Cut cauliflower and broccoli into bite-size flowerettes. Bring cauliflower, broccoli and carrots to a boil. Boil for 6 minutes. Drain vegetables and add mushrooms. Season lightly with seasoned salt and Accent.

Dressing

2 cloves garlic, minced
3/4 cup white wine vinegar
16 ounces Italian dressing

3/4 cup red or white wine
1 teaspoon crushed oregano

Combine garlic, white wine vinegar, Italian dressing, wine, and crushed oregano. Mix well. Pour over vegetables and leave overnight in the refrigerator.

Cold Vegetable Salad

16 ounces white corn, drained
17 ounces LeSeur peas, drained
16 ounces French style
  green beans, drained
16 ounces tiny limas, drained

1 small green pepper, sliced
1 small red onion, sliced
1 cup celery, chopped
2 ounces pimiento, chopped
  Dressing

Mix all ingredients.

Dressing

1 tablespoon water
1 teaspoon salt
1/2 teaspoon pepper

1 cup sugar
3/4 cup vinegar
1/2 cup oil

In saucepan, mix all ingredients and bring to a boil. Cool and pour over vegetables. Refrigerate.

French Dressing

10¾ ounces tomato soup
1 teaspoon salt
1 teaspoon pepper
1 teaspoon dry mustard
1 teaspoon paprika

1 teaspoon garlic salt
1 teaspoon onion salt
¾ cup sugar
¾ cup white vinegar
1½ cups oil

Combine all ingredients except oil in a blender. Add oil and blend well.

Piquant Salad Dressing

1 cup salad oil
3 tablespoons lemon juice
1 teaspoon sugar
1 teaspoon salt

2 teaspoons paprika
1 small onion, chopped
1 teaspoon dry mustard
1 clove garlic

Combine all ingredients in blender. Cover and blend well. Chill thoroughly. Stir before serving over salad. Yields 1⅓ cups.

"Sweet and spicy topping for garden salads."

Spinach Salad Dressing

1 cup salad oil
⅔ cup sugar
⅓ cup ketchup

¼ cup wine vinegar
1 tablespoon Worcestershire
1 small onion, finely grated

Mix all ingredients together. Pour over spinach salad.

Rainbow Parfait Salad

20 ounces pineapple chunks
1 cantaloupe
1 cup strawberries
1 cup blueberries (or other fruit), rinsed

1 cup cottage cheese
1/2 cup plain yogurt
3 tablespoons honey
1 tablespoon lemon peel, grated
4 thin lemon slices or sprigs of mint

Drain pineapple chunks well. Using a melonball scoop or teaspoon, cut cantaloupe into balls. Wash, hull, and slice strawberries; drain well. Combine cottage cheese, yogurt, honey, and lemon peel. In each tall parfait glass, spoon a layer of cottage cheese mixture. Layer cantaloupe balls, pineapple chunks, strawberry slices, and blueberries. Top with cottage cheese mixture and a pineapple chunk. Garnish glasses with lemon slices or mint, if desired. Serves 4.

"A healthy complement to any meal."

Ribbon Salad

3 ounces cherry gelatin
3 ounces lemon gelatin
1/4 cup pecans
1/2 cup sour cream

1/2 cup mayonnaise
3 ounces lime gelatin
1 cup crushed pineapple, drained

Mix cherry gelatin following instructions on package; pour into mold. Chill between layers. Mix lemon gelatin with pecans, sour cream, and mayonnaise. Place on top of cherry gelatin. Combine lime gelatin and pineapple. Place on top of lemon mixture. Refrigerate until well set. Turn out of mold.

Blueberry Salad Squares

2 cups hot water
6 ounces grape gelatin
16 ounces blueberries with juice

8¼ ounces crushed pineapple
Topping

Combine hot water, gelatin, blueberries, and pineapple. Pour into 9x13 dish. Chill until set.

Topping

4 ounces whipped topping
4 ounces cream cheese
½ cup sour cream

¼ cup confectioners sugar
½ teaspoon vanilla
½ cup pecans, chopped

Beat whipped topping, cream cheese, sour cream, confectioners sugar, vanilla, and pecans. Spread over congealed gelatin mixture. Refrigerate. Cut into squares and serve.

Strawberry Salad

8 ounces cream cheese, softened
¾ cup sugar
1 large can pineapple tidbits, drained
10 ounce package frozen strawberries, just thawed

½ cup nuts
2 bananas, sliced
1 12 ounce tub of whipped topping, thawed

Beat cream cheese and sugar together in bowl and set aside. Mix remaining ingredients and combine with cream cheese mixture. Put in paper baking cups and freeze. Makes approximately 15 individual cups.

"A great after-dinner dessert!"

Spicy Fruit Salad

32 ounces mixed fruit chunks
20 ounces pineapple chunks
1/2 cup red hots

1/2 cup white vinegar
1/2 tablespoon whole cloves

Drain fruit, reserving liquid. Place fruit in bowl. Combine liquid, red hots, vinegar, and cloves. Heat until candies dissolve. Cool mixture and pour over fruit. Cover and refrigerate overnight before serving.

Strawberry Salad Mold

1 cup water
15 1/2 ounces crushed pineapple
6 ounces cherry gelatin
1/2 cup pecans, chopped

3 bananas, mashed
2 1/2 cups fresh strawberries
with juice and sugar
8 ounces sour cream

Drain pineapple, reserving juice. Boil water and pineapple juice. Add gelatin and stir until dissolved. Combine pecans, bananas, and strawberries. Add to gelatin mixture. Stir and pour half of mixture into a mold. Refrigerate until set. Do not refrigerate remaining portion of mixture. Spread sour cream over top of gelatin mold. Add remainder of gelatin mixture and refrigerate until congealed. Unmold on a bed of lettuce and garnish with fresh strawberries.

Cranberry Salad

3 ounces strawberry gelatin
1 cup boiling water
1 cup jellied cranberry sauce

1/2 cup tart apples, chopped
1/2 cup celery, chopped
1/4 cup pecans, chopped

Dissolve gelatin in water and cool. Add cranberry sauce, apples, celery, and nuts. Chill until firm.

Festive Cranberry Mold

2⅓ cups water
2 cups fresh cranberries
¾ cup sugar
6 ounces lemon gelatin

8½ ounces crushed pineapple
¼ cup pecans, chopped
½ cup tokay grapes,
   halved and seeded

In a medium saucepan, combine water, cranberries, and sugar. Bring to a boil; reduce heat and simmer about 5 minutes or until berries pop. Add gelatin and stir until dissolved. Stir in undrained pineapple and chill until partially set. Fold in pecans and grapes. Turn into a 5 cup ring mold. Chill until firm. Garnish with fresh grapes and cranberries.

Grape Nut Whip

2 eggs, well beaten
½ cup sugar
2 tablespoons lemon juice
1 cup heavy cream, whipped
1 cup pineapple chunks
1 cup tokay (red) grapes, halved

1 cup green seedless
   grapes, halved
11 ounces Mandarin oranges
2 cups miniature marshmallows
½ cup slivered almonds

Combine eggs, sugar, and lemon juice in top of double boiler. Cook until slightly thickened. Remove from heat and cool. Fold in cream, pineapple, red and green grapes, mandarin oranges, marshmallows, and almonds. Chill 5 to 6 hours. Serves 12 as a salad or 8 as a dessert. More fruit may be added if desired.

"A traditional holiday favorite."

Hawaiian Pie

20 ounces crushed pineapple
¾ cup sugar
2 teaspoons flour
3 large bananas, sliced

1 cup coconut
½ cup pecans, chopped
2 pie shells, baked
   Whipped topping

Combine pineapple, sugar, and flour. Cook until thickened and then cool. Blend in bananas, coconut, and pecans. Divide mixture between 2 baked pie shells; refrigerate. To serve, top with a whipped topping.

Mandarin Orange Salad

22 ounces mandarin
   oranges, drained
20 ounces crushed
   pineapple, drained

8 ounces cottage cheese
6 ounces orange gelatin

Mix mandarin oranges, pineapple, cottage cheese, and orange gelatin together and chill. Serves 10.

"Can also be served as a dessert."

Peaches and Cream Salad

6 ounces peach gelatin
2 cups boiling water
15¼ ounces crushed pineapple

21 ounces peach pie filling
Topping

Dissolve gelatin in boiling water. Add pineapple and peach pie filling. Chill until set.

Topping

8 ounces cream cheese
½ pint sour cream
½ cup sugar

1 teaspoon vanilla
½ cup nuts, chopped

Combine cream cheese, sour cream, sugar, vanilla, and nuts. Spread over gelatin mixture. Refrigerate.

Pretzel Salad

2 cups pretzels, crushed
¾ cup margarine, melted
¼ cup sugar
1½ cups whipped topping
8 ounces cream cheese, softened

1 cup sugar
6 ounces strawberry gelatin
2 cups pineapple juice
20 ounces frozen strawberries, partially thawed

Mix and press pretzels, margarine, and sugar into a greased 9x13 pan. Bake at 350 for 10 minutes. Cool. Combine whipped topping, cream cheese, and cup of sugar. Spread on cooled pretzel crust and chill. Dissolve gelatin in hot pineapple juice. Add strawberries and pour on cream cheese layer. Refrigerate about 1 hour.

COASTAL
COOLERS

Beverages

Cold, Alcoholic
91 Amaretto Breeze
91 Batch of Bloody Marys
91 Bellinis
92 Best Ever Daiquiris
89 Bourbon Slush
92 Champagne Delight
92 Cranberry Rum Slush
85 Frosty Margaritas
84 Frozen Peach
       Berry Pizzazz
84 Fuzz Buzz
85 Homemade Kahlua
86 Lemon Berry Splash
87 Midori Cooler
87 Peach Champagne
       Punch
90 Simply Super Dessert Drink
87 Sparkling Wine Punch
90 Summer White Wine
84 Tangy Rum Delight
89 Tequila Slush
89 White Sangria

Cold, Non-Alcoholic
82 Christmas
       Cranberry Punch
85 Citrus Cooler
81 Cranberry Smoothie
82 Frosted Mocha Punch
83 Orange Macaroon
86 Orange Sour
86 Peach Frosty
79 Sparkling Lemonade
79 Spring Cooler
82 Strawberry Whip
81 Summer Slush
80 Sunshine Fruit Punch
81 Sunshine Shake

Hot, Alcoholic
88 Chalet Cafe
88 Farmer's Bishop
88 Hot Buttered Rum

Hot, Non-Alcoholic
80 French Hot Chocolate
83 Hot Cider Punch
80 Hot Spiced
       Cranberry Punch
90 Mocha Cocoa
83 Russian Tea

Sparkling Lemonade

1 12 ounce frozen lemonade,
   thawed in refrigerator
1 12 ounce frozen pink lemonade,
   thawed in refrigerator
1 2 liter bottle lemon-lime
   sparkling water, chilled
1 1 liter bottle ginger ale, chilled

1 750 ml bottle sparkling
   cider, chilled
1 28 ounce bottle club soda, chilled
   Ice cubes
   Orange slices
   Lime slices

Mix all ingredients, except fruit and ice cubes, in a large container. Transfer into a pitcher for serving. Add ice cubes and fruit slices for garnish. 22 cups

Spring Cooler

1½ cups sugar
1½ cups water
 4 3 inch sticks cinnamon
 6 whole cloves
 1 46 ounce can pineapple
    juice, chilled

2 cups orange juice
1 cup lemon juice
1 33.8 ounce bottle
   ginger ale, chilled
   Orange wedges
   Maraschino cherries

Combine sugar, water, cinnamon sticks, and cloves in a saucepan; bring to a boil. Reduce heat; simmer 30 minutes. Refrigerate 8 hours or overnight; discard spices. Combine sugar syrup and fruit juices; stir well. To serve, combine juice mixture with ginger ale; stir well. Serve over crushed ice. Place orange wedges and maraschino cherries on skewers and place in each glass. 3½ quarts

Sunshine Fruit Punch

1   6 ounce can frozen lemonade
1/2   6 ounce can frozen orange juice
2   46 ounce cans pineapple juice

2   small cans apricot juice
2   bottles ginger ale, chilled

Mix first four ingredients and chill. Just before serving, add ginger ale. Add a frozen fruit mold for that party touch.

French Hot Chocolate

4   squares semisweet chocolate
1/4   cup light corn syrup
1/2   teaspoon vanilla

4   cups milk
1   cup whipping cream

In double boiler, over hot, not boiling water, heat chocolate and syrup until melted and smooth, stirring occasionally. Cover and chill 30 minutes. Stir in vanilla. Heat milk over medium low heat until small bubbles form on the edge. DO NOT BOIL! Beat at medium low speed chocolate and cream until soft peaks form. Pour milk into mugs filled with whipped cream mixture. 8 servings

Hot Spiced Cranberry Punch

1/2   cup brown sugar, packed
1/2   teaspoon cloves
1/4   teaspoon cinnamon
1/8   teaspoon salt
16   ounces pineapple juice

1/2   cup water
1/4   teaspoon allspice
1/8   teaspoon nutmeg
1   quart cranberry juice

Combine sugar, water, spices, salt and bring to a boil. Add fruit juices and heat to boiling. Serve hot. Serves 16

Summer Slush

1 46 ounce can pineapple juice
2 6 ounce cans frozen lemonade
6 ounces lemon juice
2 envelopes powdered
   raspberry punch, unsweetened

4 cups sugar
1 package frozen raspberries
   Water

Mix all ingredients and add enough water to make 2 gallons. Freeze until "slush" consistency.

Sunshine Shake

2 quarts orange juice
1 cup instant dry milk
2 teaspoons sugar
2 teaspoons vanilla

2 8¼ ounce cans
   crushed pineapple, undrained
4 bananas, sliced

Combine all ingredients in container of electric blender; process until smooth. Chill before serving. 8 servings

Cranberry Smoothie

2 cups cranberry juice
1 8 ounce carton vanilla yogurt

1 pint fresh strawberries
1 banana, sliced

Combine half of all ingredients in container of electric blender; process until smooth. Repeat with remaining ingredients; combine mixtures. Pour into individual glasses. 4 cups

Strawberry Whip

½ cup strawberries, frozen
1 medium ripe banana
¾ cup skim milk

½ cup plain yogurt
½ teaspoon vanilla

Add ingredients to container of electric blender and process until smooth. 2 cups

Christmas Cranberry Punch

2 pints raspberry sherbet
2 cups orange juice
½ cup lemon juice
¾ cup sugar

1½ quarts cranberry juice cocktail
2 28 ounce bottles
   ginger ale, chilled

Soften 1 pint sherbet in a punch bowl. Blend in orange juice, lemon juice, and sugar, stirring until sugar dissolves. Add cranberry juice; refrigerate up to 5 hours. Just before serving, add ginger ale; mix well. Scoop remaining sherbet into balls and float on top of punch. Serves 30

Frosted Mocha Punch

1½ ounces instant coffee
2 cups hot water
1 cup sugar

4 quarts milk
2 quarts vanilla ice cream
2 quarts chocolate ice cream

Dissolve coffee and sugar in hot water. Cool. Add milk and ice creams. Serve. Serves 40

Russian Tea

3/4 cup sugar
1/3 cup dry lemonade mix
2/3 cup instant tea
1 teaspoon cinnamon

1/2 teaspoon ground cloves
1/2 teaspoon ginger
2 cups Tang
1/3 box of apricot jello

Mix ingredients and store in a clean, dry jar. Use 2 heaping teaspoons per cup of hot water.

Hot Cider Punch

2 cups water
1 tablespoon ground ginger
1 tablespoon ground nutmeg
6-10 whole cloves
6-10 whole allspice
3-4 2 inch sticks cinnamon

1/2 gallon apple cider
1 1/2 cups sugar
1 1/2 cups light brown sugar, firmly packed
1 large orange, sliced and each slice quartered

Combine water and spices in a large saucepan. Cover and bring to a boil. Boil 10 minutes. Add apple cider and sugar. Simmer over low heat for 10 minutes, stirring frequently. Stir in the orange slices during the last five minutes. Serve hot. May refrigerate and reheat to serve. Yields 5 pints.

Orange Macaroon

2 cups orange juice
2 cups ice, crushed
1/2 cup canned coconut cream

3/4 teaspoon almond extract
Whipped cream
Orange peel, shredded

In blender, combine orange juice, ice, coconut cream, and almond extract. Cover and blend. Serve in chilled glasses garnished with whipped cream and shredded orange peel. 4 servings

Frozen Peach Berry Pizzazz

1 cup frozen unsweetened
   peach slices
1 cup frozen unsweetened
   strawberries
1 cup peach schnapps
1 6 ounce can frozen strawberry
   daiquiri mix

1 6 ounce can frozen orange juice
1/2 cup vodka or rum
3 cups ice cubes
1 28 ounce bottle carbonated
   water, chilled
   Whole strawberries

In a large mixing bowl stir together peaches, frozen strawberries, schnapps, daiquiri mix, orange juice concentrate, and vodka or rum. Place half of the fruit mixture in a blender container. Cover and blend till combined. Add half of the ice cubes. Cover; blend till slushy. Pour into a 1 1/2 or 2 quart pitcher; add half of carbonated water. Repeat with remaining fruit mixture, ice cubes, and carbonated water in another pitcher. Garnish with whole strawberries. Serve punch immediately. 10 servings

Fuzz Buzz

1 6 ounce can frozen limeade
3/4 cup vodka
3 ounces peach schnapps

2 medium peaches,
   unpeeled and sliced
   Ice

Combine first 4 ingredients in container of electric blender and process until smooth. Gradually add ice until desired consistency is reached. 4 cups

Tangy Rum Delight

3 6 ounce cans limeade
2 1/4 cups white rum, chilled

1 2 liter bottle 7-Up, chilled
14 ounces club soda, chilled

Mix together in a punch bowl or pitcher. Add a fruited frozen ice ring or fruit frozen in ice cubes, if desired.

Homemade Kahlua

4 cups water
4 cups sugar
3/4 cup instant coffee

1 fifth vodka
1 vanilla bean

Boil water and sugar for 10 minutes. Cool. Add coffee and vodka. Using 2 empty fifth bottles place 1/2 of vanilla bean, cut fine, in each. Pour in liquid. Shake once a day for 3 weeks.

Citrus Cooler

1 1/2-2 cups sugar
2 1/2 cups water
1 46 ounce can pineapple juice
1 46 ounce can orange juice

1 1/2 cups lemon juice
1 1/2 quarts ginger ale or champagne
Pineapple wedges
Orange wedges

Combine sugar and water in saucepan. Bring to a boil, stirring until sugar dissolves. Pour mixture into 4 1/2 quart freezer container. Stir in fruit juices. Freeze until firm. Remove from freezer 1 1/2-2 hours before serving. Mixture should be slushy. Stir in ginger ale or champagne. Garnish with pineapple and orange wedges. 5 1/2 quarts

Frosty Margaritas

1/4 cup plus 2 tablespoons tequila
3 tablespoons Triple Sec
2 tablespoons sweet and sour beverage mix

1 6 ounce can frozen limeade, thawed
4 cups ice cubes

Combine first 4 ingredients in container of electric blender; process until smooth. Gradually add ice, processing until mixture reaches desired consistency. Serve immediately. 1 quart

Lemon Berry Splash

1 bottle rose wine, chilled
2 28 ounce bottles
  ginger ale, chilled

1 lemon, sliced
1 pint strawberries, washed,
  with caps left on

Mix wine and ginger ale in a punch bowl. Add the lemon slices and strawberries, stirring carefully.

Orange Sour

1 cup orange juice
3/4 cup apricot nectar
1 9/16 ounce envelope
  instant whiskey sour drink mix

1/2 cup ice, crushed
  Orange slices
  Maraschino cherries

In blender, combine orange juice, apricot nectar, drink mix, and ice. Process 15 seconds. Pour over ice in 2 tall glasses. Garnish with orange slices and cherries, if desired. 2 servings

Peach Frosty

1 8 1/2 ounce can unsweetened
  sliced peaches, drained
2 cups orange juice
1 pint vanilla ice milk

1/4 cup plain yogurt
1/8 teaspoon cinnamon
1/8 teaspoon nutmeg

Add ingredients to container of electric blender and process until smooth. 5 cups

Peach Champagne Punch

1 16 ounce can sliced peaches
   in light syrup, chilled
1 pint strawberries
1 cup peach-flavored
   brandy, chilled

1 2 liter bottle
   lemon-lime soda, chilled
2 bottles champagne, chilled

Drain peaches; reserve syrup. Place peach slices and strawberries in the compartments of ice cube trays, fill with water and freeze until solid. Just before serving, combine in large punch bowl reserved peach syrup, brandy, soda, and champagne; stir. Add fruit ice cubes and serve. About 32 servings

Sparkling Wine Punch

2 bottles champagne, chilled
1 bottle sparkling cider, chilled
1 liter bottle ginger ale, chilled

4 cups white grape juice, chilled
1 liter bottle orange-flavored
   sparkling water

Mix all ingredients in a 7-8 quart punch bowl and serve. Add a fruited ice ring for a decorative touch. 22 servings

Midori Cooler

¼ cup Midori liqueur
¼ cup vodka
¼ cup pineapple juice
¼ cup orange juice
1 cup ginger ale

Crushed ice
Watermelon or
honeydew melon balls
Fresh mint sprigs

Combine first 5 ingredients; stir well. Pour over crushed ice. Garnish with melon balls and mint sprigs.

Chalet Cafe

1½ cups hot coffee
2 ounces brandy
⅛ teaspoon allspice

⅛ teaspoon cinnamon
Whipped cream
Freshly ground nutmeg

Combine coffee, brandy, allspice, and cinnamon. Pour into mugs. Top with whipped cream. Sprinkle with nutmeg. 2 servings

Hot Buttered Rum

1 pound butter, softened
1 pound light brown sugar
1 pound powdered sugar
2 teaspoons nutmeg

2 teaspoons cinnamon
1 quart vanilla ice cream, softened
Hot water
Rum

Combine butter, sugars, and spices. Beat until light and fluffy. Add ice cream. Spoon into a 2 quart container and freeze. To serve, spoon 3 tablespoons of mixture into each mug. Add hot water and rum to taste. 25 cups

Farmer's Bishop

2 quarts apple cider
2 2 inch cinnamon sticks
1 orange, cut into ½ inch thick slices

24 whole cloves
1½ cups apple schnapps
1½ cups brandy

In a large saucepan, combine apple cider and cinnamon sticks. Heat until almost boiling. Pour into a 4 quart heat-proof bowl. Stud orange slices with cloves and float on top of cider. In small saucepan heat schnapps and brandy until warmed. Do not boil. Ignite liquor with a match and pour slowly into bowl. Ladle into warmed mugs. 20 servings

Tequila Slush

4½ cups water
2 6 ounce cans frozen
   limeade, thawed
1 6 ounce can frozen
   orange juice, thawed

¾ cup lime juice
1 28 ounce bottle grapefruit soda
1 cup tequila

Combine first 4 ingredients, mixing well; stir in soda and tequila. Pour mixture into a freezer container; freeze overnight or until firm. Remove from freezer 30 minutes before serving. Stir until slushy. Yields 3 quarts.

White Sangria

1 cup sugar
1½ cups water
1 cup orange juice
½ cup brandy
1 orange, sliced

1 lime, sliced
1 cup honeydew melon balls
1 cup cantaloupe balls
3¼ cups dry white wine, chilled

Mix sugar and water in large pitcher until sugar is dissolved. Add other ingredients, except wine, and let stand 2 hours before serving. Add chilled wine and serve over ice.

Bourbon Slush

1 6 ounce can frozen limeade
¾ cup bourbon

1-2 tablespoons honey
   Cracked ice

Add first 3 ingredients to container of electric blender. Add ice until container is about three-quarters full and blend until smooth.

Simply Super Dessert Drink

1 cup whipping cream
1 cup Kahlua
1/2 cup creme de cacao
1/2 cup Amaretto

1 teaspoon Galliano
2 teaspoons instant coffee granules
8 ice cubes
Shaved chocolate

Combine first 7 ingredients in container of electric blender; process until smooth.
Serve in chilled champagne glasses. Garnish with shaved chocolate,
if desired. 4 cups

Summer White Wine

1 bottle dry white wine, chilled
1 orange, washed and quartered
1 lemon, washed and quartered
2 peaches, peeled, pitted,
and quartered

5-6 large whole strawberries
1 small piece cucumber skin
2 tablespoons sugar
2 cups carbonated water, chilled

Pour wine into 2 quart pitcher. Add fruit and cucumber skin. Stir in sugar. Just before
serving add carbonated water and ice cubes, if desired. Stir very gently.

Mocha Cocoa

3 tablespoons sugar
3 tablespoons cocoa
3 tablespoons instant coffee
1/2 cup water

1 3 inch stick cinnamon
6 1/2 cups skim milk
1 teaspoon vanilla
Additional cinnamon sticks

Combine first 5 ingredients in a large saucepan. Cook over medium heat, stirring
constantly, until mixture comes to a boil. Add milk and vanilla; cook until
thoroughly heated. Serve each cup with a cinnamon stick. 7 servings

Amaretto Breeze

1 quart vanilla ice cream
¼ cup brandy

¼ cup Amaretto

Combine all ingredients in container of electric blender; process until smooth. Serve immediately. 4¼ cups

Batch of Bloody Marys

1 fifth of vodka
2 large cans of V-8 juice
  Juice of 4 limes
⅓ cup plus 4 teaspoons
  Worcestershire sauce

30 shakes celery salt
 8 teaspoons Texas Pete,
   or 4 teaspoons Tabasco

Mix all of the ingredients and stir. Serves 40.

Bellinis

6 cups sliced fresh or
  frozen peaches
2 cups apricot nectar

6-7 cups champagne, chilled
    Lime slices

Combine half of peaches and half of apricot nectar in container of electric blender. Blend until smooth. Repeat procedure with remaining peaches and nectar. Freeze. Remove frozen mixture about 30 minutes before serving. Use a spoon or an ice cream scoop to put mixture in stemmed glasses. Add cold champagne. Garnish with a twist or slice of lime.

Champagne Delight

1 pint raspberry sherbet, softened
¼ cup plus 2 tablespoons cognac

1 25.4 ounce bottle
   champagne, chilled

Spoon about ⅓ cup sherbet into each of 6 champagne glasses. Add 1 tablespoon cognac to each; stir well. Slowly fill each glass with champagne; stir gently. Serve immediately. 6 servings

Cranberry Rum Slush

1 12 ounce can frozen
   cranberry juice
1½ cups rum

Juice of 1 lemon
About 8 cups ice, crushed

Combine half of first 3 ingredients in container of electric blender; process until smooth. Gradually add ice and blend until right consistency is reached. Be careful not to add too much ice which dilutes the taste. Repeat with the remaining half of ingredients. 7 cups

Best Ever Daiquiris

2 6 ounce cans frozen
   limeade, thawed
1 6 ounce can frozen
   lemonade, thawed
4½ cups rum

4½ cups water
1 teaspoon sweetened
   reconstituted lime juice
   Lime slices

Combine all ingredients, except lime slices, in a large container. Cover and freeze 12 hours or overnight. To serve, place 3-4 cups frozen mixture in blender. Blend until smooth. Serve immediately. Garnish with lime slices. Store remaining mixture in freezer until needed.

MAIN
SAILS

Main Dishes

Crab and Spinach Casserole

1 package frozen
   spinach, chopped
1 cup sharp cheese, grated
1/4 cup butter plus 2 tablespoons
   butter, melted
2 tablespoons onion, minced
2 tablespoons flour

1 cup milk
1/8 teaspoon curry powder
1/2 teaspoon salt
1 tablespoon lemon juice
1 pound crabmeat
1/2 cup bread crumbs

Cook spinach and drain well. Put in the bottom of a greased casserole dish. Sprinkle cheese over spinach. Melt 1/4 cup butter and saute onions until transparent. Melt the remaining 2 tablespoons of butter and stir in flour. Add milk, stirring constantly, until thickened. Add curry powder and salt. Stir lemon juice and crabmeat into sauce. Pour over spinach and cheese. Add bread crumbs on top. Bake at 350 for 30 minutes.

Crab-Artichoke Bake

2 cups fresh crabmeat
2 cans artichoke hearts, drained;
   or 2 frozen packages, cooked
1 cup Swiss cheese, grated
2 cups cheddar cheese, grated
1/2 cup green pepper, chopped
1/2 cup onion, chopped

4 teaspoons lemon juice
   Salt and pepper
1 can cream of celery
   or chicken soup
   Bread crumbs
   Parmesan cheese

Blend ingredients except bread crumbs and Parmesan cheese. Fold into a well greased 4-quart casserole. Top with bread crumbs mixed with Parmesan cheese. Bake until bubbly, about 30-35 minutes, in a preheated 375 oven.

Crabmeat and Broccoli Casserole

1 bunch fresh *or* 1 package
  frozen broccoli
½ pound fresh *or* 1 package
  frozen crabmeat, flaked
  and shells removed
½ pint sour cream

¼ cup chili sauce
1 small onion, chopped fine
1 cup sharp cheddar cheese, grated
2 tablespoons fresh lemon juice
1 tablespoon lemon peel, grated
  Salt and pepper

Cook broccoli until tender and break into small pieces. Mix with other ingredients. Pour into a small, shallow, buttered casserole. Bake in a 350 oven about 20 minutes or until cheese is melted and top is browned. This can be made early in the day, or the day before, and refrigerated.

Crab Imperial

1 tablespoon butter
1 tablespoon flour
1 cup milk
  Salt and pepper
16 ounces backfin crabmeat
  (well picked to remove shells)

1 tablespoon mayonnaise
½ teaspoon Worcestershire sauce
1 lemon, juiced
  Bread crumbs
  Butter

In a small saucepan, melt butter and stir in flour. Add milk, salt, and pepper and simmer over medium-low heat until thickened. Cool. Combine white sauce with crabmeat. Add mayonnaise, Worcestershire sauce, and juice of 1 lemon. Mix well and spoon into large scallop shells (for individual servings) or a casserole dish. Cover with buttered bread crumbs. Bake in 350 oven until top browns and heated to taste.

"Scallop shells for individual servings are often found in gift shops featuring 'beachy' items."

Crab Mornay

1 onion, minced
7 tablespoons butter
4 tablespoons flour
1½ cups half and half
1 cup chicken stock

¾ teaspoon salt
3 egg yolks
1 pound crabmeat
¼ cup Parmesan cheese
   Puff pastry shells

Preheat oven to 350. Lightly saute onion in 4 tablespoons butter until translucent, but do not brown. Stir in flour and heat until bubbly. Whisk in 1 cup half and half, chicken stock, and ¼ teaspoon salt, stirring until mixture is smooth. Simmer 3 minutes. Remove from heat. In bowl, mix egg yolks with remaining ½ cup half and half. Stir into hot mixture along with remaining 3 tablespoons butter and ½ teaspoon salt. Gently fold in crabmeat. Pour mixture into greased 1½ quart casserole dish. Sprinkle with Parmesan cheese. Bake 45 minutes or until lightly browned. Serve in cooked pastry shells.

Hot Stuffed Avocados with Crab

2 tablespoons green
   onions, minced
3 tablespoons butter, melted
3 tablespoons flour
½ cup milk

12 ounces crabmeat
1 tablespoon lemon juice
1 teaspoon salt
2 avocados

Saute onions and butter until tender. Blend in flour. Add milk and cook over low heat until thick and bubbly, stirring constantly. Stir in crab, lemon juice, and salt and set aside. Cut avocados in half. Carefully remove pulp to within ¼ inch of edge. Reserve shells. Chop pulp and stir into crab mixture. Spoon crab mixture into shells and bake at 325 for 20 minutes. You may sprinkle ½ cup grated cheddar cheese on top. May be made the night before if you brush the avocados with lemon juice.

"Scrumptious!!"

Creamed Crab

½ cup butter
1 small bunch of green
  onions, chopped
½ cup parsley, chopped
2 tablespoons flour
1 pint cream

½ pound Swiss cheese, grated
1 tablespoon sherry
  Red pepper
1 pound white crabmeat
  Pastry shells

Melt butter and saute onions over low heat with parsley. Blend in flour. Add cream, cheese, sherry, and red pepper, stirring until cheese melts. Add crabmeat and mix well. Serve hot over pastry shells as a main dish, or serve from chafing dish with toast points as an hors d'oeuvre.

Gourmet Seafood

2 large onions, chopped
1 green pepper, chopped
¾ cup celery, chopped
  Butter
1 can cream of celery soup
1 can cream of mushroom soup
1 box frozen green peas, cooked
  2 minutes, optional
2 cups cooked rice

2 cups cooked Uncle Ben's wild rice
2 cups half and half
2 pounds crabmeat
1 pound shrimp
  Pepper
2 tablespoons sherry, optional
2 cups cheddar cheese, grated
  Sliced almonds

Saute onions, green peppers, and celery in butter. Add celery soup, mushrooms soup, peas, rice, wild rice, half and half, crabmeat, shrimp, pepper, and sherry. Mix well. Pour into 13x9 casserole. Sprinkle with cheddar cheese and almonds. Bake at 350° for 35 minutes or until hot and bubbly.

May substitute chicken for part of crabmeat. If so, add 1 can cream of shrimp soup and use only 1 cup half and half.

Soft Shell Crab Batter

2 cups self-rising flour
2 eggs, beaten
1/2 cup cornstarch

Salt, pepper, and garlic
Beer, enough to thin batter

Mix all ingredients together except beer. Add beer just before you are ready to dip crabs. Fry in large skillet in about 1 1/2 inches of oil. Be sure oil is very hot and crabs are dry and cleaned. Enough batter for 20-30 crabs.

Soft Shell Crab Sauce

1 tablespon onion, finely chopped
1 cup mayonnaise
   Juice of 1 lime
   Juice of 1/2 lemon

1 tablespoon horseradish
   Tabasco or Texas Pete
   Worcestershire sauce

Mix all ingredients and chill well. Serve in small individual containers on each plate or pass in larger serving bowl to accompany fried soft shell crabs.

Crab with Smithfield Ham

2 pounds crabmeat
1/4 cup butter, melted
   Lemon juice

1/2 pound Smithfield ham,
   thinly sliced
12 ounces Swiss cheese, sliced

Put crab in 9x13 baking dish. Pour melted butter on top. Sprinkle with lemon juice. Spread Smithfield ham slices on top and then layer with Swiss cheese slices. Bake at 350 for 30 minutes. Serves 8.

Grandma Lindsey's Crab Cakes

1 pound crabmeat
1 egg
1 medium onion, chopped
1 cup or less saltine
   crackers, crushed
1/2 teaspoon black pepper

1/4 teaspoon salt
1/2 teaspoon dry mustard *or*
   1/2 teaspoon prepared mustard
1/2 teaspoon fresh parsley, chopped
   or 1 teaspoon dry parsley
1 tablespoon mayonnaise

Mix together all ingredients and form into patties. Broil until brown or pan fry in margarine until brown.

Microwave Fish Fillets

1 pound flounder fillets
1 can cream of shrimp soup
1 can small shrimp

1/2 cup Swiss cheese, shredded
1/3 cup white wine (or milk)
   Pepper

Roll up fish fillets and secure with toothpicks. Combine soup, shrimp, cheese, pepper, and wine and pour over the fillets. Microwave for 8 to 10 minutes on medium. Serve with rice.

"By rolling fillets, they cook evenly."

Dill Sauce

1 cup sour cream
3/4 cup mayonnaise
1 tablespoon dried parsley flakes

1 tablespoon dried onion flakes
1 teaspoon dill weed
1 teaspoon seasoned salt

Mix together all ingredients and refrigerate for several hours before using. Serve as a sauce for broiled fish. This will keep in the refrigerator for approximately 2 weeks.

Fish Fillets with Lynnhaven Sauce

Flounder, grouper, orange
roughy, trout fillets or fish
of preference

Lynnhaven Sauce

Put fillets in shallow baking dish. Spread prepared sauce over fillets to cover. Broil
10 minutes; then bake at 350 for 15-20 minutes.

Lynnhaven Sauce

1/2 cup mayonnaise
1 tablespoon Old Bay Seasoning

1/2 teaspoon thyme
2 teaspoons horseradish

Mix sauce ingredients well.

*Lynnhaven Sauce is from Anchor Inn Restaurant.

Orange Roughy

1 large bell pepper, cubed
1 large onion, cubed
1/2 cup olive oil
1-1 1/2 pounds orange roughy
Garlic powder

Seafood seasoning
Crushed pepper
Melted butter, plus
2 drops lemon juice

Saute pepper and onion in olive oil over high heat. When bubbling, turn to
medium. Push vegetables to side of pan and put fish in center of pan. Cook
4-5 minutes and turn. Add seasonings and cook 4-5 additional minutes or until fish
flakes with a fork. Place fish and vegetables on a platter and drizzle
with lemon butter.

Flounder with Butter Sauce

3 tablespoons flour
1/2 teaspoon salt
1/8 teaspoon white pepper
1/8 teaspoon ground mace
6 fresh flounder fillets

1/4 cup butter
1 tablespoon vegetable oil
Chopped parsley
Butter Sauce

Combine first 4 ingredients in a bowl. Dredge each fillet in flour mixture. Melt oil and butter in pan over medium heat. Saute fillets on both sides until lightly browned and flakes with a fork. Place on warm serving platter and top with butter sauce and parsley.

Butter Sauce

2 shallots, minced
1/2 cup white wine
2 teaspoons white wine vinegar

1/2 cup butter, softened
Salt
Pepper

Combine shallots, wine, and vinegar in small saucepan. Cook over medium heat until reduced to 3 tablespoons. Add butter, 1 tablespoon at a time, and whisk over low heat until sauce thickens. Add salt and pepper to taste. Serve over warm fish fillets.

Flounder-Scallop Bake

1/2 pound flounder, skinned
1 pound scallops
Butter
1 small onion, chopped

1/2 green pepper, chopped
1 pound fresh mushrooms, sliced
6 ounces sharp cheddar cheese, grated

Place skinned flounder in a 6x6 glass dish. Layer with scallops. Dot butter over scallops. Layer onion, green pepper, and mushrooms over scallops. Top with cheese. Bake 45 minutes, uncovered, at 350. Serves 2-3.

Baked Flounder with Mornay Sauce

4 pounds flounder fillets
1 cup crabmeat
2 tablespoons bacon fat
1 onion, chopped fine
1 shallot, chopped
2 garlic cloves, minced
2 tablespoons celery, chopped

2 tablespoons green
    pepper, chopped
1 tablespoon salt
1/2 teaspoon pepper
1 egg
3/4 cup bread crumbs
    Mornay Sauce

Butter shallow dish 1½ inches deep. Cover bottom with half of flounder. Mix all ingredients for crab filling and place generous portion on top of fish. Cover with remaining fish.

Mornay Sauce

3 tablespoons butter
3 tablespoons flour
1 cup chicken stock

1/2 cup light cream
1/4 cup Swiss cheese, grated

Melt margarine in a saucepan. Blend in flour and slowly add chicken stock and cream, stirring constantly. Bring to boil, lower heat, and simmer 5 minutes. Add cheese and cook until melted. Pour sauce over fish. Bake at 375 for 30 minutes or until fish is tender.

Tuna Steaks

Tuna steaks, 1-1¼ inch thick
1 bottle Italian dressing

1/2 cup soy sauce
    Oregano (optional)

Mix dressing and soy sauce. Marinate tuna steaks in mixture for 2-3 hours, turning occasionally, keeping refrigerated. Grill over charcoals, basting with marinade mixture. Sprinkle with small amount of oregano, if desired, and serve. May substitute swordfish or chicken for tuna.

"The whole family will love this dish!"

Quick and Easy Maryland Fried Fish

½ pound pan-dressed fish or
    ⅓ pound fish fillets, per person
    Salt
    Lemon and pepper seasoning

1-2 cups dry pancake mix
     Fat or oil for frying

Wash and dry fish. Dip fish into clean, cool water; sprinkle lightly with salt and lemon and pepper seasoning. Then coat lightly with pancake mix. Fry in deep fat at 350 for 4-5 minutes, or fry in 1½ inches hot fat in fry pan, 4-5 minutes on each side. (Fish is done when browned on both sides and flakes easily when tested with a fork. Be careful not to overcook.) Remove fish from pan and drain on paper towels. Serve with cocktail or tartar sauce. Note: If desired, fish may be pan-fried over medium to low heat, in just enough fat or oil to keep from sticking, until done as described above.

Bluefish Mull

2 large bluefish fillets
5-6 potatoes, cubed to
     1½ inch pieces
1 stalk celery, cubed to
   1 inch pieces

1 onion, chopped
1 large can V-8 juice

Clean and skin 2 large bluefish fillets. In a deep metal pan, place potatoes, celery, and onion. Place fillets on top of vegetables. Pour V-8 juice over all ingredients. Cover with foil, cook at 450 for 45 minutes or until potatoes are tender. Remove foil and continue to cook for 5-10 minutes to dry fish.

"Even non-bluefish eaters will love this one!"

Shrimp-Stuffed Fish Rollups

14 fresh or frozen shrimp,
cooked and peeled
1 small onion, minced
1 clove garlic, crushed
2 tablespoons butter, melted
1/4 cup soft bread crumbs
1 tablespoon fresh
parsley, chopped

1/2 teaspoon salt
1/8 teaspoon pepper
6-8 sole or flounder fillets
(about 1 1/2 pounds)
1/4 cup butter, melted
Blender Hollandaise Sauce

Chop 8 shrimp and set aside. Reserve remainder for garnish. Saute onion and garlic in 2 tablespoons butter until tender. Add chopped shrimp, bread crumbs, parsley, salt, and pepper. Mix well and remove from heat. Divide mixture evenly and spread over fillets. Roll up each fillet and secure with a wooden toothpick. Pour half of remaining butter into a 10x6x2 baking dish. Add fillets to dish and brush with remaining butter. Bake at 350 for 25-30 minutes or until fish flakes with a fork. Remove fillets to serving dish. Top with blender Hollandaise sauce and garnish with reserved shrimp. Serves 6.

Blender Hollandaise Sauce

3 egg yolks
2 tablespoons lemon juice

Dash of salt and pepper
1/2 cup butter, melted

Combine all ingredients except butter in blender pitcher. Set on high and process until thick and lemon colored. Turn blender to low and add butter in a slow steady stream. Turn to high and process until thick. Yields 3/4 cup.

Lobster Casserole

2 tablespoons butter
2 tablespoons flour
1/2 teaspoon salt
1/8 teaspoon pepper
1 cup milk
   Dash of nutmeg
1/2 teaspoon paprika
2 egg yolks, slightly beaten

1 cup sharp cheddar
   cheese, shredded
2 6 ounce cans button
   mushrooms, drained
1 pound lobster meat,
   canned or fresh
2 tablespoons sherry

Combine butter, flour, salt, pepper, and milk. Cook until thickened. Add nutmeg and paprika. Add egg yolks and cook about 3 minutes. Add 1/2 cup cheese, mushrooms, lobster, and sherry. Place in a greased 1 1/2 quart casserole. Sprinkle remaining cheese over top. Bake at 350 for 45 minutes or until cheese is melted and bubbly.

Oyster Pie

1 pint oysters
1/2 cup celery, diced
1/2 cup green pepper, diced
4 tablespoons butter
5 tablespoons flour

1 3/4 cups milk
1 teaspoon salt
1/8 teaspoon pepper
2 tablespoons pimientos, chopped
   Pastry

Cook oysters in their liquor for about 5 minutes or until edges begin to curl. Drain. Cook celery and green pepper in butter until tender. Blend in flour; add milk. Cook until thick, stirring constantly. Add oysters, seasonings, and pimientos. Pour into casserole and top with pastry. Bake for about 15 minutes or until crust is brown in 425 oven. Serves 6.

Scalloped Oysters

1 pint oysters
2 cups medium coarse
  cracker crumbs
1/2 cup butter or margarine, melted
1/2 teaspoon salt

Pepper
3/4 cup light cream
1/4 cup oyster liquor
1/4 teaspoon Worcestershire sauce

Drain oysters, reserving 1/4 cup liquor. Combine crumbs, butter, and salt. Spread 1/3 of the crumbs in greased loaf pan. Cover with half the oysters. Sprinkle with pepper. Using another 1/3 of the crumbs, spread second layer. Cover with remaining oysters. Sprinkle with pepper. Combine cream, oyster liquor, and Worcestershire sauce. Pour over the oysters. Top with remainder of crumbs. Bake at 350 about 40 minutes.

"Very tasty!"

Creamy Scallops and Mushrooms

1/2 pound fresh mushrooms, sliced
1 medium onion, sliced
4 tablespoons butter or margarine
1 pound fresh scallops
1/4 cup dry sherry

1/4 cup all purpose flour
1 cup half and half
1/2 teaspoon salt
1/8 teaspoon white pepper
4 frozen patty shells, baked

Saute mushrooms and onion in 1 tablespoon butter until tender. Add scallops and sherry and bring to a boil. Reduce heat and simmer, uncovered, 8 minutes, stirring occasionally. Melt remaining 3 tablespoons butter in a medium saucepan over low heat. Add flour, stirring until smooth. Cook 1 minute, stirring constantly. Gradually add half and half. Cook over medium heat, stirring constantly, until mixture is thickened and bubbly. Stir in salt and pepper. Partially drain scallops and mushrooms and add to sauce, stirring gently. Cook uncovered, just until heated. Spoon mixture into patty shells.

Scallops Imperial

1 pound sea scallops, not
  bay scallops
  Flour
  Butter
  Salt and pepper to taste

1 small onion, finely minced
1 carrot, shredded
1-2 ounces gin
2-3 ounces heavy cream

Cut scallops in half, if necessary, to make all approximately same size. Dredge in flour and remove excess flour with fingers. Saute scallops in butter. Add salt and pepper. Remove scallops from pan and brown onion and carrot in same pan. Return scallops to pan and heat. Add gin and boil a few minutes. Add cream and heat thoroughly.

"Excellent taste and appearance!"

Seafood Brochettes

6 medium shrimp, shelled
  and deveined
3/4 pound scallops
12 cherry tomatoes

1 large green pepper, cut in
  1 inch pieces and blanched
  for 3 minutes
1/2 pound fresh pineapple wedges
1 medium onion, cut in 6 wedges

Marinade

1/2 cup dry sherry
2 tablespoons sesame seed oil
1 tablespoon sesame seed, crushed

1 garlic clove, chopped
1/4 teaspoon black pepper
2 tablespoons ginger

Combine all ingredients for marinade in a shallow bowl. Coat shrimp and scallops and let stand at room temperature for 30 minutes. Drain, reserving the marinade. Thread the skewers, alternating with vegetables and pineapple. Broil on grill 8-10 minutes. Turn several times and brush often with reserved marinade. Serve with cooked rice.

Barbecued Shrimp

2 pounds fresh jumbo shrimp, in shell
1 cup olive or vegetable oil
1 cup dry sherry

1 cup soy sauce
1 clove garlic, mashed
Butter Sauce

Combine all ingredients and marinate in the refrigerator for 3-4 hours. Shell and devein shrimp and cook over a hot charcoal fire for 2-3 minutes per side or until just barely cooked. Serve with Butter Sauce.

Butter Sauce

1/2 pound butter
Juice of 1 lemon
1/2 teaspoon salt

1 tablespoon Worcestershire sauce
1 tablespoon soy sauce
3-4 dashes Tabasco sauce

Melt butter in small saucepan, add remaining ingredients, and keep warm.

"The best you'll ever eat!!"

Linguine with White Clam and Shrimp Sauce

4 tablespoons oil
2 cloves garlic, diced
1 large onion, diced
1 tablespoon dried parsley flakes

8 large fresh clams, diced, juice reserved
1 pound medium shrimp, cleaned
1 pound linguine, cooked

Heat oil in deep frying pan over medium heat. Add garlic and saute one minute. Add onion and saute 3 to 5 minutes until onion appears translucent. Add parsley and diced clams with juice. Cook over medium-low heat about 4 minutes. Add shrimp and cook just until pink, about one minute. Remove from heat. Do not overcook shrimp. Serve over cooked linguine. Serves 6.

Herbed Shrimp with Basil Mayonnaise

2 pounds shrimp
3/4 cup olive oil
1 tablespoon parsley, minced
2 garlic cloves, crushed

1 teaspoon salt
1/2 teaspoon oregano
Pepper
2 tablespoons lemon juice

Rinse shrimp. With scissors, slit on underside and devein shrimp. Do not shell shrimp. Using six 10 or 12 inch skewers, thread each shrimp at the wide end, then curl shrimp into rounds; secure through tail ends. Arrange skewers in long shallow dish. Combine oil, parsley, garlic, salt, oregano, pepper, and lemon juice in small bowl. Pour over shrimp. Allow shrimp skewers to marinate 2-3 hours. Grill or broil shrimp for 3 minutes each side. Serve on skewers or remove and arrange on platter. Serve with basil mayonnaise.

Basil Mayonnaise

1 cup mayonnaise
2 cups basil leaves or
    4 tablespoons dried basil
1 garlic clove, crushed

1/2 teaspoon salt
Pepper
1 teaspoon lemon juice

Whisk all ingredients together. This sauce can be refrigerated 7 days.

Shrimp in a Shell

1 stick butter
1 pound jumbo shrimp
1 teaspoon garlic powder

1/4 cup soy sauce
1/8 cup sherry or sake

Melt butter in large fry pan or wok. Add shrimp in shell to butter and stir fry until red on both sides. Add remaining ingredients. Turn heat to low. Cover and cook for 5 minutes. Peel and eat using sauce to dip.

Malay Shrimp

2 tablespoons green onion, sliced
1 small clove garlic, minced
2 teaspoons cooking oil
3/4 cup chicken broth
3 tablespoons peanut butter
1 tablespoon soy sauce
1/2 teaspoon lemon peel,
   finely shredded

1 tablespoon lemon juice
1 teaspoon chili powder
1/2 teaspoon brown sugar
1/4 teaspoon ground ginger
1 pound (20-21) large
   shrimp, uncooked

Cook onion and garlic in hot oil until tender, but not brown. Stir in broth, peanut butter, soy sauce, lemon peel, lemon juice, chili powder, brown sugar, and ginger. Simmer, uncovered, about 10 minutes, stirring frequently. Remove from heat and cool. Peel shrimp, leaving tail attached, and devein. Marinate shrimp in peanut mixture at room temperature for 1 hour. Turn to coat shrimp well. Drain shrimp, reserving peanut mixture. Thread shrimp onto 4 bamboo skewers. Grill over hot coals for 8-10 minutes or until done. Reserved peanut mixture may be used for basting or heated and served as a sauce.

"Nice change of pace!"

Shrimp in Mustard Cream Sauce

1 pound large shrimp
2 tablespoons salad oil
1 shallot, minced
3 tablespoons dry white wine

1/2 cup heavy or whipping cream
1 tablespoon Dijon mustard
   with seeds
Salt

Shell and devein shrimp. Over medium heat, heat oil in 10-inch skillet and cook shallot 5 minutes, stirring often. Increase heat to medium-high. Add shrimp and cook 5 minutes or until shrimp turn pink, stirring often. With slotted spoon, remove shrimp to bowl. To drippings in skillet, add wine and cook 2 minutes. Add cream and mustard and cook an additional 2 minutes. Return shrimp to skillet and stir until heated thoroughly. Add salt to taste.

Shrimp and Feta in Casserole

4 dozen medium shrimp, peeled
  and deveined
  Melted butter
  Garlic
  Shrimp Sauce

Feta cheese
4 individual ovenproof
  au gratin casseroles
  Scallions, chopped

Blanch shrimp slightly in melted butter and garlic for approximately 1-2 minutes. Shrimp will be barely pink. Set aside. Prepare shrimp sauce (below).

Divide shrimp into 4 individual ovenproof casseroles. Cover generously with sauce and crumble feta cheese generously on top. Bake at 450 for 20 minutes or until sauce is bubbly. Finish quickly under broiler to slightly brown cheese. Garnish with chopped scallions. Serve immediately.

Shrimp Sauce

1/3 pound butter
1/2 ounce fresh garlic
2 tablespoons Madeira
1/2 teaspoon leaf oregano
1/2 teaspoon leaf basil
1 tablespoon tarragon vinegar
3/4 cup very good
  commercial marinara sauce

1 ounce grated Parmesan cheese
2 egg yolks
1/2 tablespoon roux (mixture
  of flour and butter of
  equal amounts, thickened)

Use a 3 quart saucepan and slowly simmer butter, garlic, wine, oregano, and basil over very low heat just until hot; do not boil nor let butter separate. Add vinegar and marinara sauce and bring back to a slight simmer. Add egg yolks and Parmesan cheese. Stir with wire whisk. Add roux and stir until sauce barely bubbles. Remove from heat.

Shrimp Linguine

4½ cups water
1½ pounds shrimp, unpeeled,
    medium-size, and fresh
  1 16 ounce package linguine
    (use fresh, if possible)
  1 6 ounce package frozen
    snow peas, thawed and drained
  6 green onions, chopped
  4 medium tomatoes, peeled,
    chopped, and drained

¾ cup olive oil
¼ cup fresh parsley, chopped
⅓ cup wine vinegar
  1 teaspoon dried whole oregano
1½ teaspoons dried whole basil
½ teaspoon garlic salt
½ teaspoon ground black pepper

Bring water to a boil, add shrimp, and cook 3-5 minutes. (Do not overcook.) Drain, rinse, chill, peel, and devein shrimp. Cook linguine according to directions, but omit salt. Drain, rinse with cold water, and rinse again. Combine shrimp, pasta, and rest of ingredients. Toss gently. Cover and chill at least 2 hours. Good served warm, also. Serves 10.

Shrimp Tempura

  1 pound shrimp (about 15)
    Garlic salt, optional
    Monosodium glutamate, optional
1½ cups white flour
  1 tablespoon baking powder

½ teaspoon salt
½ cup vegetable oil
  1 cup ice water
    Oil for frying

Clean and devein shrimp. Pat dry. If desired, sprinkle with garlic salt and monosodium glutamate, then refrigerate. Mix flour, baking powder, and salt. Add oil a little at a time, while stirring with a wooden spoon. Stir until all ingredients form a ball and sides of bowl are clean. Add water, a little at a time while stirring, until dough is consistency of pancake batter. Dip shrimp in batter and fry shrimp, 2 or 3 at a time, in oil heated to 350-360 degrees. Serve with sweet and sour sauce.

Shrimp Zucchini Boats

4 zucchini, large
3 tablespoons butter
1 cup fresh mushrooms, sliced
1 cup green celery, chopped
1/2 cup scallions, chopped
6 tablespoons flour
1/2 teaspoon salt
1/2 teaspoon oregano
1/4 teaspoon fresh ground pepper
2 cups Muenster cheese, shredded

1/2 cup water chestnuts, chopped
3/4 pounds fresh medium shrimp, peeled, deveined, and cut in half
1 2 ounce jar chopped pimientos, drained
2 tablespoons Parmesan cheese, grated
Bacon, cooked and crumbled, optional

Cut a wide oval shape out of side of each zucchini and scoop out center (leave 1/4-inch shell). Chop scooped-out zucchini and reserve. Melt butter in skillet. Saute mushrooms, celery, and scallions one minute. Stir in flour and seasonings. Remove from heat. Stir in Muenster cheese, water chestnuts, shrimp, pimientos, and chopped zucchini. Fill shells with mixture. Place in buttered or Pammed shallow baking dish or pan. Bake at 325 for 20 minutes. Sprinkle on Parmesan cheese and bake until melted and zucchini is tender, about 5 to 10 minutes. (Do not overcook. Zucchini should be crisp-tender.) Optional: sprinkle bacon on top of Parmesan cheese and bake.

"Wonderful! Tastes very fresh and crispy. The simple flavorings make a remarkable statement."

Shrimp and Crabmeat Casserole

1 1/2 pounds shrimp, cooked and deveined
1 pound crabmeat
2 medium onions, chopped fine
2 medium green peppers, chopped fine

2 cups celery, diced
2 cups mayonnaise
2 teaspoons Worcestershire sauce
Salt and pepper to taste
Bread crumbs, buttered

Mix together all ingredients. Pour into a large casserole. Top with buttered bread crumbs. Bake at 300 for 30 minutes. Serves 10-12.

Shrimp Creole

1 tablespoon flour
1 tablespoon bacon fat
2 onions, minced
1 large green pepper, minced
3 tablespoons celery, minced
2 tablespoons olive oil
1 large can tomatoes, peeled
2 small garlic cloves, crushed
2 teaspoons parsley, minced

¼ teaspoon red pepper
1 teaspoon salt
2 bay leaves
¼ teaspoon powdered thyme
2 pounds raw shrimp,
   peeled and deveined
2 teaspoons Worcestershire sauce
   Cooked rice (do not use
   5-minute rice)

Brown flour in bacon fat. Saute onions, green pepper, and celery in olive oil until onion browns slightly. Add tomatoes. Mix browned flour with sauteed vegetables; then add all seasonings except Worcestershire sauce. Let creole cook slowly, tightly covered, for 1 hour. Add shrimp and Worcestershire sauce. Cover and cook until shrimp turn bright pink, about 5-10 minutes. Serve over mounds of cooked rice.

Seafood Fettucini

1 stick butter
¼ cup onions, chopped
3 tablespoons flour
1½ chicken broth
1 cup half and half cream
½ teaspoon salt

¼ teaspoon red pepper
2 dozen shrimp (1½ pounds)
1 cup crabmeat or sea legs
1 16-ounce box fettucini
   noodles, cooked

Melt ½ stick butter in frying pan and saute onions. Add flour and stir. Reduce heat and cook 1 minute. In another saucepan, boil broth. Add onion mixture and remaining ½ stick butter. Cook on high until butter melts, stirring constantly. Add half and half. Mix in salt, pepper, and seafood. Layer seafood mixture and noodles in dish. Bake for 30 minutes at 350. May be frozen, unbaked.

"Truly an original dish!"

Skewered Seafood and Veggies

Marinade:

¼ cup dry white wine
2 tablespoons light olive oil
2 tablespoons fresh lemon juice
¼ cup parsley, minced

2 cloves garlic, crushed
1 tablespoon chervil
1 teaspoon rosemary
¼ teaspoon pepper

18 medium shrimp, shelled and
     deveined, leaving tails intact
12 scallops
 1 small yellow squash, sliced
     diagonally in 12 pieces
 1 small zucchini, sliced
     diagonally in 12 pieces
 1 yellow pepper, halved, seeded,
     and cut in 12 chunks

 1 green pepper, halved, seeded,
     and cut in 12 chunks
12 cherry tomatoes
 2 lemons, thinly sliced
12 long wooden skewers,
     soaked in water

In large shallow pan, combine marinade ingredients and add shrimp and scallops.
Cover and marinate for 3-4 hours, stirring occasionally. Blanch squash, zucchini, and
peppers in boiling water 1-2 minutes or until crisp tender. Drain and rinse under
cold water to prevent further cooking. Drain again. Remove seafood from
marinade and set aside. Add vegetables and tomatoes to marinade and coat.
Preheat broiler. On each of 6 skewers, thread 3 shrimp and 2 scallops alternating
with a slice of folded lemon between. On remaining 6 skewers, thread 2 slices of
yellow squash, 2 slices of zucchini, 2 chunks each yellow and green pepper, and
2 cherry tomatoes. Cook under broiler 8-10 minutes or until seafood is done,
brushing with marinade and turning once or twice during cooking time. Can
also be grilled outside.

"Light and tasty!"

Chicken Champagne

1 chicken
Flour
1/2 cup butter or margarine
1/2 teaspoon seasoned salt
1/4 teaspoon seasoned pepper
1/4 teaspoon powdered herbs

1 tablespoon chives, chopped
1 tablespoon parsley, chopped
1 small can chicken broth
1/2 split domestic champagne

Cut up chicken into serving pieces; dip into flour and fry until golden brown. Place in baking dish and sprinkle with salt, pepper, and herbs. Sprinkle parsley and chives over mixture. Add chicken broth and champagne. Bake 1 1/2 hours at 325, basting every 20 minutes. Do not cover.

"This tasty dish has a delicious and delicate sauce."

Peachy Sweet-Sour Chicken

2 tablespoons oil
2 1/2-3 pounds chicken, skinned
1 8 1/4 ounce can pineapple chunks
1 pound peaches, peeled
and sliced
1/2 cup onion, diced
1 small green pepper, cut into strips

1 1/2 cups ketchup
1/2 cup cider vinegar
2 tablespoons sugar
1 1/2 teaspoons dry mustard
1 teaspoon salt
1/2 teaspoon ground ginger
Hot cooked rice

In a large skillet, heat oil over medium heat. Add chicken and brown well on all sides. Remove and set aside, leaving drippings in skillet. Meanwhile, drain juice from pineapple (reserving pineapple) and toss with sliced peaches. Set aside. Saute onion and green pepper in reserved drippings in skillet for about 3 minutes. Add ketchup, vinegar, sugar, dry mustard, salt, ginger, and drained liquid from peaches. Stir and heat through. Return chicken pieces to skillet and simmer for 35 minutes, turning chicken occasionally. Skim off excess fat. Add peaches and pineapple to skillet and simmer for an additional 5 minutes, stirring occasionally. Serve hot with rice. Serves 4.

Chicken Cordon Bleu

6 chicken breasts,
   skinned and boned
1 8 ounce package of
   cooked ham, sliced
1 8 ounce package of Swiss cheese
3 tablespoons flour

1 teaspoon paprika
6 tablespoons margarine
1 chicken bouillon cube
1/2 cup dry white wine or sherry
1 tablespoon cornstarch
1 cup heavy cream

Pound chicken breasts until flattened. Place slice of ham on chicken piece and then a slice of cheese. Roll each up and secure with toothpicks. Mix flour and paprika on waxed paper. Roll chicken pieces in the mixture to coat. Melt margarine over medium heat and brown chicken pieces. Mix bouillon cube and wine and add to chicken. Reduce heat to low, cover, and simmer chicken for 30 minutes. The cheese will melt to help form the sauce. Remove chicken to serving platter. Blend cornstarch and heavy cream until smooth. Gradually stir into the sauce remaining in skillet. Stir until thickened. Serve sauce over the chicken.

Baked Chicken Breasts

8 chicken breasts, boned
8 slices Swiss cheese
1 10¾ ounce can cream
   of chicken soup, undiluted

1/4 cup dry white wine
1 cup herb seasoned stuffing
   mix, crushed
1/4 cup margarine, melted

Arrange chicken in lightly greased 9x13 pan. Top with cheese slices. Combine soup and wine, stirring well. Spoon evenly over chicken and sprinkle with stuffing mix. Drizzle melted margarine over the top. Bake at 350 for 45-55 minutes.

"This is a great dish for company."

Grilled Lemon Chicken

3-3½ pounds chicken, skinned
  ⅔ cup lemon juice
  ⅓ cup oil
  3 cloves garlic, crushed
  1 teaspoon grated lemon peel

  ¾ teaspoon salt
  ¼ teaspoon pepper
  ½ cup apple jelly
  ¼ teaspoon ground ginger

In casserole dish, combine lemon juice, oil, garlic, lemon peel, salt, and pepper. With sharp knife, cut several slashes, about ⅛-inch deep, in each piece of chicken. Place chicken skin-side down in marinade. Cover and refrigerate at least 2 hours or up to 6 hours. About 10 minutes before chicken is done, in small saucepan over low heat, combine apple jelly and ginger. Heat until jelly is melted, stirring constantly. Keep warm. Serves 4.

To barbecue: Place chicken, skin-side down, on grill over medium coals. Cook 30 to 35 minutes or until fork-tender, turning and brushing frequently with marinade. During last 5 minutes of grilling, brush often with jelly glaze.

To broil: Place chicken skin-side up on broiler pan. Broil 15 minutes, basting occasionally with marinade. Turn and broil 15-20 minutes more, basting, until fork-tender. Brush with jelly glaze during last 5 minutes of broiling.

Chicken Divan

  2 whole chicken breasts
  1 small onion
  1 celery stalk
    Salt and pepper
  1 can cream of chicken soup
  ½ cup mayonnaise
  ¼ teaspoon curry powder

  ½ tablespoon lemon juice
  1 package frozen broccoli spears,
    cooked and drained
  ½ cup cheddar cheese, shredded
    Almonds, toasted and
    sliced, optional

Simmer chicken in water with onion, celery, salt, and pepper for 1 hour. Cool and break into pieces. Mix soup, mayonnaise, curry powder, and lemon juice. Layer broccoli, chicken, soup mixture, and cheese in casserole. Repeat layers. Bake for 45 minutes at 350. Sprinkle toasted, sliced almonds on top.

Baked Chicken

3-3½ pounds chicken, skinned
¼ cup flour
¼ cup butter, melted
⅔ cup evaporated milk, undiluted
1 10½ ounce can cream
 of mushroom soup
1 cup American cheese, grated

½ teaspoon salt
⅛ teaspoon pepper
2 cups (1 pound can) whole
 onions, drained, optional
¼ pound mushrooms, sliced
 Dash paprika

Coat chicken with flour. Melt butter in a 13x9x2 baking dish. Arrange chicken in a single layer with skins down in dish. Bake uncovered at 425 for 30 minutes. Turn chicken; bake until brown, 15 to 20 minutes longer or until tender. Remove from oven and reduce temperature to 325. Pour off excess fat. Combine evaporated milk, soup, cheese, salt, and pepper. Add onions and mushrooms to chicken. Pour milk mixture over chicken. Sprinkle with paprika. Cover dish with foil and bake an additional 15-20 minutes.

"This special dish makes its own wonderful gravy!"

Party Baked Chicken Breasts

4 whole chicken breasts, split
 and boned
8 strips of bacon

1 small jar chipped beef
½ pint sour cream
1 can mushroom soup

Wrap 1 strip of bacon around each chicken breast. Cover bottom of casserole dish with the chipped beef. Place chicken in casserole on top of beef. Mix sour cream and soup and pour over chicken. Cook in 300 oven for 3 hours. May be prepared well in advance. May be left in the oven 1 hour after turned off.

Monterey Chicken

8 large, whole chicken breasts, skinned and boned
1 7 ounce can mild green chilies, chopped
1/2 pound Monterey Jack cheese, cut into 8 strips
1/2 cup fine bread crumbs
1/4 cup Parmesan cheese, freshly grated

1-3 teaspoons chili powder
1/4 teaspoon cumin
1/2 teaspoon salt
1/4 teaspoon freshly ground pepper
6 tablespoons butter, melted
Tomato Sauce (recipe follows)
Sour cream
Limes

Pound the chicken breasts between 2 sheets of waxed paper until thin. Spread each breast with 1 tablespoon of the chilies. Put a cheese strip on top of the chilies. Roll up each breast and tuck ends under. Secure with a toothpick, if necessary. Combine the bread crumbs, Parmesan cheese, chili powder, cumin, salt, and pepper in a shallow dish. Dip each stuffed breast into the melted butter and roll in the bread crumb mixture. Place the breasts in a baking dish, seam side down. Drizzle with remaining butter. Cover and chill at least 4 hours or overnight. Preheat oven to 400. Bake for 25-40 minutes, or until done. Serve with the tomato sauce. Garnish with sour cream and fresh limes.

Tomato Sauce

1 15 ounce can tomato sauce
1/3 cup green onions, sliced
1/2 teaspoon cumin

Salt and freshly ground pepper
Hot pepper sauce, if desired

In a small saucepan, combine all ingredients. Bring to a boil and cook, stirring constantly, until slightly thickened.

Russian Chicken

1 bottle Russian dressing
7 ounces apricot preserves
1 package Lipton Onion Soup mix

1/2 pound fresh mushrooms, sliced
8 chicken breasts, boned and skinned

Heat dressing, preserves, and soup in skillet until thoroughly mixed. Add mushroom slices. Arrange chicken breasts in a 13x9 pan; pour sauce over. Cover tightly with foil. Bake at 350 for 35 minutes; remove foil and bake an additional 10 minutes, or until hot and bubbly. Serves 8.

Chicken and Green Bean Casserole

1 16 ounce box long grain and wild rice
2 2 1/2 pound fryers, cooked and boned
1 10 3/4 ounce can condensed cream of celery soup
1 onion, minced
1 2 ounce jar pimientos

2 cups mayonnaise
1 8 ounce can water chestnuts, sliced
2 16 ounce cans French-style green beans, drained
Paprika
Grated Parmesan cheese

Cook rice as directed on box. Add all ingredients except paprika and cheese, and mix thoroughly. Pour into greased, shallow 3-quart baking dish. Sprinkle with paprika and Parmesan cheese. Bake at 350 until bubbly, approximately 30-40 minutes. Freezes well. When frozen, remove from freezer at least 4 hours before heating.

Hot Peanutty Chicken Salad

¾ cup peanuts, chopped
2½ cups chicken, cooked
and chopped
¼ cup green pepper, chopped
¼ cup onion, chopped
1½ cups cooked rice

¾ cup mayonnaise
1 3 ounce can mushrooms, drained
2 cans cream of mushroom soup
1 cup cheddar cheese, shredded
Salt and pepper

Reserve ¼ cup peanuts. Mix remaining ingredients thoroughly. Turn into a 2 quart casserole. Sprinkle with reserved peanuts. Bake at 400 for 30-40 minutes or until hot and bubbly. Serves 6-8.

Hot Chicken Salad

2 cups chicken, cooked and diced
1 can cream of chicken soup
1 cup celery, diced
¾ cup mayonnaise
1 cup cooked rice
1 teaspoon onion, grated
1 tablespoon lemon juice

1 can water chestnuts, sliced
½ teaspoon salt
3 eggs, hard-boiled and diced
½ cup butter
1 cup corn flakes, crushed
½ cup blanched almonds

Mix chicken, soup, celery, mayonnaise, rice, onion, lemon juice, water chestnuts, and salt. Place half the chicken mixture in a greased 13x9 casserole. Place eggs over top and add remaining chicken mixture over eggs. Melt butter; stir in corn flakes and almonds. Spread over casserole. Cover with foil and bake for 25 minutes. Uncover and bake 5 minutes longer. Makes 8 servings.

Company Chicken 'N' Bread

1   large round loaf French bread
    (long may be substituted)
8-10 boneless chicken breasts
½   cup butter
2   3 ounce cans mushrooms,
    drained and sliced
1   large onion, chopped
½   teaspoon onion salt

½   teaspoon garlic salt
1   cup white wine
½-1 teaspoon of each:
    Oregano
    Basil
    Thyme
    Rosemary
    Curry powder

Cut off the top of the bread and scoop out the inside. Lightly brown chicken in butter about 10 minutes on each side; remove from pan. Saute mushrooms, onion, onion salt, garlic salt, wine, oregano, basil, thyme, rosemary, and curry powder. Place chicken in bread and top with mushroom mixture. Place top slice of bread to close. Wrap bread in foil and bake at 325 for 2 hours. Serves 6-8.

Buttermilk Fried Chicken

1   fryer, cut up
2   tablespoons lemon juice
2   teaspoons Worcestershire sauce
1   teaspoon paprika
2   cups buttermilk
2   cloves garlic, crushed

1½ teaspoons celery seed
1   teaspoon salt
1   teaspoon pepper
1   cup flour
    Oil for frying

Arrange chicken pieces, one layer deep, in baking dish. Combine next 8 ingredients and pour over chicken. Cover and refrigerate overnight. Drain chicken and roll in flour. Fry in about 1 inch of hot oil until golden brown.

Deep Dish Chicken Pot Pie

½ cup celery, chopped
6 tablespoons margarine or butter
⅓ cup unsifted flour
7 teaspoons chicken-flavor instant
   bouillon or 7 chicken-flavor
   bouillon cubes
¼ teaspoon pepper
6 cups milk

3 cups chicken, cooked and
   cut into small pieces
1 cup carrots, cooked and sliced
1 cup potatoes, cooked and diced
1 cup frozen green peas, thawed
3 cups biscuit baking mix
1 egg yolk, plus 1 tablespoon water

In large saucepan, cook celery in margarine until tender. Stir in flour, bouillon, and pepper. Add 5 cups milk. Cook and stir until thickened and bubbly. Stir in chicken, carrots, potatoes, and peas. Remove from heat. In medium bowl, combine remaining milk and biscuit mix. Mix well. Turn two-thirds of dough into well-greased 13x9 baking dish and sprinkle with flour. With floured hands, pat evenly over bottom and up sides of dish. Pour chicken mixture into prepared dish. Turn remaining dough onto a well-floured surface. Knead until smooth. Roll out to ⅛-inch thickness. Cut into eight 3-inch rounds. Arrange on top of casserole. Beat together egg yolk and water. Brush on rounds. Bake in 375 oven for 25-30 minutes or until crust is golden. Serves 8-10.

Parmesan Chicken Bites

4 chicken breasts, boned and
   cut in strips or bite-size pieces
1 cup toasted bread crumbs
¾ cup Parmesan cheese

Pepper
Garlic
½ cup butter or margarine,
   melted

Mix bread crumbs, Parmesan cheese, pepper, and garlic. Dip chicken in butter or margarine and roll in bread crumb mixture. Spread chicken in glass casserole dish and dot with butter. Do not turn chicken. Cover with foil while baking for 1 hour at 350. Chicken may be breaded the night before. Ingredients may need to be doubled for more chicken.

Chicken Zucchini Stir Fry

3 tablespoons soy sauce
2 tablespoons cornstarch
1/2 teaspoon sugar
1 small clove garlic, minced
1 whole chicken breast, boned and cut into thin strips
1 8 ounce can pineapple chunks in juice

2 tablespoons oil
1/2 teaspoon curry powder
2 stalks celery, diagonally cut into 1/4 inch thick slices
1 medium zucchini, sliced
1 medium onion, cut into 1 inch squares

Combine 1 tablespoon each cornstarch and soy sauce with sugar and garlic. Stir in chicken to coat and let stand 15 minutes. Drain pineapple, reserving all juice. Add enough water to pineapple juice to measure 1 cup. Combine with remaining 2 tablespoons soy sauce and 1 tablespoon cornstarch. Heat 1 tablespoon oil in large frying pan or wok over medium-high heat. Add chicken and curry and stir-fry 2-3 minutes, or until tender. Remove. Heat remaining 1 tablespoon oil in same pan. Add vegetables and stir-fry until tender, yet crisp. Stir pineapple juice mixture into pan along with chicken and pineapple. Cook until mixture boils and thickens. Serve immediately over hot rice. Serves 4.

"Add 2 tablespoons of soy sauce to your rice for a pleasing taste!"

Soupreme Skillet Chicken

2 medium zucchini
2 pounds chicken, skinned
2 tablespoons oil
1 can cream of celery soup
1 teaspoon paprika

1/2 teaspoon basil leaves, crushed
1 medium clove garlic, minced
1/2 cup canned tomatoes, drained and chopped

Cut zucchini in half lengthwise and slice diagonally in 1/2 inch pieces. In large skillet, brown chicken in oil. Pour off fat. Add soup and seasonings. Cover and cook over low heat for 30 minutes, stirring occasionally. Add zucchini and tomatoes. Cook an additional 15 minutes or until tender. Serves 4.

Glazed Cornish Hens

2 1 to 1½ pounds Cornish
   hens, thawed
½ cup apricot nectar
1 tablespoon apricot jam
½ teaspoon grated orange peel

1 tablespoon brown sugar
2 whole cloves
   Dash cinnamon
4 teaspoons dry white wine
½ teaspoon cornstarch

Clean hens and salt insides lightly. Combine nectar, jam, orange peel, sugar, cloves, and cinnamon in small saucepan. Bring to boil over moderate heat, stirring occasionally. In a small bowl, combine wine and cornstarch. Stir into hot apricot mixture. Cook, stirring frequently, until mixture is smooth and thickened. Remove from heat. Stuff hens, if desired. Place hens on rack of broiler pan and baste with glaze. Roast in 350 oven for one hour or until leg joints move freely, basting frequently. Hens can also be put on spit of gas grill and barbecued for one hour. Serves 2.

"Wonderfully moist and tender!"

Cornish Hens with Apple-Walnut Dressing

2 Cornish hens
   Paprika
   Salt
   Pepper
   Oil
1 cup wild rice, cooked

2 tablespoons celery, minced
2 tablespoons onion, minced
¼ cup walnut pieces
1 apple, cored and chopped
2 tablespoons port wine
1 teaspoon parsley

Preheat oven to 350. Wash hens and pat dry. Season with salt, paprika, and pepper. Rub lightly with oil. Combine wild rice, celery, onion, walnut pieces, apple, port wine, and parsley; toss lightly. Stuff hens and truss. Place hens in uncovered roast pan and roast for 1 hour or until tender.

Beef Brisket

3-4 pounds straight or first-cut
    beef brisket
    Salt and pepper
1 medium onion, sliced

1 large can tomato sauce
    Juice of 1 lemon
4 tablespoons brown sugar

Tear two good-sized pieces of aluminum foil. Crease together to make one larger piece. Put in baking pan. Place brisket on foil in pan, fat side up. Sprinkle with salt and pepper. Add sliced onions, tomato sauce, lemon juice, and brown sugar. Fold ends up, enclosing brisket except for a small hole in the center which will allow steam to escape. Bake at 350 for 3 hours or until tender. Remove meat to platter. Put sauce in bowl and refrigerate both for a couple of hours. Remove excess fat from meat and slice very thin across the grain. Skim fat from sauce. Alternate layers of sauce and meat in baking dish. Refrigerate overnight (or longer) for best flavor. Reheat and serve.

"This make-ahead dish is easy, and yet it is special enough for company."

Corned Beef

3-4 pounds corned beef
1 orange, sliced
1 large onion, quartered
2 stalks celery
2 cloves garlic
1 teaspoon dill seed

1/2 teaspoon rosemary
6 whole cloves
3 sticks cinnamon
1 bay leaf
    Light corn syrup or honey

Cover corned beef with water. Add remaining ingredients except corn syrup or honey. Cover and simmer 1 hour per pound. Remove meat from liquid. While hot, brush with light corn syrup or honey.

"Meat that melts in your mouth!"

Stuffed Eye of Round Roast

1 4-5 pound eye of round roast   Sauce
  Stuffing

Preheat oven to 350. Split roast, leaving 1/2 inch unsplit at each end. Tightly stuff and tie roast. Place roast on a rack in a shallow roasting pan. Roast uncovered 1 1/2 hours at 350. After removing roast from oven, let it sit for 20 minutes. Slice roast. Drizzle half of sauce on slices and serve remaining sauce on the side.

Stuffing

1 large Granny Smith apple, peeled, cored, and chopped
3 cups crumbled cornbread
6 ounces ground pork
1/2 cup apple cider
1/4 cup fresh parsley, chopped

1 tablespoon fresh thyme, chopped, *or* 1 teaspoon dried thyme
1/8 teaspoon rosemary
Salt and white pepper

Mix stuffing ingredients to a very smooth texture by hand or in a food processor, adding more cider if not moist enough.

Sauce

1 cup apple cider
2 shallots, chopped
1/4 pound butter

3/4 cup demi glace
1 jigger Apple Jack brandy

Pour 1 cup cider into saucepan and cook until reduced to 1/2 cup. In saute pan or small skillet, saute shallots in butter until clear. Add cider and demi glace. Bring to a boil and add Apple Jack brandy. Reduce to simmer and continue cooking until sauce has consistency to coat the back of a spoon.

Creole Roast Beef

1 large onion, chopped
1 whole garlic, chopped
6 celery stalks, chopped
2 medium green peppers, chopped
  Oil

2 bay leaves
1 heaping tablespoon chili powder
2 8 ounce cans tomato sauce
1 3-5 pound eye of round roast

Saute onions, garlic, celery, and peppers in oil that just covers bottom of pan. Add remaining ingredients; cook and stir to mix seasonings well. Taste and add hot sauce or more chili to taste. Pour creole sauce over roast beef. Cover and cook for 3 hours at 325. Slice roast thin. Serve with rice because sauce is excellent over rice or noodles. Other roasts may be substituted.

"Excellent company dish—cannot be overcooked!"

Spicy Pot Roast

2 tablespoons olive oil
1 4-5 pound pot roast
1 cup tomato sauce
1 cup dry red wine
2 pieces orange peel, orange part only, each about 1x2 inches

5 whole cloves
2 cinnamon sticks
1 clove garlic, minced
12 small white onions, peeled
¼ teaspoon sugar

Heat olive oil in a large Dutch oven, add pot roast, and brown on all sides. Add tomato sauce, ½ cup of wine, orange peel, cloves, cinnamon, and garlic. Cover and bake at 300 for 3 hours. Add remaining ingredients, cover and cook 1 hour longer, or until meat is tender. Remove meat to a warm platter and let stand for 15 minutes before slicing. Skim grease from pan juices. Serve remaining pan juices as a sauce over meat slices. Serves 6-8.

"Nice change of taste for a pot roast."

Pot Roast Supreme

1 3 pound bottom round beef roast
1/4 cup butter
3 carrots, chopped
4 stalks celery, chopped
1/2 cup onion, chopped
1 clove garlic, minced
1/4 pound mushrooms, chopped
1 10 1/2 ounce can consomme

1/2 cup dry red wine
2 teaspoons salt
1/8 teaspoon pepper
1/2 teaspoon paprika
1 tablespoon capers
1/4 cup flour (optional)
1 cup sour cream

Brown roast in butter in a large Dutch oven. Add carrots, celery, onion, and garlic to pan and cook until onion is limp. Add mushrooms. Combine half of the consomme with the wine, salt, pepper, paprika, and capers. Add to beef. Cover and bake at 350 for 2 hours, or until meat is tender. Remove meat to a heated platter. With a slotted spoon, remove most of the vegetables from the pan liquids and puree them in a food processor or blender. Return the puree to the pan. Combine flour, if desired, with remaining consomme and stir into pan liquids. (If not using flour, just add consomme.) Cook until sauce boils and thickens. Stir in sour cream and heat, but do not boil. Serve the sauce over the sliced meat. Serves 4 to 6.

"The sauce makes the dish!"

Bourbon Steak

Porterhouse steak, 2 inches thick (about 3 pounds)
1/2 cup bourbon
6 tablespoons soy sauce
Juice of 1/2 lemon

2 tablespoons salad oil
1 garlic clove, crushed
1/2 teaspoon crushed black peppercorns

Place steak on a platter. Combine bourbon, soy sauce, lemon juice, oil, garlic, and peppercorns. Mix thoroughly and pour over the steak. Cover and allow to remain in the refrigerator for 4-12 hours before broiling. Remove steak from the marinade mixture. Broil in a preheated broiler or cook on an outside barbecue.

Marinated Round Steak

London broil or round steak,
3 inches thick

Lemon pepper
Sauce

Prepare sauce. Place meat in pan and pierce with fork. Pour sauce over steak. Bake at 350 or on grill until pink, turning and basting meat with sauce. Sprinkle with lemon pepper. Slice and serve on poppy seed rolls.

Sauce

- 1 cup cooking oil
- 1/2 cup vinegar
- 1/2 garlic knob, chopped
- 1/4 cup salt
- 1/4 teaspoon red pepper

- 2 tablespoons black pepper
- 2 tablespoons paprika
- 1/2 cup A-1 sauce
- 1/2 cup Worcestershire sauce

Blend ingredients.

"Superb!"

London Broil Marinade

- 2 teaspoons salt
- 1 teaspoon pepper
- 1/2 teaspoon basil
- 1/2 teaspoon rosemary

- 1 onion, chopped
- 2 tablespoons wine vinegar
- 4 tablespoons salad oil

Combine all ingredients and pour over meat in a shallow glass pan. Pierce meat and turn. Marinate from 1-5 hours, depending on strength of flavor desired.

Marinated Flank Steak

1 flank steak, approximately
  1 1/2 pounds
Pepper, freshly ground
Parsley, freshly chopped

Garlic, freshly chopped
Soy sauce
1/2 pound bacon
Toothpicks

Pound steak until thin. Lay flat and score diagonally, making diamond-shaped cuts. Sprinkle cut side with garlic, pepper, parsley, and soy sauce. Cook bacon until crisp. Lay bacon strips lengthwise on steak and roll up like a jelly roll. Skewer with wooden toothpicks at 1-inch intervals. Prepare marinade. Pour marinade over rolled steak in a dish. Marinate 2 days in a refrigerator, basting frequently. Sear steak in a buttered skillet on all sides, then roast for 15 minutes in a 450 oven. To cook on the grill, sear each side for 2 minutes, then grill 6 more minutes on each side.

Marinade

2 tablespoons dry English mustard
1/4 cup wine vinegar
2 garlic cloves, minced
1 1/2 cup corn oil
2 tablespoons parsley, chopped

1 teaspoon pepper, freshly ground
1/4 cup Worcestershire sauce
3/4 cup soy sauce
1/3 cup fresh lemon juice

Combine marinade ingredients and mix well.

Fool Proof Beef Tenderloin

Whole beef tenderloin,
approximately 4 pounds

Salt and pepper

Preheat oven to 500. Salt and pepper a butcher-prepared tenderloin, rubbing in spices on all sides. Place in shallow baking dish. Cook uncovered at 500 for 12 minutes. After 12 minutes, turn oven off but do not open door. Leave in oven for 45 minutes more. This cooking time gives a medium-rare tenderloin.

Italian Beef Bake

2 pounds beef chuck, 1 inch thick
1 envelope onion soup mix
1 green pepper, chopped
1/4 cup onion, chopped
1 1 pound can tomatoes

1/4 teaspoon salt
   Dash pepper
1 tablespoon bottled steak sauce
1 tablespoon cornstarch
2 tablespoons parsley, chopped

Cut beef into serving size portions and arrange in a shallow pan, with pieces overlapping. Sprinkle with soup mix, green pepper, and onion. Drain and chop tomatoes, saving liquid. Add tomatoes, salt, and pepper to beef. Combine tomato liquid, steak sauce, and cornstarch. Pour over beef. Cover and bake at 350 for 2 hours. Serve with parsley sprinkled on top.

Sweet and Sour Beef Stew

1 1/2 pounds beef stew meat
2 tablespoons cooking oil
1 cup carrots, chopped
1 cup onions, sliced
1 8 ounce can tomato sauce
1/4 cup brown sugar

1/4 cup vinegar
1 tablespoon Worcestershire sauce
3/4 cup water
1 teaspoon salt
4 teaspoons cornstarch

Brown meat in hot oil. Add next 6 ingredients, 1/2 cup water, and salt. Cover and cook over low heat about 2 hours, or until the meat is tender. Combine the cornstarch and 1/4 cup cold water. Add to the beef mixture. Cook and stir until thick and bubbly. Serve over noodles and garnish with carrot curls and parsley. Good over toast, also. Serves 6.

Stir-Fried Beef with Broccoli

1/2 pound boneless beef sirloin or flank steak, cut into strips	1 bunch broccoli or 2 frozen packages of broccoli
1 tablespoon cornstarch	6 small onions
2 tablespoons soy sauce	2 tablespoons oil
1 tablespoon dry sherry	1 teaspoon salt
1 teaspoon sugar	1/2 cup water

Combine meat, cornstarch, soy sauce, sherry, and sugar in medium-sized bowl. Cut broccoli into pieces, 3 inches long. Rinse in water. Cut onions into 6 to 8 wedge shapes. Heat skillet for 30 seconds. Add 2 tablespoons of oil and coat pan. Drop in meat and vegetables and stir fry for 1 minute. Sprinkle with salt and add water. Cover pan and cook over low heat 2 minutes, or until beef is done and vegetables are crisp tender.

Hamburger Pie

1 pound ground hamburger	1 deep dish pie shell
1 8 ounce can tomato sauce	1 egg
1/4 cup onion, chopped	1/4 cup milk
1/4 cup green pepper, chopped	1/2 teaspoon dry mustard
1/4 teaspoon oregano	1/2 teaspoon Worcestershire sauce
Sprinkle of "Crazy Salt"	2 cups cheddar cheese, grated
1/2 cup breadcrumbs	

Brown meat and drain. Add tomato sauce, onions, green pepper, and oregano. Sprinkle with "Crazy Salt" and saute for 5 minutes. Add bread crumbs and mix well. Pour in defrosted pie shell. Mix remaining ingredients and spread on top of pie. Bake at 400 for 30 minutes.

"Great family dinner!"

Eggplant Casserole

1 package spaghetti sauce mix
1 pound ground beef, cooked
1 eggplant, peeled and sliced

1 12-ounce or larger package Mozzarella cheese, grated

Prepare spaghetti sauce mixture according to package directions. Add cooked ground beef. Cover the bottom of an 8x8 pan with a small amount of sauce. Next, place a layer of sliced eggplant, a layer of sauce, and a layer of grated cheese. Repeat layers (the more cheese the better). Bake at 350 for 45 minutes. This freezes very well.

"Even the children will love this!"

Very Italian Lasagna

1 pound Italian sausage
4 cloves garlic, crushed
2 teaspoons sweet basil
1 teaspoon oregano
1½ teaspoons salt
½ cup dry white wine
5 drops of Tabasco sauce
4 1 pound cans Italian tomatoes, undrained
2-3 6 ounce cans tomato paste, according to preferred sauce thickness

¾ pound lasagna
1 pound ricotta cheese or small curd cottage cheese
½ cup Parmesan cheese, grated
1 tablespoon parsley
2 eggs
1 package frozen chopped spinach
½ pound mozzarella cheese, grated Parmesan cheese

Remove sausage from casing, crumble, and cook in skillet until done. Add next 8 ingredients and mix well. Cover and simmer for 45 minutes. Cook lasagna according to package directions and drain. Mix thoroughly the ricotta cheese, ½ cup Parmesan cheese, parsley, eggs, and spinach. In a large oblong casserole dish, arrange a layer of sauce, lasagna noodles, and the cheese and spinach mixture. Repeat layers ending with sauce. Top with mozzarella cheese and Parmesan cheese. Bake for 45 minutes at 350.

Enchilada Pie

2 pounds ground beef
1 can Old El Paso tomatoes and green chilies
1 package enchilada sauce mix
1 can cream of mushroom soup

1 can cream of chicken soup
1 pound cheddar cheese, grated
1 cup milk
12 regular tortillas or 6 large tortillas

Brown meat and drain. Add tomatoes, chilies, and enchilada sauce mix. Simmer over low heat while preparing sauce. In saucepan, heat soups, cheese (reserve some to sprinkle on top), and milk until cheese is melted. In a greased baking dish, layer tortillas, meat, and sauce until all are used. Top with reserved cheese. Bake for 30 minutes at 350. Serves 8.

Italian Sausage Casserole

1/2 pound mild Italian sausage
1/2 cup onion, chopped
1 clove garlic, crushed
2 tablespoons butter
2 tablespoons flour
1/2 teaspoon Italian seasoning
1/8 teaspoon salt

1/8 teaspoon pepper
1 cup milk
2 cups mozzarella cheese, shredded
2 cups noodles, cooked and drained
1/2 cup zucchini, halved and sliced
1/2 cup tomatoes, chopped

Cook sausage, onion, and garlic in skillet until sausage is brown and crumbly. Drain and set aside. Melt butter; stir in flour and seasonings until smooth. Remove from heat and stir in milk. Bring to a boil over medium heat, stirring constantly for one minute. Reduce heat to low. Stir in half of the cheese. Stir in cooked sausage mixture, noodles, zucchini, and tomatoes. Turn into a buttered 1 quart casserole. Bake at 350 for 25-30 minutes or until hot and bubbly. Remove from oven and sprinkle with remaining cheese. Return to oven to melt cheese.

Festive Baked Ham

1 cup apple cider	1 cup firmly packed brown sugar
1/2 cup water	1 21 ounce can cherry pie filling
1 5 pound uncooked ham half	1/2 cup raisins
12 whole cloves	1/2 cup orange juice

Combine apple cider and water in a saucepan; bring to a boil. Set aside. Remove skin from ham. Place ham, fat side up, on a cutting board. Score fat in a diamond design, and stud with cloves. Place ham in a shallow baking pan, fat side up; coat top with brown sugar. Insert meat thermometer, making sure it does not touch fat or bone. Bake, uncovered, at 325 about 2 hours (22-25 minutes per pound) or until meat thermometer registers 160, basting every 30 minutes with cider mixture. Combine remaining ingredients in a saucepan and bring to a boil. Serve sauce with sliced ham.

"Sauce is excellent. Great for the holidays!"

Raisin Sauce for Ham

1 cup raisins	1/4 teaspoon dry mustard
1 3/4 cups water	1/4 teaspoon ground cloves
1/2 cup brown sugar	1/4 teaspoon salt
1 1/4 tablespoons cornstarch	1 tablespoon butter
1/4 teaspoon cinnamon	1 tablespoon vinegar

Boil raisins in water for 5 minutes. Mix dry ingredients. Add to raisin mixture. Cook 15 minutes. Stir in butter and vinegar. Yields 2 cups.

Sweet and Sour Pork

2 pounds boneless pork loin, cut
　　into 1/2 inch cubes
1/4 cup soy sauce
　　Cornstarch
2 or more eggs, beaten
　　Flour
　　Oil for frying
1 large onion, cut into eighths

1 large green pepper, cut into
　　1 inch squares
1 cup pineapple chunks, drained
　　(reserve juice)
2 small tomatoes, cut into
　　thin wedges
　　Sweet and sour sauce

Toss pork cubes with soy sauce. Roll the cubes in cornstarch, then in beaten egg, then in flour. Fry in hot oil until golden brown. Drain on paper towels and keep warm in 350 oven. Heat 1 tablespoon oil in wok over high heat. Add onion and stir-fry for 2 minutes. Add green pepper and stir-fry an additional 2 minutes. Add pineapple and tomatoes and stir-fry 1 minute. Return pork cubes to wok, add sauce, and stir until thoroughly heated. Serve with hot, steamed rice.

Sweet and Sour Sauce

1/2 cup pineapple juice (use juice
　　from canned pineapple chunks)
1/4 cup wine vinegar
2 tablespoons oil
2 tablespoons brown sugar

1 tablespoon soy sauce
1/2 teaspoon pepper
1 teaspoon cornstarch
2 teaspoons water

Combine pineapple juice, vinegar, oil, brown sugar, soy sauce, and pepper in saucepan. Bring to a boil and add cornstarch which has been mixed with water. Stir until clear and slightly thickened.

"Zesty sauce!"

Szechwan Pork and Cabbage

12 ounces lean boneless pork
1 tablespoon cornstarch
¾ cup water
1 tablespoon lite soy sauce
1-2 teaspoons Szechwan chili sauce *or*
   ½ teaspoon ground red pepper
   and 2 tablespoons soy sauce
1 tablespoon cooking oil
1 clove garlic, crushed

1 teaspoon ginger root, grated
4 cups cabbage or Chinese
   cabbage, cut into 1 inch pieces
4 green onions, cut into
   1 inch pieces
1 medium green pepper, cut
   into strips
2 cups hot cooked rice

Partially freeze pork. Slice thinly into bite-size strips. Combine cornstarch, water, lite soy sauce, and chili sauce in a small bowl and set aside., Preheat wok or large skillet over high heat. Add oil, garlic, and ginger root. Stir-fry 15 seconds. Add cabbage and stir-fry 3-4 minutes or until crisp-tender. Remove. Add onions and green pepper. Stir-fry 3-4 minutes. Remove. Stir-fry meat 3-4 minutes. Push meat to side of pan and add cornstarch mixture. Cook and stir about 1 minute. Return all vegetables to pan. Stir to coat with sauce. Cook 1 minute more. Serve immediately over rice.

Pork Bar-B-Que

4-6 pounds fresh pork shoulder
6 cloves garlic, minced
1 large onion, finely chopped
1 16 ounce can whole tomatoes
1 small bottle Worcestershire sauce
2½ cups cider vinegar

3 tablespoons yellow
   prepared mustard
2½ teaspoons crushed red pepper
   Tabasco sauce
   Salt

Trim shoulder of fat and skin. Place in Dutch oven on top of range. Add remaining ingredients. Cover and simmer for 5-6 hours or until meat is tender and stringy. Remove meat from pot. Discard all fat and bone. Mince meat, return to pot, and simmer until sauce is cooked down to desired consistency. Skim fat and adjust seasonings to taste. Serve on buns with fresh cole slaw.

Pork Tenderloins

4 medium pork tenderloins
1/2 pound bacon
String
1 small bottle of soy sauce
1 tablespoon onion, grated

1 garlic clove, crushed
1 1/2 tablespoons vinegar
1/2 teaspoon cayenne pepper
1/2 teaspoon sugar

Wrap tenderloins with bacon and tie with string. Combine other ingredients in large bowl to make a marinade. Soak meat in marinade for approximately 3 hours, turning frequently. Remove meat from marinade. Bake at 300 uncovered for approximately 2 hours. Baste with marinade frequently, using all of the marinade.

Pork Chops with Cabbage and Pears

2 pork chops (1 1/2 inches thick)
Salt and pepper
2 tablespoons vegetable oil
1/2 small head of red cabbage, cored and shredded
2 scallions (or more for garnish), sliced

1/2 teaspoon crumbled thyme
1/2 teaspoon crumbled sage
2 tablespoons red wine vinegar
2 tablespoons butter
1 teaspoon sugar
1 large pear, peeled, cored, and cut into wedges

Trim pork from bones, then tie into small rounds. Add salt and pepper. Heat oil in a Dutch oven and brown the pork on all sides. Add cabbage, scallions, thyme, sage, and vinegar. Simmer, covered, for 30 minutes. In another small skillet, heat butter and stir in the sugar. Saute pear wedges for 3-4 minutes or until lightly browned. Arrange red cabbage on serving plates. Top with pork medallions and pear wedges. Garnish with additional sliced scallions. Serves 2.

"Very tasty!"

Pork Chops and Apples

8 pork chops, ¾ inch thick
½ cup apple juice
½ cup light raisins
1 teaspoon salt
¼ cup brown sugar, packed

¼ teaspoon ground nutmeg
¼ teaspoon ground cinnamon
3 large red apples, each cut
   into 6 to 8 wedges
½ cup water

Brown chops in a greased skillet over medium heat. Arrange chops in a shallow 2 quart baking dish. Pour apple juice over chops and sprinkle with raisins and salt. Cover and bake at 350 for 45 minutes. Turn chops. Combine brown sugar, nutmeg, and cinnamon and coat apple wedges with this mixture. Arrange apples around chops. Sprinkle apples with the remaining sugar mixture and pour water over all. Cover and bake an additional 15 minutes. Serves 4 to 6.

Teriyaki Pork Chops

1 cup soy sauce
¾ cup water
½ cup sweet vermouth
½ cup honey

Garlic, to taste
1 teaspoon ginger
8 pork chops

Combine ingredients and pour over pork chops. Marinate overnight. Grill over charcoals for 15-20 minutes on each side, basting with marinade.

Pork Chops Florentine

6 loin pork chops (1/2 to 3/4 inch thick)
1 1/2 pounds fresh spinach, washed, chopped, and lightly steamed
2 tablespoons onion, grated
6 tablespoons butter
6 tablespoons flour
1 1/4 cups strong chicken stock

1 3/4 cups milk
Salt and white pepper
Dash of nutmeg
2 egg yolks, lightly beaten
1 cup Swiss cheese, grated
3 tablespoons Parmesan cheese, freshly grated

Brown pork chops in a lightly greased skillet. Lower heat, cover, and cook about 30 minutes or until tender. Keep warm. Combine the cooked spinach with the grated onion and set aside. In a medium saucepan melt butter. Stir in the flour and cook over low heat for 3 minutes. Slowly stir in chicken stock and milk and continue to stir until thickened. Add salt, pepper, and nutmeg. Stir a little of this sauce into egg yolks and then return the yolk mixture to the sauce, stirring until smooth and thick. Mix 1 cup sauce with spinach mixture and spread it over the bottom of a large, greased shallow casserole. Arrange pork chops on top of the spinach. Meanwhile, stir the Swiss cheese into the sauce and stir over low heat until cheese is melted. Pour sauce over pork chops, sprinkle with Parmesan cheese, and bake uncovered at 400 for 15 minutes or until bubbling and the cheese is lightly browned. Serves 6.

"Great dish for a buffet."

Glen's Duck

2 ducks, cleaned
1 bottle Sauer's Bar-B-Que sauce

1/2 cup vinegar
Wild rice, cooked

Place all ingredients in a crock pot. Cook for six hours and serve over wild rice.

Veal Scallopini Marsala

1 pound veal scallopini	1/2 cup butter
1/2 teaspoon salt	1/2 cup Marsala wine
1/2 teaspoon pepper	Juice of one lemon
2 tablespoons flour	

Season pieces of veal with salt and pepper and dust with flour. Melt butter in a skillet and saute the veal quickly over moderately high heat. Drain off any excess butter and add Marsala wine to veal. Bring to a boil. Arrange scallopini on a platter. Mix lemon juice with drippings and pour on top of the veal.

Veal Strips in Wine Sauce

1/2 cup oil	Salt and pepper
3 pounds very thin veal, cut in small serving pieces	3/4-1 cup dry vermouth
Garlic salt	Lemon juice
Seasoned bread crumbs	Parsley, chopped
1 8 ounce jar mushrooms, sliced or whole	White rice, cooked
	Wild rice, cooked

Heat oil in skillet until hot. Brown veal strips which have been sprinkled on both sides with garlic salt and seasoned bread crumbs. Do not drain oil. Lower heat; cover veal strips with drained mushrooms, salt, pepper, and vermouth. Cover. Simmer slowly for 20 minutes. Add more vermouth and 2-4 tablespoons of water, if necessary, to keep moist and make gravy. When serving, sprinkle with lemon juice and chopped parsley. Serve over white and wild rice, combined half and half.

Veal and Smithfield Ham Swirls

1/2 cup green onions, chopped
1/2 cup butter, melted
 2 cups soft bread crumbs
 2 cloves garlic, minced
 1 cup fresh parsley, chopped
 1 egg, beaten
 2 tablespoons chicken broth
 4 1/2 inch thick boneless
   veal steaks (about 1 3/4 pounds)

 2 teaspoons Dijon mustard
1/2 pound cooked Smithfield ham,
   thinly sliced
 1 tablespoon butter, melted
1/2 cup white wine
   Onion butter

Saute green onions in 1/2 cup butter in large skillet until tender. Remove from heat.
Add bread crumbs and next 4 ingredients. Stir well and set aside. Flatten veal to
1/4 inch thickness with a meat mallet. Spread mustard evenly over veal and top
with a ham slice. Pat 1/4 cup onion mixture evenly over ham. Roll up jelly-roll
fashion and secure with a wooden pick. Place rolls, seam side down, on a rack in a
shallow pan. Brush with 1 tablespoon melted butter. Bake at 325 for 30-35 minutes
or until tender. Remove veal from pan to serving platter. Remove pick and cut into
1/2 inch slices. Add white wine to pan and bring to a boil, stirring to loosen pan
drippings. Pour over veal steaks. Top with onion butter.

Onion Butter

 1 cup purple shallots, chopped
 1 cup red wine

1/2 cup butter, softened

Combine shallots and wine in a saucepan. Cook over medium heat about
5 minutes. Cool. Combine with butter. Place onto waxed paper and shape into a
log 2 inches in diameter. Chill well. Cut into 1/2 inch slices to serve.

"This is a delightful way to serve veal as a company dish."

Veal alla Maria

1 pound veal fillet, sliced into 2 cutlets
All-purpose flour
6 mushrooms, sliced
3 tablespoons water, warm
2 slices prosciutto, diced
5 parsley sprigs, chopped

Pinch of black pepper
3 heaping tablespoons butter
2 tablespoons virgin olive oil
3 tablespoons dry vermouth
2 slices of mozzarella or Fontina cheese

Pound the cutlets thin and sprinkle with flour. Soak the mushrooms in the water for ten minutes. Drain mushrooms, reserving liquid, and chop coarsely. Mix prosciutto, parsley, mushrooms, and black pepper together. Place butter and olive oil in a skillet and heat. Add the veal and cook for 2 minutes; turn over. Add parsley mixture and cook for 4 minutes. Add vermouth and reserved liquid. Cover and cook for 2 minutes. Shake the skillet and place the cheese on the cutlets. Cover and cook slowly for 2 minutes longer. Shake pan well and serve immediately.

Veal with Crabmeat

3 tablespoons all-purpose flour
1/2 teaspoon salt
1/4 teaspoon pepper
1 1/2-1 3/4 pounds boneless veal cutlets (1/4 inch thick)
1/3 cup butter or margarine

1/4 cup lemon juice
3/4 pound lump crabmeat
1 tablespoon fresh parsley, chopped, optional
Microwave Hollandaise, page 170
Paprika

Combine flour, salt, and pepper; dredge veal in flour mixture. Melt butter in a large skillet over medium heat. Add veal, cooking 1 minute on each side or until lightly browned. Add lemon juice to skillet and cook an additional 30 seconds. Remove veal to serving platter. Discard all but 1 tablespoon of pan drippings. Add crabmeat to reserved drippings and sprinkle with parsley, if desired. Saute until heated. Spoon crabmeat evenly over cutlets. Top with Hollandaise sauce and sprinkle with paprika. Serve immediately. Serves 6.

"A wonderfully tasty dish."

Veal Scallops with Mushrooms and Ham

4 veal scallops, ¼ inch thick
Flour for dusting scallops
4 tablespoons butter
Salt and pepper
2 medium onions, chopped
2 shallots, minced
½ pound fresh
mushrooms, chopped

1 4 ounce ham slice, cut
in julienne strips
2 tablespoons flour
1 cup milk
¾ cup Gruyere or other
Swiss cheese, grated
2 tablespoons cream, warmed

Dust the scallops with flour. Heat butter in a skillet over moderately high heat. Add scallops and brown lightly. Season with salt and pepper and place in an ovenproof baking dish. Add onions and shallots to the skillet and saute for 5 minutes. Add mushrooms and cook an additional 2 minutes. Add ham to the skillet. Stir in 2 tablespoons flour and slowly add milk. Bring the sauce to a boil, stirring constantly, then lower heat and cook until thick. Sprinkle half of the cheese on the veal scallops, cover with sauce, and top with the remaining cheese. Bake uncovered at 425 for 15 minutes. Just before serving, sprinkle with cream. Serves 4.

Marinated Lamb Chops

8 loin lamb chops, cut 1 inch thick
and trimmed
2 tablespoons wine vinegar
1 tablespoon lemon juice
2 teaspoons mustard
3 tablespoons olive oil

1 clove garlic, minced
¼ teaspoon ground ginger
1 teaspoon rosemary
¼ teaspoon salt
1 small onion, sliced

Place lamb chops in a deep ceramic or glass bowl. Combine remaining ingredients and pour over chops. Marinate in the refrigerator, covered, for 4-5 hours. Broil over a hot charcoal fire or under an oven broiler for 5 minutes per side for medium rare. Serves 4.

Lamb and Artichoke Stew

1 tablespoon butter
2 pounds lamb, cut into cubes
3 onions, chopped
2 cloves garlic, crushed
1/2 cup parsley, chopped
  Salt and pepper
1 6 ounce can tomato paste

1 cup dry white wine
2 14 ounce cans artichokes
  in brine, drained
1/2 teaspoon dried dill weed
3 tablespoons lemon juice
  Rice pilaf

Using a large frying pan, melt butter and saute lamb until lightly browned. Remove. Saute onion, garlic, and parsley in same pan. Place meat, onions, garlic, and parsley in a Dutch oven or heavy kettle. Add salt, pepper, tomato paste, and wine. Cover and simmer 1 1/2 hours. Add artichokes, dill, and lemon juice. Simmer 1 1/2 hours. Serve over rice pilaf.

Lamb Curry

5 tablespoons butter
1 teaspoon mild fresh curry
1 cup onions, sliced
2 medium-sized apples, cored,
  peeled, and sliced
2 cups lamb, cut into cubes

2 tablespoons flour
1 chicken bouillon cube, mixed
  with 2 cups hot water
1 tablespoon lemon juice
  Salt and pepper

Melt 3 tablespoons butter in large frying pan. Add curry. Saute onions and apples until onions are tender. Remove from pan. Brown lamb in pan. Remove lamb from pan. In same pan, melt 2 tablespoons butter and stir in 2 tablespoons flour. Let this bubble for a minute but do not brown. Add hot bouillon all at once. Stir until sauce is smooth and thick. Add onions, apples, and meat. Stir in lemon juice and add salt and pepper to taste. Simmer for 30 minutes. Serves 4. This can, and should be made ahead of time. Reheat when ready to serve, but do not overcook, as apples will become too mushy.

STARBOARD
SIDES

Vegetables

Asparagus and Peas Casserole

2 14½ ounce cans
   asparagus spears
1 17 ounce can green peas
4 hard cooked eggs, peeled
   and sliced

½ cup bread crumbs, buttered
   Cheese Sauce

Preheat oven to 350. Drain asparagus and peas, reserving the liquid. Cut the asparagus into 1 inch pieces. Set aside.

Cheese Sauce

6 tablespoons butter
¼ cup plus 3 tablespoons flour
1½ cups reserved vegetable liquid

1 pound processed American
   cheese, cut into 1 inch cubes

Melt butter over medium heat. Stir in flour. Whisk in reserved vegetable liquid. Stir until thick. Add cheese; stir until melted.

Arrange half of the vegetables in a 2 quart casserole. Place 2 sliced eggs on top. Pour half of cheese sauce over eggs. Repeat layers. Add bread crumbs on top. Bake for 30 minutes.

Asparagus Casserole

2 cups asparagus, or 2 15 ounce
   cans long stemmed asparagus
1 cup celery, chopped

1 can cream of celery soup
1 cup grated Mozzarella cheese
4 ounces slivered almonds, toasted

Preheat oven to 350. Place asparagus in casserole dish. Add chopped celery followed by cream of celery soup. Place Mozzarella on top. Place in oven for about 20 minutes. Remove and place toasted almonds on top. Return to oven for 10 minutes or until bubbly. Serves 4.

Asparagus with Avocado Dressing

3½ pounds thin asparagus
1 egg
1 ripe avocado, peeled and
    cut into chunks
1 teaspoon salt

1 teaspoon extra fine sugar
½ cup lime juice
2 teaspoons chives, minced
½ teaspoon Tabasco sauce
4 tablespoons buttermilk

Rinse asparagus and snap off butts where they bend. Set asparagus on steamer rack over boiling water. Steam for 5-8 minutes. Set aside until cooled. Combine egg, avocado, salt, sugar, lime juice, chives, and Tabasco in blender. Make a puree. Add buttermilk gradually. Scoop into a serving dish. Cover tightly and refrigerate. To serve, arrange asparagus on plates and spoon dressing over each.

"This dish is excellent for a luncheon served with quiche and crusty French bread."

Oven Baked Fresh Asparagus

2 pounds fresh asparagus
3 tablespoons fresh parsley, minced
2 tablespoons olive oil

2 tablespoons butter, melted
    Salt and pepper

Preheat oven to 400. Wash, drain, and break ends off asparagus. Arrange in one layer in baking dish. Sprinkle with parsley. Combine oil and melted butter; drizzle over asparagus. Add salt and pepper. Cover with foil and bake at 400 for 15 minutes.

Brandied Bean Casserole

1 15 ounce can
   kidney beans, drained
1 16 ounce can pork and
   beans, drained
1/2 cup California brandy

1/4 cup molasses
1/4 cup ketchup
1/4 cup minced dried onions
1 cup ham, cubed (optional)
1 cup cheddar cheese, cubed

Drain beans. Mix all ingredients except cheese. Bake at 375 for 40 minutes. Remove from oven and stir cheese cubes into casserole. Continue baking 10 more minutes. Serve hot.

Mexican Broccoli

1 package chopped
   broccoli, thawed
1/2 cup onion, chopped
1/2 cup celery, chopped
1 cup Minute Rice, uncooked
1 cup water

1 can cream of mushroom soup
1/4 cup margarine, melted
1 small jar of Cheese Whiz
1 tablespoon Cheese Whiz with
   jalapeño peppers

Mix all ingredients together. Bake at 325 for 30-45 minutes until bubbly.

Broccoli with Cashews

1 large bunch fresh broccoli
2 tablespoons onion, minced
2 tablespoons butter
1 cup sour cream
2 teaspoons sugar

1 teaspoon vinegar
1/2 teaspoon poppy seeds
1/4 teaspoon salt
1/2 teaspoon paprika
1 cup cashews, toasted

Cook broccoli in water until crisp. Saute onion in butter. Stir in sour cream and remaining ingredients, except cashews. Layer broccoli in a buttered 1 1/2 quart baking dish and cover with sauce. Sprinkle with cashews and bake uncovered at 325 for 25 minutes.

Italian Broccoli Casserole

2 10 ounce packages
frozen cut broccoli
2 eggs, beaten
1 can condensed
cheddar cheese soup

1/2 teaspoon dried oregano, crushed
1 8 ounce can stewed
tomatoes, cut up
3 tablespoons Parmesan
cheese, grated

Cook broccoli in unsalted boiling water 5-7 minutes or until tender; drain well. Combine eggs, cheddar cheese soup, and oregano. Stir in stewed tomatoes and cooked broccoli. Pour vegetable-cheese mixture into a 10x6x2 baking dish. Sprinkle with Parmesan cheese. Bake at 350 for 30 minutes until bubbly.

Barbecued Corn on the Cob

6 ears fresh corn
1/2 cup butter or margarine, melted
2 envelopes instant
tomato soup mix

1/2 cup water
1 medium onion, finely chopped

Remove husks and silks from corn just before cooking. Combine remaining ingredients; stir well. Place each ear on a piece of aluminum foil and spoon 2 tablespoons of sauce over each. Wrap foil tightly around corn. Bake at 425 for 12-15 minutes.

Corn Pudding

1 onion, finely chopped
1/4 cup margarine
1 large can cream-style corn
2 eggs, beaten
2 teaspoons salt
3 tablespoons sugar

1 teaspoon black pepper
2 jalapeno peppers, chopped
2 tablespoons Worcestershire sauce
1 teaspoon dry mustard
1 cup milk
1 cup sharp cheddar cheese, grated

Brown onion in margarine. Add remaining ingredients. Mix well. Pour into a greased casserole dish and bake at 375 for 50-60 minutes.

Microwave Creole Corn

2 cups fresh cut corn
2 slices bacon
1 small onion, minced
1 16 ounce can stewed
   tomatoes, drained

1 bay leaf
1/8 teaspoon pepper
   Dash of Tabasco sauce

Pour corn into covered casserole. Microwave on high 4-5 minutes. Dice bacon and arrange in 1 quart casserole. Cover and microwave on high for 3 minutes. Remove bacon and add onion to drippings. Cover and microwave for 2 minutes. Add corn, stewed tomatoes, bay leaf, pepper, Tabasco sauce, and reserved bacon. Mix well. Microwave before serving.

Smothered Cabbage Wedges

1 medium head of cabbage,
   cut in 8 wedges
1/2 cup green pepper,
   finely chopped
1/4 cup onion, finely chopped
4 tablespoons margarine
1/4 cup all purpose flour

1/2 teaspoon salt
1/8 teaspoon pepper
2 cups milk
1/2 cup mayonnaise
3/4 cup cheddar cheese, grated
3 tablespoons chili sauce

In Dutch oven or large skillet, cook cabbage wedges in small amount of boiling salted water until tender, or about 12 minutes. Drain well. Place cooked cabbage wedges in 13x9x2 baking dish. In saucepan, cook green pepper and onion in margarine until tender, but not brown. Blend in flour, salt, and pepper. Add milk all at once; cook and stir until mixture thickens and bubbles. Pour over cabbage. Bake uncovered at 375 for 20 minutes. Combine mayonnaise, cheese, and chili sauce. Spoon over wedges. Bake 5 more minutes. Serves 8.

Company Carrot Casserole

12 carrots, peeled and sliced
 1 small onion, sliced
½ cup flour
¼ cup margarine
 1 teaspoon salt
¼ teaspoon celery salt

¼ teaspoon dry mustard
¼ teaspoon pepper
 2 cups milk
 1 cup sharp cheddar
   cheese, shredded
 2 cups fresh bread crumbs, buttered

Cook the carrots until tender. Add the onion and cook for 2-3 more minutes. Set aside. Make a cream sauce of the flour, margarine, salt, celery salt, mustard, pepper, and milk. Heat until thick; then stir in cheese and stir until melted. Pour over carrots in a casserole dish. Top with buttered bread crumbs. Serve hot.

Nutty Carrots

  5 cups carrots, cut into 3 inch sticks
1½ cups water
 ½ teaspoon salt
 ½ cup butter, melted
  2 teaspoons honey
  1 teaspoon salt

¼ teaspoon coarse ground pepper
 2 tablespoons fresh lemon juice
¼ teaspoon lemon peel,
   freshly grated
½ cup walnuts, broken in pieces

Cook carrots in water with ½ teaspoon salt until just tender. Drain thoroughly. In the meantime, heat all remaining ingredients, except walnuts. Pour sauce over hot carrots. Toss with walnut pieces.

Marinated Carrots

5 cups carrots, sliced
1 medium sweet onion,
   cut in round slices
1 small green pepper,
   cut in round slices
1 can tomato soup
1/2 cup salad oil

3/4 cup sugar
3/4 cup vinegar
1 teaspoon mustard
1 teaspoon Worcestershire sauce
1 teaspoon salt
1 teaspoon pepper

Cook carrots; drain and cool. Mix carrots and remaining ingredients. Cover and marinate 12 hours in refrigerator. Drain before serving. Serves 8-10.

String Bean Casserole

1 1/2 cups butter, melted
1 large onion, chopped
1 pound fresh mushrooms, sliced
1/4 cup flour
2 cups milk
3/4 cup cheddar cheese, grated

1/3 teaspoon Tabasco sauce
1 teaspoon salt
1/2 teaspoon pepper
3 cans French green beans, drained
1 cup sliced water chestnuts
1/4 cup slivered almonds

Saute onions and mushrooms in butter. Stir in flour. Add milk while stirring. Add cheese. Do not boil. Add Tabasco, salt, and pepper; stir. Add beans and water chestnuts and stir. Pour into 1 1/2 quart casserole and bake at 350 for 40 minutes. Sprinkle almonds on top for last 15 minutes of baking.

Frozen Cucumbers

7-8 cups cucumbers, unpeeled
     and thinly sliced
  1 cup onion, diced
  1 cup green peppers, diced

1 tablespoon salt
2 cups sugar
1 cup vinegar
1 teaspoon celery seed

Combine cucumbers, onions, green peppers, and salt. Allow ingredients to marinate for 1 hour. Mix sugar, vinegar and celery seed; pour over cucumber mixture. Freeze until ready to use; thaw before serving. Served chilled.

Baked Mushrooms with Cheese

  1 pound fresh mushrooms
1/2 cup butter
  2 shallots, finely chopped

Salt and pepper
1/2 cup sour cream
  4 ounces cheddar cheese, grated

Wash and slice mushrooms, removing ends of stems. Melt butter in skillet and add shallots and mushrooms. Cook slowly until tender. Add salt and pepper. Drain mushroom mixture. Put in a casserole and cover with sour cream. Sprinkle with cheese and broil until lightly browned. Serve immediately.

Cold Dill Peas

  1 10 ounce package
     frozen tiny peas
  1 cup sour cream
1/2-1 tablespoon dill weed
  1 teaspoon chives, chopped

1/2-1 teaspoon curry powder
     Salt and pepper
     Fresh lemon juice
     Fresh dill or chives for garnish

Cook and thoroughly drain peas. Combine all remaining ingredients and mix well. Gently stir in peas and chill. Garnish with fresh dill or chives.

"Great summertime vegetable to use for a cookout."

Peas with Rosemary and Toasted Pine Nuts

½ cup chicken stock
2 spring onions, 2 inches of
   green part included
½ teaspoon sugar
3 pounds fresh peas, shelled
6 large lettuce leaves

3 tablespoons butter
10 tablespoons pine nuts
1 tablespoon fresh rosemary,
   minced, or 1 teaspoon dried
   and crumbled
Salt and pepper

Bring stock, green onions, and sugar to simmer in medium saucepan. Add peas. Simmer 5-10 minutes, or until tender. Drain, discarding liquid. Arrange lettuce leaves on a platter. Over medium heat, melt butter in heavy skillet. Add pine nuts and toast until golden brown approximately 2-3 minutes. Mix in rosemary and cook 1 minute. Add peas and green onions. Stir until hot. Season with salt and pepper. Spoon mixture onto lettuce leaves and serve.

Basil Oven Fries

3-4 medium baking potatoes,
   peeled and cut ¼ inch thick
⅓ cup olive oil

1 teaspoon salt
   Freshly ground black pepper
⅓ cup fresh basil, chopped

Wash, peel and slice potatoes into ¼ inch slices. Line baking sheet with heavy-duty foil. Drizzle 3 tablespoons of olive oil on foil, spreading evenly. Place slices on baking sheet taking care to overlap as little as possible. Season with salt and pepper. Turn slices to coat with oil and seasonings. Broil potatoes 6 inches from heat until brown, about 13 minutes. Carefully turn potatoes over; broil 12 minutes on this side or until golden brown. Remove from oven; sprinkle with basil and toss. Serve hot. Serves 3-4.
"*Great for summer supper with grilled steaks and sliced tomatoes.*"

Potatoes Supreme

1-2 pound package frozen
    hash brown potatoes
1 can cream of celery soup
1 can cream of potato soup
1/2 cup onion, chopped
8 ounces sour cream
1/2 cup milk
1 tablespoon parsley

1/4 teaspoon pepper
1/2 teaspoon salt
1 green pepper,
    chopped (optional)
8 ounces cheddar cheese,
    shredded
8 strips bacon, cooked
    and crumbled

Preheat oven to 350. Thaw potatoes. Combine potatoes, soups, onion, sour cream, milk, parsley, pepper, and salt. Add green pepper if desired. Put mixture in oblong pan. Cover with foil and bake 45 minutes. Remove foil and put cheese and bacon on top. Bake an additional 15 minutes.

Savory New Potatoes

1 3/4 pounds tiny new potatoes
1 egg, room temperature
2/3 cup corn oil
1/4 cup cider vinegar
1 1/2 teaspoons Dijon mustard
1 1/2 teaspoons fresh savory
    or chives, minced

1/2 teaspoon sugar
1 teaspoon salt
1/4 teaspoon white pepper,
    freshly ground

Boil potatoes until just tender. Set aside and cool. Whisk egg in small bowl to blend. Slowly whisk in oil, beginning with a few drops. After mixture starts to blend, add oil in a slow steady stream. Blend in remaining ingredients. Arrange potatoes on a platter. Drizzle with dressing mixture. Serve at room temperature.

Fantastic Potatoes

12 potatoes
1 8 ounce container sour cream
1 8 ounce package cream cheese
1 garlic clove, minced

2 teaspoons pepper
1/4 cup chives, minced
1 tablespoon butter
1/2 teaspoon paprika

Peel, dice, and cook potatoes. Mash potatoes and add sour cream, cream cheese, garlic, and pepper. Stir in chives. Spoon into greased casserole. Dot with 1 tablespoon butter and 1/2 teaspoon paprika. Bake at 350 for 1 hour.

Herbed Potato Bake

1/4 cup margarine, melted
1 envelope onion soup mix
1 teaspoon rosemary

3 baking potatoes, unpeeled and cut into 1/2 inch slices

Preheat oven to 350. Combine margarine, soup mix, and rosemary. Scrub potatoes and cut into 1/2 inch slices. Toss potatoes in soup mixture and arrange in a shallow baking dish. Cover and bake at 350 for 1 hour. Serves 4.

"Great with grilled meats."

Fresh Garden Mix

1 medium zucchini, sliced
1 medium yellow squash, sliced
1 medium onion, sliced
6-12 Chinese pea pods
1 cup fresh green beans

1 small green pepper, chopped
4 tablespoons butter
3/4 teaspoon seasoned salt
2 tablespoons seasoned pepper
1/2 teaspoon dill weed

Saute all vegetables in melted butter. Cover pan tightly and heat on low for 10-12 minutes, stirring occasionally. Sprinkle with seasoning salt, seasoning pepper, and dill weed before serving.

Grilled Mixed Vegetables

2 garlic cloves, crushed
1 teaspoon salt
1 teaspoon rosemary
  Pepper
1 cup olive oil

12 large mushrooms
6 1¼ inch slices Spanish onion
6 1¼ inch slices eggplant
6 plum or cherry tomatoes
3 green peppers, quartered

Combine garlic, salt, rosemary, and pepper in a large shallow pan. Whisk in olive oil. Cut stems from mushrooms; add to marinade along with onion, eggplant, tomatoes, and green peppers. Toss to coat and marinate for at least 2 hours. Put the vegetables on skewers or hinged broiling racks set over grill and broil for 8 minutes. Turn and grill 6 minutes more until tender. Transfer to a heated platter and serve.

Winter Vegetables Julienne

1 leek
2 large carrots
2 medium white turnips
3 medium zucchini
5 tablespoons unsalted butter

5 teaspoons Dijon mustard
1 teaspoon salt
2 tablespoons green peppercorns
  Freshly ground black pepper

Wash, peel, and julienne vegetables. Over medium high heat, melt butter in 10 inch heavy skillet. Stir in mustard and salt. Add vegetables except zucchini to skillet; toss to coat. Saute vegetables until slightly softened, about 3-5 minutes. Add zucchini to skillet and cook, stirring and tossing about 3 more minutes. Add peppercorns and pepper; toss again. Serve immediately.

Vidalia Onion Casserole

4-5 Vidalia onions, sliced
Butter
Salt and pepper

1½ cups Longhorn cheese, grated
½ cup Ritz crackers, crushed

Saute onion in butter only until transparent; add salt and pepper. Place half of onions in a 1½ quart casserole. Sprinkle half of cheese on this layer of onions. Place remaining onions in dish and sprinkle with remaining cheese. Cover top with crackers and dot with butter. Bake at 325 for 30 minutes.

Bleu Cheese Crusted Onions

2 large Spanish onions, thinly sliced
6 ounces bleu cheese
6 tablespoons unsalted butter, room temperature

2 teaspoons Worcestershire sauce
½ teaspoon dried dill weed
Freshly ground black pepper

Generously butter 9x13 baking dish. Position rack in center of oven and preheat to 425. Peel and wash onions. Slice onions thin, being sure to leave slice intact. Transfer to buttered dish, spreading evenly over bottom. Combine remaining ingredients in mixing bowl. Blend well. Spread cheese mixture over onions in pan using a flexible spatula. Bake 20 minutes, then broil briefly until top is brown and bubbly. Serve hot.

Chili Squash

1 medium onion, chopped
2 tablespoons butter, melted
1 zucchini, cut into ¼ inch slices
1 4 ounce can chopped green chilies, drained

1 medium tomato, peeled and chopped
½ teaspoon salt
⅛ teaspoon pepper

Saute onion in butter in large skillet for 2 minutes. Add remaining ingredients. Stir gently. Cover and cook 5 minutes or until crisp and tender; stir occasionally. Serves 6.

Zucchini Sticks

3-4 medium zucchini, cut into 2 inch lengths	1/4 cup whipping cream
Oil for frying	1/4 teaspoon salt
4 eggs	1/2 teaspoon freshly ground pepper
	3/4 cup seasoned bread crumbs

Slice zucchini into French fry-sized sticks. Preheat oil to 350. In blender or processor, mix eggs, whipping cream salt, and pepper; transfer to bowl. Dip zucchini pieces into egg mixture, then coat with bread crumbs. Add to hot oil in batches and fry until brown and crisp, about 3-4 minutes. Drain on paper towels. Serve hot.

Zucchini Au Gratin

2 pounds zucchini	2 tablespoons flour
2 1/2 cups hot zucchini juices	1/4 teaspoon savory
1 teaspoon salt	1/2 cup rice, cooked
3 tablespoons olive oil	2/3 cup grated Parmesan cheese
1 cup onions, minced	2 tablespoons olive oil

Prepare and grate zucchini. Sprinkle salt over zucchini and toss. Let zucchini drain in colander over bowl. Heat juices left in bowl. Heat 3 tablespoons olive oil in large skillet; add onions and cook slowly until onions are translucent. Remove zucchini from colander; squeeze and pat dry. Increase heat under skillet with onions and brown them while stirring. Add zucchini. Cook and stir 5 minutes until zucchini is almost tender. Sprinkle on flour and stir to coat. Add hot liquid (zucchini juices) gradually while stirring. Add savory and cook until simmering and smooth. Remove from heat. Stir in rice and all but 2 tablespoons cheese. Put in buttered baking dish and sprinkle with reserved cheese. Drizzle the 2 tablespoons olive oil evenly over cheese. Bake at 425 for 30 minutes or until liquid is absorbed.

Summer Squash Casserole

3-4 cups squash, cooked
    and mashed
1 cup sour cream
1 can cream of chicken soup
¾ cup onion, chopped

1 carrot, grated
    Salt and pepper
1 package Pepperidge Farm
    herb dressing
1 stick butter, melted

Mash squash. Mix sour cream, soup, onion, carrot, and salt and pepper. Fold in mashed squash. Add dressing to melted butter and mix thoroughly. In 2 quart casserole, layer squash mixture with dressing, starting with squash and ending with dressing. Bake at 350 for 30 minutes.

Sunshine Casserole

2 pounds yellow squash, sliced
1 medium onion, sliced
½ teaspoon garlic salt
¼ teaspoon ground cumin
1 teaspoon salt
¼ teaspoon pepper

1 10 ounce package frozen whole
    kernel corn, cooked and drained
2 cups sharp cheddar
    cheese, grated
    Seasoned bread crumbs

In large covered skillet, steam squash and onion in small amount of water. When vegetables are tender, drain. Gently stir in seasonings and corn. Cover and cook an additional 5 minutes. Stir in cheese and pour into 1½ quart casserole. Top with bread crumbs. Bake at 350 for 25-30 minutes. Can be microwaved on high for 10 minutes and placed under broiler until golden brown.

Mock Crab Cakes

2 cups zucchini, peeled and grated
1 cup bread crumbs
2 eggs
2 tablespoons onion, grated

1 teaspoon Old Bay seasoning
1 tablespoon mayonnaise
Oil for frying

Drain zucchini for 2 hours to remove as much water as possible. Mix zucchini with remaining ingredients. Form into cakes. Using only enough oil to cover bottom of non-stick pan, fry on both sides until golden brown.

Baked Spinach and Artichoke Hearts

1 can artichoke hearts, drained
2 packages frozen chopped
   spinach, thawed and drained
2 tablespoons mayonnaise

7 tablespoons milk
1/2 teaspoon garlic salt
1 8 ounce package cream cheese
   Grated Romano cheese

Grease 8x8 baking dish and line bottom with quartered artichoke hearts. Cover with spinach. Blend mayonnaise, milk, and garlic salt with cream cheese. Mix well. Spread cream cheese mixture over spinach. Sprinkle top with grated Romano cheese. Bake at 350 for 30 minutes. Serves 8.

Grated Sweet Potato Pudding

2 cups raw sweet potatoes, grated
1 1/2 cups milk
2 eggs, beaten
1 cup sugar

4 tablespoons butter, melted
1 teaspoon vanilla
   Dash cinnamon

Peel and grate raw sweet potatoes. Add cold milk and mix well. Add beaten eggs, sugar, butter, and vanilla. Pour into greased baking dish. Sprinkle with cinnamon. Bake at 350 for 1 hour or until golden brown.

Vegetable Rice Ring

2 cups rice, cooked
1/2 cup Italian salad dressing
1/2 cup mayonnaise
1 cup radishes, chopped
1 cucumber, seeded and chopped
2 tomatoes, seeded and chopped
1 green pepper, chopped

1 red pepper, chopped
1 carrot, chopped
1/2 cup celery, diced
1/2 cup green onions, chopped
  Lettuce
  Cherry tomatoes

Cook rice a day ahead. Marinate overnight in Italian salad dressing. Cover and chill. Add mayonnaise to undrained rice mixture and blend well. Fold in vegetables and press into bundt pan or large ring mold. Cover and refrigerate at least 3 hours. Unmold onto platter. Garnish with lettuce leaves and fill center with cherry tomatoes. Serves 12.

Cheese and Broccoli Rice

2 eggs
1 cup milk
4 green onions, chopped
1 clove garlic, minced
1 cup broccoli, chopped and
  partially cooked

1/4 cup bacon drippings
1 cup cheddar cheese, grated
2 cups rice, cooked
  Salt and pepper

Mix eggs with milk. Add green onions, garlic, broccoli, bacon drippings, and cheese. Add mixture to cooked rice. Add salt and pepper. Bake in casserole at 350 for 45 minutes or until firm.

Cheese and Rice Puffs
with Vegetable Sauce

3 cups rice, cooked and cooled
3 eggs, slightly beaten
1/2 cup all purpose flour
1/2 teaspoon salt
1/4 teaspoon pepper

3 ounces Edam or cheddar cheese, cut into 1/2 inch cubes
1/2 cup crackers, finely crushed
Cooking oil for frying
Vegetable Sauce

Combine rice, eggs, flour, salt, and pepper. Shape 2 tablespoonfuls of rice mixture around each cheese cube. Shape in cracker crumbs. Fry rice balls, 4 or 5 at a time, in 1/2 inch hot oil for 2 1/2-3 minutes; turn once. Remove, drain, and keep warm. Serve with vegetable sauce poured over rice puffs.

Vegetable Sauce

2 tablespoons green pepper, chopped
2 tablespoons onion, chopped
2 tablespoons carrot, shredded
2 tablespoons butter or margarine

2 tablespoons all purpose flour
1/2 teaspoon salt
Dash pepper
1 1/2 cups milk
Excess cheese from rice puffs

Cook green pepper, onion, and carrot in butter until tender. Stir in flour, salt, and pepper. Add milk. Cook and stir until bubbly; cook 1 minute more. Stir in remaining cheese from rice puffs and cook until melted.

Sweet Potato Souffle

3-5 cups sweet potatoes,
       cooked and mashed
1½ cups sugar
 ½ pound butter
       or margarine, melted
 3 eggs, beaten
 ¾ cup milk

1 cup brown sugar
1 cup pecans, chopped
1 cup coconut
⅓ cup flour
½ pound butter or
     margarine, melted

Combine first five ingredients and pour into greased baking dish. Blend together brown sugar, pecans, coconut, flour, and butter. Sprinkle over souffle. Bake at 375 for approximately 25 minutes, until slightly browned.

"Excellent for a holiday dinner."

Broccoli Stuffed Tomatoes

6 medium tomatoes
    Salt and pepper
1 package frozen chopped
    broccoli, cooked
1 cup Swiss cheese, grated

1 cup soft bread crumbs
½ cup mayonnaise
2 tablespoons onion, chopped
2 tablespoons Parmesan
    cheese, grated

Cut tops from tomatoes. Scoop out pulp leaving shells intact. Sprinkle cavities with salt and pepper. Invert on wire rack to drain. Cook broccoli and drain well. Combine broccoli and next four ingredients. Mix well. Stuff tomatoes with broccoli mixture. Sprinkle with Parmesan cheese. Bake at 350 for 30 minutes.

Vera Cruz Tomatoes

6 strips bacon
1/4 cup onion, chopped
1/2 pound fresh spinach, snipped
1/2 cup sour cream

Dash Tabasco
4 medium tomatoes
1/2 cup Mozzarella cheese, shredded

Cook bacon; crumble and set aside. Cook onion in 2 tablespoons bacon drippings till tender; stir in spinach and cook, covered, 5 minutes. Remove from heat; stir in sour cream, bacon, and Tabasco. Cut tops from tomatoes, remove centers, leaving shells. Drain. Salt shells and fill with spinach mixture. Place in 8x8x2 baking pan. Bake at 375 for 20-25 minutes. Top with shredded cheese; bake 2-3 more minutes or till cheese is melted. Serves 4.

Microwave Hollandaise

1/4 cup butter
2 egg yolks, beaten
1/4 cup half and half

1 tablespoon lemon juice
1/2 teaspoon dry mustard
1/4 teaspoon salt

Place butter in 2 cup glass casserole. Microwave on high for 30-45 seconds, or until melted. Mix together egg yolks, half and half, lemon juice, dry mustard, and salt. Stir a little hot mixture into egg mixture; then stir egg mixture into hot mixture. Microwave on high for 1-1 1/2 minutes, or until thickened, stirring every 15 seconds. Remove from microwave and beat until light. Yields 2/3 cup.

GALLEON GRAINERY

Breads

Peach Spread

1 6 ounce package cream cheese
1/2 cup fresh peaches, peeled and
    chopped, or frozen peaches,
    thawed and drained
1/4 cup slivered almonds, toasted

2 tablespoons honey
1/2 teaspoon vanilla
    Dash of ground cinnamon
    Dash of ground ginger

Place cream cheese, peaches, almonds, honey, vanilla, cinnamon, and ginger in bowl of food processor fitted with steel blade and process until smooth. Serve with warm bread or muffins. This may be stored covered in the refrigerator.

Strawberry Butter

1 cup butter, softened
2/3 cup strawberries, chopped

3 tablespoons powdered sugar

Whip ingredients in blender until light. Serve with warm biscuits.

Banana Bread

2 cups all purpose flour, sifted
1 teaspoon baking soda
1/2 teaspoon salt
1/2 cup butter
1 cup sugar
2 eggs

1 cup bananas, very ripe
    and mashed
1/3 cup milk
1 teaspoon lemon juice or vinegar
1/2 cup nuts, chopped

Preheat oven to 350. Sift flour, baking soda, and salt. Cream butter and gradually add sugar. Mix well. Add eggs and bananas, blending thoroughly. Combine milk and lemon juice, which will curdle a bit. Slowly and alternately fold in dry ingredients and milk mixture, beginning and ending with the dry ingredients. Blend well after each addition. Stir in nuts, then pour the batter into a heavily buttered 9x5x3 pan. Bake for 1 hour, or until bread springs back when lightly touched in the center.

Quick Blueberry Bread

5 cups flour	4 eggs
1½ cups sugar	2 cups milk
¾ cup butter or margarine	2 teaspoons vanilla extract
1 teaspoon salt	3 cups blueberries
2 tablespoons baking powder	1½ cups pecans or walnuts, chopped

Preheat oven to 350. Blend flour, sugar, butter, salt, and baking powder in a mixer or food processor. Beat eggs, milk, and vanilla together. Add to flour mixture and blend well. Gently add blueberries and nuts. Pour into loaf pans (5 mini pans or 2 bread pans). Bake one hour and 20 minutes or until brown. Cool in the pans for 1 hour. Remove from pans and continue to cool on racks.

Blueberry Pumpkin Muffins

1½ cups all purpose flour	½ cup canned solid pack pumpkin
⅔ cup sugar	½ cup milk
2 teaspoons baking powder	1 egg
¾ teaspoon salt	¼ cup butter or margarine, melted
½ teaspoon cinnamon	¾ cup fresh or frozen blueberries
½ teaspoon nutmeg	¼ cup brown sugar, firmly packed

Preheat oven to 400. Grease 12 2½ inch muffin pan cups. In medium bowl combine dry ingredients. In small bowl blend pumpkin, milk, egg, and butter. Add pumpkin mixture to dry ingredients and stir just until blended. Fold in blueberries. Fill prepared muffin cups ¾ full. Sprinkle batter evenly with brown sugar. Bake for 20 minutes. Serve warm.

"Wonderful texture!"

Carrot Bread

3 eggs
1 cup white sugar
1 cup vegetable oil
1 tablespoon vanilla
1 tablespoon cinnamon
1 teaspoon salt

2 cups carrots, coarsely grated
1 cup brown sugar, packed
2 cups flour
2 teaspoons baking soda
¼ teaspoon baking powder
1 cup nuts, chopped

Beat eggs, then add sugar, oil, and vanilla, stirring until well mixed. Add remaining ingredients and mix. Pour into 2 ungreased loaf pans and bake at 350 for 50-60 minutes. Invert on racks and let cool completely.

"Zucchini or any type of squash may be used instead of carrots."

Cherry Nut Bread

¾ cup sugar
½ cup butter
2 eggs
2 cups all purpose flour, sifted
1 teaspoon baking soda
½ teaspoon salt

1 cup buttermilk
1 cup pecans, chopped
1 10 ounce jar maraschino cherries, drained and chopped
1 teaspoon vanilla

In large bowl, cream together sugar, butter, and eggs until fluffy. Sift together flour, soda, and salt. Add dry ingredients to creamed mixture with buttermilk. Beat until blended. Stir in nuts, cherries, and vanilla. Pour into greased 9x5x3 loaf pan. Bake at 350 for 55-60 minutes.

"A family favorite."

Cranberry Bread

Grated peel and juice of 1 orange
2 tablespoons oil
2 tablespoons water
2 cups flour
1 teaspoon baking powder
1/2 teaspoon baking soda

1/2 teaspoon salt
1 egg
3/4 cup sugar
1 cup cranberries,
    coarsely chopped

Mix orange peel, orange juice, water, and oil. Combine flour, baking powder, soda, and salt in a separate container. Beat egg and sugar until light and fluffy. Stir in alternate amounts of orange mixture and dry ingredients, adding cranberries with the last addition of flour. Stir just until blended. Turn into greased 6 cup tube pan or 9x5x3 loaf pan. Bake in 325 oven for 45 minutes for tube pan or 1 hour for loaf pan or until pick comes out clean. Cool completely and wrap airtight. Keeps for approximately 3 days.

"One cup thawed frozen blueberries may be substituted for cranberries."

Cranberry Muffins

2 cups Bisquick
1/2 cup sugar
1 tablespoon orange zest, grated
1/2 cup nuts, chopped

1 egg
1/4 cup orange juice
1 8 ounce can whole
    cranberry sauce

Preheat oven to 400. Mix together Bisquick, sugar, grated orange zest, and nuts. Mix eggs, orange juice, and cranberry sauce together. Combine egg mixture with dry ingredients, stirring until ingredients are just moistened. Line muffin tins with paper cupcake liners. Fill tins 2/3 full and bake for 25 minutes.

Lemon Poppy Seed Miniature Muffins

½ cup butter, softened
¾ cup sugar
 2 large eggs, separated
 1 teaspoon lemon zest
1½ teaspoons vanilla
1⅓ cups all purpose flour

1¼ teaspoons baking powder
½ teaspoon baking soda
¼ teaspoon salt
½ cup buttermilk
 3 tablespoons poppy seeds

Cream butter and sugar together, beating the mixture until light and fluffy. Add egg yolks one at a time, beating after each addition. Add lemon zest and vanilla. Blend well and set aside. Into another bowl sift together flour, baking powder, baking soda, and salt. Gradually add sifted dry ingredients to butter mixture, alternately with buttermilk. Blend until just combined. Fold in poppy seeds. Beat egg whites to soft peaks and fold egg whites into mixture. Spoon batter into ⅛ cup muffin tins, filling ¾ full. Bake in a preheated 350 oven for 15 minutes. Turn muffins out onto racks and let them cool. Paper muffin tin liners should be used.

Oat Muffins

 1 cup buttermilk
 1 cup quick cooking oats
 1 egg, well beaten
½ cup brown sugar, packed
⅓ cup oil

 1 cup flour
½ teaspoon salt
 1 teaspoon baking powder
½ teaspoon soda

Mix buttermilk and oats in a bowl and refrigerate overnight. Add egg, brown sugar, and oil. Mix well. Sift flour, salt, baking powder, and soda together. Stir sifted ingredients into oats mixture. Place in greased muffin tins. Bake at 400 for 15-20 minutes. Makes 12 muffins.

"A favorite with men!"

Chunky Pecan Muffins

1½ cups all purpose flour
2 teaspoons baking powder
¼ teaspoon salt
½ cup brown sugar, firmly packed
   Pinch of allspice
1 egg, slightly beaten
⅓ cup milk

¼ cup maple flavored syrup
½ cup margarine, melted
1 cup pecans, coarsely chopped
1 teaspoon vanilla extract
¼ cup sugar
¼ teaspoon ground cinnamon
¼ cup margarine, melted

Combine flour, baking powder, salt, brown sugar, and allspice. Make a well in center of mixture. Combine egg, milk, syrup, and ½ cup margarine. Add to dry ingredients, stirring just until moistened. Stir in pecans and vanilla. Fill paper lined muffin pans ⅔ full. Bake at 400 for 15-20 minutes. Combine sugar and cinnamon. Dip tops of warm muffins in remaining margarine, then in sugar and cinnamon mixture. Serves 12.

Pumpkin Bread

1½ cups sugar
2 eggs
½ cup salad oil
1⅔ cups flour
1¼ teaspoon baking powder
1 teaspoon baking soda

¾ teaspoon salt
1½ teaspoons cinnamon
1½ teaspoons cloves
1½ teaspoons nutmeg
1 cup pumpkin, fresh or canned

Stir sugar, eggs, and salad oil together. Sift flour, baking powder, soda, salt, cinnamon, cloves, and nutmeg together. Combine sugar mixture and dry ingredients, mixing well. Stir in pumpkin. Pour batter into greased and floured loaf pan. Bake at 325 for 1 hour 15 minutes.

"A Christmas tradition."

Harvest Pumpkin Loaf

1/2 cup butter, softened
1 cup sugar
2 eggs
1¾ cups all purpose flour
1 teaspoon baking soda
1/2 teaspoon salt
1 teaspoon cinnamon

1/2 teaspoon ground nutmeg
1/4 teaspoon ground ginger
1/4 teaspoon ground cloves
¾ cup pumpkin, cooked
   and mashed
¾ cup semisweet chocolate morsels
¾ cup pecans, chopped

Cream butter. Gradually add sugar and beat well. Add eggs, one at a time, beating well after each addition. Combine flour, soda, salt, cinnamon, nutmeg, ginger, and cloves. Add to creamed mixture alternately with pumpkin, beginning and ending with flour mixture. Stir in chocolate morsels and 1/2 cup pecans. Spoon mixture into a 9x5x13 greased and floured loaf pan. Sprinkle top with remaining 1/4 cup pecans. Bake at 350 for 1 hour and 5 minutes or until wooden pick inserted in center comes out clean. Cool in pan 10 minutes. Remove from pan and cool on wire rack.

Glaze

1/2 cup powdered sugar, sifted
1 tablespoon half and half

1/8 teaspoon ground nutmeg
1/8 teaspoon cinnamon

Combine sugar, half and half, nutmeg, and cinnamon. Stir until smooth. Yields 1/4 cup. Drizzle on cooled cake.

Poor Man's Pudding Loaf

15 ounces raisins
1 cup water
1 cup cold water
3 cups all purpose flour
1 teaspoon cinnamon

1 teaspoon allspice
1 teaspoon ginger
1 teaspoon baking soda
2 cups sugar
1 cup margarine, halved

In a large saucepan, boil raisins in 1 cup water for 15 minutes. Add cold water and set aside. Combine flour, cinnamon, allspice, ginger, baking soda, and sugar. Add dry ingredients to raisin mixture and stir. Melt butter in 2 loaf pans. Pour batter into loaf pans and stir well. Bake at 350 for approximately 1 hour. Cool 15 minutes and remove from pans.

Zucchini Bread

3 eggs
1 cup salad oil
1¾-2 cups sugar
2 cups zucchini, grated
1 tablespoon vanilla
3 cups flour
1 teaspoon salt

1 teaspoon soda
½ teaspoon baking powder
¼ teaspoon allspice
3 teaspoons cinnamon
½ cup nuts, chopped
1 cup raisins or ½ cup dates, finely chopped

Beat eggs until light and fluffy. Add oil, sugar, zucchini, and vanilla, mixing thoroughly. Sift together flour, salt, soda, baking powder, allspice, and cinnamon. While stirring egg mixture gradually add sifted dry ingredients. Add nuts to mixture. Pour into two 9x5x2 loaf pans. Bake at 325-350 for 1 hour.

Zucchini do not need to be peeled before grating unless skin is tough. Very large zucchini may need to have seeds removed before using.

Carrot Bran Muffins

- 1 cup bran flakes cereal, crushed
- 1 cup all purpose flour
- 1/2 cup light brown sugar, firmly packed
- 2 teaspoons baking powder
- 1/2 teaspoon baking soda
- 1/2 teaspoon salt
- 1/2 teaspoon cinnamon
- 1/4 teaspoon nutmeg, freshly grated
- 1 cup milk
- 1 egg
- 3 tablespoons butter
- 1 cup carrots, grated
- 1/2 cup nuts, chopped
- 1/2 cup raisins

Preheat oven to 400. Prepare muffin tins with paper liners or grease. Combine bran flakes, flour, brown sugar, baking powder, baking soda, salt, cinnamon, and nutmeg and sift together into a medium sized mixing bowl. Blend in milk, egg, and butter. Stir until ingredients are moistened. Add carrots, nuts, and raisins. Spoon mixture into prepared tins. Bake until golden, approximately 15-20 minutes.

Easy Bran Muffins

- 1 cup shortening
- 3 cups sugar
- 4 eggs
- 2 cups boiling water
- 2 cups Nabisco 100% bran cereal
- 5 cups flour, sifted
- 1 quart buttermilk
- 5 teaspoons baking soda
- 1 teaspoon salt
- 4 cups Nabisco 100% bran cereal

Cream shortening, sugar, and eggs. In separate container combine boiling water and 2 cups of cereal. Pour cereal mixture over creamed mixture. Add flour, buttermilk, baking soda, salt, and remaining 4 cups of cereal, mixing well. Spoon mixture into muffin tin. This can be stored in refrigerator for up to 4 weeks (in sealed container). Bake as much as you want at a time. Bake 15 minutes at 450.

"Before baking, muffins may be garnished with fresh chopped fruit of the season."

Nutty Strawberry Bread

3 cups all purpose flour
1 teaspoon salt
1 teaspoon soda
1 tablespoon ground cinnamon
2 cups sugar
3 eggs, well beaten

1¼ cups salad oil
20 ounces fresh strawberries, capped and chopped, or frozen, thawed and drained
1¼ cups chopped pecans

Combine flour, salt, soda, cinnamon, and sugar. Make a well in center of dry ingredients. Add eggs and oil, stirring mixture until dry ingredients are moistened. Stir in strawberries and pecans. Spoon mixture into 2 lightly greased 8x4x2⅝ loaf pans. Bake at 350 for 1 hour or until done. Allow to stand overnight before slicing. Yields 2 loaves.

Bread Sticks

4 cups all purpose flour
1⅓ cups warm water
1 envelope dry yeast
2 tablespoons olive oil

1 egg, beaten with
  2 tablespoons water
Coarse salt

Mix 2 cups of flour with water and yeast in a large bowl until smooth. Add oil to 2 tablespoons of egg mixture, reserving remainder for glaze. Mix in enough of the remaining flour, ½ cup at a time, to form soft dough. Knead on floured surface until smooth and elastic, adding more flour if sticky, about 8 minutes. Grease large bowl. Add dough, turning to coat entire surface. Cover and let rise 30 minutes. Preheat oven to 400. Prepare greased baking sheet. Punch down dough and divide in half. Roll each half into an 18 inch long rope. Cut each into 14 pieces. Then roll each piece into a 12 inch long rope. Twist together 2 ropes. Arrange twisted ropes on baking sheet. Repeat with remaining dough. Brush with reserved egg mixture. Lightly sprinkle with coarse salt and bake until golden, about 20 minutes. Cool on wire rack.

"Two tablespoons fresh rosemary, minced and two tablespoons fresh dill, minced may be added to the oil for a tasty variation."

Golden Crust Bread

1 cup sour cream
¼ teaspoon soda
1¼ cup hot water
1 cake yeast (compressed or dry,
    dissolve as directed on package)

2 tablespoons sugar
1 tablespoon salt
2 tablespoons butter, melted
    (no substitute)
6½ cups flour

Combine sour cream and soda. Add hot water, yeast, sugar, salt, and butter. Stir until dissolved. Gradually add flour. Mix until well blended. Knead dough on floured board 5 to 7 minutes. Place in greased bowl and cover. Let rise in warm place (85 to 90 degrees) until double in bulk, about 2 hours. Divide dough in 2 parts, forming each into a ball. Allow to rest loosely covered for 10 minutes. Shape into loaves. Place in greased pans and cover to let rise in warm place until double in bulk, about 1½ hours. Bake at 375 for 40-45 minutes.

Herb Cheese Biscuits

3 ounces sharp cheddar
    cheese, shredded
1½ cups all purpose flour
1¼ teaspoon salt
4 ounces unsalted butter,
    chilled and cut into 8 slices

1 tablespoon fresh minced basil
    leaves or 1 teaspoon dried basil
1½ teaspoons baking powder
¼ cup milk

Preheat oven to 425. Mix flour, salt, butter, basil, and baking powder. Add milk and stir. Turn out on lightly floured surface. Knead 2 to 3 minutes. Form a ball and roll out to ¾ inch thickness. Using a 1½ inch or 2 inch biscuit cutter, cut biscuits and place on baking sheet. Bake 12 minutes or until golden brown.

"For a variation, use mozzarella cheese and 1 teaspoon dry rosemary instead of cheddar cheese and basil."

Southern Ham and Cheese Biscuits

2 cups all purpose flour
5 teaspoons baking powder
1/2 cup Smithfield ham,
   finely chopped
1/2 cup Swiss cheese

2 tablespoons shortening
3/4 cup milk, more if necessary
1/4 cup fresh minced chives *or*
   3 tablespoons dried chives

Preheat oven to 400. Sift flour and baking powder together. Add ham, cheese, and chives, mixing well. Cut in shortening with knife until resembles coarse meal. Add milk. Handle as little as possible. Pat out on floured surface and cut with biscuit cutter. Place on greased baking sheet and bake until brown, about 12 minutes. Yields 12.

"These are very easy to make."

Sweet Potato Biscuits

1 1/2 cups sweet potatoes
   (2 to 3 medium)
1/2 cup margarine
1/2 cup sugar

1 teaspoon salt
3 1/2-4 cups plain flour
4 1/2 teaspoons baking powder

Boil, peel, and mash potatoes. While hot, measure 1 1/2 cups of mashed potato into large bowl. Add margarine, sugar, and salt. Mix well. Sift together flour and baking powder; add to potato mixture. Work with hands to make soft dough, adding only necessary extra flour. Chill dough if you like or roll out and cut into biscuits. Bake on greased cookie sheet (unsalted grease, like shortening) at 400 on top shelf of oven about 15-20 minutes until light golden brown. For variety, 1 cup of raisins rolled in a little cinnamon sugar may be worked into dough.

"The one important thing to remember when you make these is to have good, tasty sweet potatoes and use no aluminum utensils."

Sweet Potato Rolls

2 cups sweet potatoes,
   cooked and mashed
1 cup sugar
2/3 cup shortening
2/3 cup warm water
2/3 teaspoon salt

1 large egg
1 yeast cake dissolved in
   warm water
6-7 cups sifted plain flour to make
   proper consistency to knead

Mix all ingredients. Knead. Let rise; then make into rolls and let rise again. Bake at 400 about 20 minutes. Dough will keep in refrigerator for at least a week.

Corn Bread

3 eggs
1/2 cup oil
8 ounces creamed corn

8 ounces sour cream
12 ounce box corn muffin mix
1 teaspoon salt

Mix eggs and oil. Add remaining ingredients and mix. Bake in 9 x 13 pan at 375 for 25-35 minutes. Do not overcook. Freezes well.

Spoon Bread

1/2 cup boiling water
1 cup cornmeal
2 tablespoons shortening, melted
3 eggs, well beaten

1 1/2 cups milk
2 teaspoons sugar
1/2 teaspoon salt
1 tablespoon baking powder

Add boiling water to cornmeal, stirring until well mixed. Allow mixture to cool. When cool, add shortening, eggs, milk, sugar, salt, and baking powder, in that order. Blend thoroughly. Pour into well greased baking dish. Bake at 400 for 30 minutes. Serve hot.

Old Fashioned Pan Rolls

1/2 cup sugar
2 teaspoons salt
2 packages active dry yeast
6-7 cups all purpose flour

2 cups warm milk
1/2 cup butter or margarine
2 eggs
Salad oil

In a large bowl combine sugar, salt, yeast, and 2 1/2 cups flour. In a saucepan over low heat, heat milk and butter or margarine until very warm (120-130 degrees). With mixer at low speed, gradually beat liquid into dry ingredients until just blended. Increase speed to medium; beat 2 minutes, occasionally scraping bowl. Beat in eggs and 3/4 cup flour to make a thick batter; continue beating 2 minutes, scraping bowl often. With spoon stir in enough additional flour, about 2 1/4-2 1/2 cups, to make a soft dough. Turn dough onto lightly floured surface and knead until smooth and elastic, about 10 minutes. Shape dough into large ball and place in a greased bowl, turning dough so that top of dough is greased. Cover with a towel; let rise in a warm place (80-85 degrees) away from drafts, until doubled, about 1 1/2 hours. Dough is doubled when 2 fingers pressed lightly into dough leave a dent. Punch down dough. Grease 15 1/2x10 1/2 open pan. Cut dough into 30 pieces; shape into balls and place in pan. Cover with towel and let rise in a warm place until doubled, about 1 1/2 hours. Preheat oven to 425. Bake rolls 15-20 minutes until golden brown. Brush with melted butter or margarine. Remove from pan and serve.

Buttermilk Biscuits

2 cups all purpose flour
2 1/2 teaspoons baking powder
1/2 teaspoon salt

1/2 teaspoon baking soda
1/3 cup butter, cold
3/4 cup buttermilk

Preheat oven to 450. Combine flour, baking powder, salt, and baking soda and sift into a medium-sized mixing bowl. Add butter and blend into flour mixture until it resembles coarse crumbs. Stir in buttermilk and blend until it forms a ball. Turn out on a lightly greased surface and pat into a circle 1/2 inch thick. Cut out biscuits; dip them in butter. Arrange on a baking sheet and bake for 12-15 minutes. Serve immediately with butter.

Fresh Corn Popovers

1/3 cup fresh corn	1/2 teaspoon salt
1/3 cup water	1/8 teaspoon freshly ground
2 eggs	white pepper
1/2 cup milk	1 cup all purpose flour
1 tablespoon corn oil	1/4 cup whole kernel corn
1 teaspoon sugar	Vegetable oil for custard cups

Preheat oven to 425. Place corn and water in container of food processor. Process until corn is finely chopped. Drain through sieve into measuring cup. Add more water if necessary to make 1/2 cup corn liquid. Whisk 1/2 cup corn liquid, eggs, milk, corn oil, sugar, salt, and pepper in medium bowl until well blended. Whisk in flour until batter is smooth. Stir in corn. Generously grease deep heavy 6 ounce popover cups or custard cups. Pour mixture into hot custard cups. Bake in oven for 15 minutes. Reduce oven to 400 and bake 20 minutes longer. Bake until popovers are firm and brown. Remove from oven. Pierce one side of each popover just above rim of cup with the tip of a small knife. Carefully remove from cups and place on sides on baking sheet. Bake until crisp, about 5 minutes. Yields 6.

"If you like popovers, you'll love these."

Corn Fritters

2 eggs	1 teaspoon sugar
1 cup milk	1/4 teaspoon paprika
2 cups flour	2 cups drained corn
3 teaspoons baking powder	2 tablespoons shortening
1 teaspoon salt	Oil

Beat eggs and stir in milk, flour, baking powder, salt, sugar, paprika, corn, and shortening. Drop from spoon in deep fat and fry until brown.

Parsley Cream Biscuits

2⅔ cups pastry flour
1 tablespoon sugar
3 teaspoons baking powder
1 teaspoon salt
1½ cups whipping cream

3 tablespoons sour cream
1 tablespoon butter, melted
1 tablespoon fresh parsley, minced
2 tablespoons butter, melted

Preheat oven to 375. Line baking sheets with parchment paper. Combine flour, sugar, baking powder, and salt in a large bowl. Add cream, sour cream, and butter, mixing with a fork until soft dough forms. Divide dough in half. Roll out one portion on a lightly floured surface to 1/2 inch thickness. Brush with melted butter. Sprinkle with parsley. Roll out second portion to 1/2 inch thickness. Set atop first half. Using a 1 inch cutter cut into rounds. Arrange on baking sheets. Bake at 375 until lightly colored or approximately 15 minutes. Serve immediately.

"Fantastic!"

Crusty Dill Butter Bread

1 long loaf French bread
1/2 cup butter, melted
1 teaspoon fresh dill, chopped, *or*
  1/2 teaspoon dried

4 tablespoons grated
  Parmesan cheese

Cut bread in half lengthwise. In a small bowl, combine butter and dill weed. Spread over both halves, then sprinkle with Parmesan cheese. Just before serving place bread on grill with other foods to heat and toast lightly. Bread may be placed on baking sheet under broiler until lightly toasted.

"Perfect for those who enjoy outdoor grilling."

Cheese Rolls

18 Brown & Serve rolls
1 pound sharp cheddar
  cheese, grated
1 can ripe olives, chopped
1 8 ounce can tomato sauce

1/2 cup oil
1 teaspoon oregano
1 teaspoon sweet basil
  Garlic powder
  Salt and pepper

Brown rolls according to package directions, cool and hollow out. Mix all other ingredients together and stuff rolls with mixture. Wrap in foil for reheating. Bake at 350 for 10-20 minutes.

"These rolls may be frozen until needed and reheated frozen for 35-40 minutes."

Herb Bread Rolls

1/2 pound butter, softened
1 teaspoon savory
1 teaspoon sweet basil

4 tablespoons chopped chives
2 loaves white bread, fresh
  and thinly sliced

Combine butter and herbs. Remove crust from bread and spread with butter mixture. Roll slices and secure with a toothpick. Bake at 350 for 35 minutes. Check often to be sure bread does not burn. Serve immediately.

"These may be frozen before baking and used as needed."

Mozzarella Melt

1 loaf French bread
1/4 cup butter, softened
1/2 cup mayonnaise

6 green onions, chopped
1/8 teaspoon garlic powder
1 cup mozzarella cheese, shredded

Split bread lengthwise. In bowl, mix butter and mayonnaise. Stir in onions and garlic. Spread evenly over bread halves. Top with mozzarella cheese. Bake at 400 until cheese is melted.

French Bread Au Fromage

½ cup butter
½ cup Swiss cheese, grated
¼ cup bacon, cooked
  and crumbled
1 tablespoon chopped chives,
  fresh or dried
2 tablespoons poppy seeds

1 tablespoon mustard
½ teaspoon grated lemon rind
1½ teaspoons lemon juice
  Dash of pepper
1 loaf French bread,
  12-14 inches long

Combine all ingredients except the bread. Cut bread on the diagonal at 1 inch intervals, almost through to bottom. Spread filling between slices and on top of the bread. Place bread in center of heavy duty foil, large enough to twist ends and seal. Grill over medium coals, turning often, for about 20 minutes or in oven at 350 until cheese melts.

"Oui, oui!"

Cheese Stuffed Bread

1 loaf Italian bread
2½ cups cheese, shredded
¾ cup mayonnaise

¼ cup scallions, chopped
¼ teaspoon Italian seasoning

Cut loaf in half lengthwise. Hollow the top portion out. Mix cheese, mayonnaise, scallions, and Italian seasoning. Spread mixture into top of loaf. Replace top onto bottom half of loaf. Cut loaf into 1 inch slices. Slide loaf onto aluminum foil and wrap completely. Bake at 300 until cheese melts or about 30 minutes.

SUNRISE
SPECIALTIES

Brunch

Oatmeal Breakfast Cake

Batter

1¼ cups boiling water
1 cup oatmeal
½ cup margarine
1 cup brown sugar
1 cup sugar
2 eggs

1 teaspoon baking soda
¾ teaspoon cinnamon
¼ teaspoon ground nutmeg
½ teaspoon salt
1½ cups all purpose flour

Pour boiling water over oatmeal; cool. Add margarine and sugars. Beat together. Beat in eggs. Sift soda, cinnamon, nutmeg, salt, and flour together. Beat into batter. Turn into a greased and floured 9x13 pan. Bake at 350 for 30-40 minutes.

Topping

½ cup brown sugar
¼ cup margarine
3 tablespoons milk

¾ cup coconut
⅓ cup nuts

In saucepan, mix sugar, margarine, milk, coconut, and nuts. Bring to a boil. Spread on baked cake. Broil till bubbly. May be served warm or cold.

Swedish Apple Cake

1⅛ cups butter
2¼ cups sugar
3 eggs
2¼ cups flour

4-5 apples, peeled and sliced
½ cup brown sugar
2 tablespoons cinnamon

Cream butter and sugar. Add eggs. Gradually add flour, mixing into stiff dough. Pour into lightly greased 9x13 pan. Stand apple slices in dough. Sprinkle with cinnamon and brown sugar. Bake at 350 for 1 hour, or until done.

Overnight Cinnamon Rolls

1 package dry yeast
3 cups hot water
1 cup sugar
1 tablespoon salt
1/2 cup shortening
2 eggs
8 cups flour, sifted
1/2 cup sugar

2 teaspoons cinnamon
Per pan:
6 tablespoons butter or
  margarine, melted
1/4 cup brown sugar, packed
  Pecans or walnuts, chopped
2 cups butter or margarine, melted

At 5:00 p.m., mix first six ingredients in blender. Add 8 cups flour; last 2-3 cups need to be stirred by hand. Place dough in greased bowl and cover; let rise till double. At 8:00 p.m. punch dough down; continue to let rise. Prepare baking pans at this time. Ready 3 9x13 or 6 9-inch round cake pans by pouring 6 tablespoons butter in each; sprinkle with brown sugar. Nuts are optional. Set pans aside. Mix sugar and cinnamon thoroughly.

At 10:00 p.m., divide dough in half. Take 1/2 of dough and roll out on floured surface. Roll into 1/4 inch thick rectangle. Spread enough melted butter to cover dough lightly; sprinkle with cinnamon/sugar mixture. Starting at long side, roll dough evenly. Cut into 3/4 to 1 inch slices and place cut side up in pans—leaving a small space between slices. Continue with other half of dough. Cover all pans with dish towels and let rise overnight. In the morning, bake 15-20 minutes at 375.

"Rolls can be frozen in aluminum foil after baking and stored until ready to serve."

Cheese Danish

2 cans crescent rolls
1 egg yolk, white reserved
1 teaspoon vanilla

1/2 cup sugar, rounded
8 ounces cream cheese

Preheat oven to 350. Layer first can of rolls, rolling thinly to cover greased cookie sheet. Mix egg yolk, vanilla, sugar, and cream cheese and spread over rolls evenly. Press out remaining can of rolls and place on top. Crimp edges. Brush whipped egg white on top. Bake 20-25 minutes or until golden brown. Serves 6-8.

Streusel Coffee Cake

3/4 cup sugar
1/4 cup soft shortening
1 egg
1/2 cup milk

1 1/2 cups flour
2 teaspoons baking powder
1/2 teaspoon salt

Mix sugar, shortening and egg thoroughly. Stir in 1/2 cup milk. Sift together flour, baking powder, and salt and stir in. Spread 1/2 of mixture in greased and floured 9 inch square pan. Sprinkle 1/4 of streusel mixture. Add remaining batter and sprinkle remaining streusel mixture over top. Bake at 375 for 25-35 minutes.

Streusel Mixture

1/2 cup brown sugar
2 tablespoons flour
2 teaspoons cinnamon

2 tablespoons butter, melted
1/2 cup nuts, chopped

Mix above ingredients together.

Good Morning Coffee Cake

1 cup butter
2 cups plus 4 teaspoons sugar
2 eggs
1 cup sour cream
1/2 teaspoon vanilla

2 cups flour
1 teaspoon baking powder
1/4 teaspoon salt
1 cup pecans, chopped
1 teaspoon cinnamon

Preheat oven to 350. Cream butter and add two cups of sugar gradually, beating until very light and creamy. Beat in eggs one at a time very well. Fold in sour cream and vanilla. Fold in flour sifted with baking powder and salt. Combine remaining sugar, pecans, and cinnamon. Place approximately 1/3 of batter in a well greased and floured Bundt pan or a 9 inch tube pan. Sprinkle with 3/4 of pecan mixture. Spoon in remaining batter. Sprinkle with remaining pecans and bake at 350 for about 60 minutes. Cool on a rack.

Grandmother's Famous Cranberry Bread

2 cups sifted all purpose flour
1 cup sugar
1 1/2 teaspoons baking powder
1 teaspoon salt
1/2 teaspoon baking soda
1/4 cup butter or margarine

1 egg, beaten
1 teaspoon grated orange peel
3/4 cup orange juice
1 1/2 cups light raisins
1 1/2 cups fresh or frozen
   cranberries, chopped

Sift flour, sugar, baking powder, salt, and baking soda into a large bowl. Cut in butter until mixture is crumbly. Add egg, orange peel, and orange juice all at once; stir just until mixture is evenly moist. Fold in raisins and cranberries.

Spoon into a greased 9x5x3 loaf pan. Bake at 350 for 1 hour and 10 minutes, or until toothpick inserted in center comes out clean. Remove from pan; cool on wire rack.

"If desired, substitute cranberries for raisins to have an all cranberry bread."

Swedish Tea Ring

1 package dry yeast
1 cup warm water
3 tablespoons sugar
2 tablespoons shortening
1 egg
3/4 teaspoon salt
3-31/2 cups all purpose flour,
    divided in half

2 tablespoons butter or
    margarine, melted
1/2 cup raisins
1/2 cup pecans, chopped
1/3 cup sugar
1 teaspoon ground cinnamon
1 cup powdered sugar
11/2 tablespoons milk

Dissolve yeast in warm water in a large bowl. Add sugar, shortening, egg, salt, and half the flour. Beat at low speed of electric mixer until smooth. Stir in enough of remaining flour to make a soft dough. Place in greased bowl, turning to grease top. Let rise until doubled in bulk. Proceed to make tea ring.

Roll dough into 21x7 inch rectangle on a slightly floured surface. Brush butter evenly on dough. Combine raisins, chopped pecans, 1/3 cup sugar, and cinnamon. Spread evenly over dough. Roll up jelly-roll fashion, beginning at long side. Pinch edges to seal. Place roll on a large greased baking sheet, seam side down. Shape into a ring and pinch ends together to seal. Make cuts into ring 2/3 way through every inch around the ring. Gently turn each piece on its side, slightly overlapping. Let rise until doubled in bulk. Bake at 375 for 20-25 minutes. Combine powdered sugar and milk and drizzle over tea ring, when it has cooled.

Curried Fruit

1/3 cup butter or margarine
3/4 cup brown sugar
1 teaspoon curry powder
1 16 ounce can pear halves
1 16 ounce can peach halves

1 151/2 ounce can
    pineapple chunks
1/2 cup toasted almonds
    Few maraschino cherries

Melt butter; add sugar and curry powder. Drain and dry fruit. Place in 11/2 quart casserole dish. Add butter mixture over fruit. Sprinkle almonds and place cherries on top. Bake for 20 minutes at 425. Serves 4-6.

Apple Crunch

1 cup all purpose flour	4 cups apples, sliced
3/4 cup rolled oats	1 cup sugar
1 cup brown sugar	2 tablespoons cornstarch
1 teaspoon cinnamon	1 cup water
1/2 cup butter or margarine, melted	1 teaspoon vanilla

Preheat oven to 350. Grease an 8 or 9 inch baking pan. Mix flour, oats, brown sugar, cinnamon, and melted butter until crumbly. Press half of mixture into pan. Cover with apples. Combine sugar, cornstarch, water, and vanilla. Cook until clear and thick. Pour over fruit. Top with rest of crumbs. Bake 1 hour. Serves 6.

Pineapple Bake

2 eggs, beaten	Margarine
1/2 cup sugar	Cinnamon
1 tablespoon cornstarch	
1 large can crushed pineapple, with liquid	

Beat eggs, sugar, and cornstarch. Add pineapple. Place in quart casserole. Dot with margarine and sprinkle with cinnamon. Bake at 350 for 1 hour or microwave 10 minutes on high and run under broiler.

Baked Cheese Grits

2 eggs, beaten	1/2 teaspoon salt
3/4 cup sharp cheddar cheese	1 clove garlic, finely minced
4 tablespoons butter, melted	2 1/2 cups cooked grits, still warm
2 teaspoons dry mustard	

Preheat oven to 350. Mix eggs, cheese, butter, mustard, salt, and garlic. Stir into grits and pour into buttered 4-6 cup casserole. Bake uncovered for 50 minutes. Serve immediately while hot, directly from casserole.

Garlic Grits Souffle

1 cup grits
Salt
2 eggs

1 6 ounce roll Kraft garlic cheese*
1 4 ounce stick margarine

Cook grits in 4 cups of water according to package directions. Salt to taste. Beat egg whites until stiff. Set aside. Add slightly beaten egg yolks and margarine to the hot grits. Add Kraft garlic cheese and stir until all ingredients are thoroughly blended and smooth. Fold in egg whites. Bake in 375 oven for 35-40 minutes.

*6 ounces sharp cheddar cheese spread plus 1 teaspoon garlic powder may be substituted.

"If souffle dish is not available, a heavy ceramic bowl 4½-5 inches deep may be used."

Ham 'N' Cheese Snack Squares

1½ cups ham, finely chopped
1 8 ounce carton plain yogurt
¼ cup Swiss cheese, shredded
¼ cup saltine crackers,
    finely crushed

2 tablespoons butter or
    margarine, melted
1-2 teaspoon caraway seeds
6 eggs

In a medium bowl, combine ham, yogurt, cheese, cracker crumbs, butter or margarine, and caraway seeds. In small mixer bowl, beat eggs on medium speed about 6 minutes or until thick. Fold eggs into yogurt mixture until well blended. Pour mixture into greased 8x8x2 pan. Bake at 375 for 15-17 minutes or until evenly browned. Cut into squares and serve hot. Makes 12-16 servings.

French Toast Grand Marnier

4 eggs
1 cup milk
2 teaspoons Grand Marnier
1 teaspoon sugar

1/2 teaspoon vanilla
1/4 teaspoon salt
 8 slices French bread, 3/4 inch thick
Powdered sugar

Beat first 6 ingredients in baking dish until well blended. Arrange bread in single layer in 12x6 baking dish. Pour mixture over bread. Turn bread until each piece is well-coated. Cover and refrigerate overnight. Put 2 teaspoons butter in hot skillet. Saute bread 4-5 minutes until brown. Sprinkle with powdered sugar. Serves 4.

Chipped Beef with Wine

4 ounces dried chipped beef
2 tablespoons butter or margarine
2 tablespoons flour
1 can mushroom soup
1/2 cup dry white wine
1 3 ounce can mushroom stems
  and pieces

1/2 cup cheddar cheese, shredded
2 tablespoons chopped parsley
  (optional)
  Toast points or English muffins

Melt butter in pan and saute beef for 3 minutes. Sprinkle with flour gradually; add soup and wine while stirring. Add mushrooms, partially drained. Add cheese and parsley. Stir until cheese melts and mixture is thick and creamy. Serve over toast points or English muffins. Serves 6-8.

Artichoke and Sausage Frittata

1 large yellow onion, sliced
1 small red pepper, sliced
1 large clove garlic, minced
2 tablespoons butter
1/2 pound hot Italian sausage,,
  cooked and crumbled
1 14 ounce can artichoke hearts,
  drained and halved

8 eggs
1/2 cup heavy cream
3/4 teaspoon salt
1/4 teaspoon pepper
1/2 teaspoon dried basil
1/2 teaspoon oregano
1 cup shredded provolone
1/2 cup shredded fresh Parmesan

Preheat oven to 425. In skillet, cook onion, pepper, and garlic in butter. Spread in bottom of greased 2 quart shallow baking dish. Sprinkle with sausage. Arrange artichokes on sausage. Beat eggs, cream, salt, pepper, basil, and oregano. Mix in cheeses. Pour into baking dish. Bake for 15-20 minutes or until set. Let stand 5 minutes before serving. Serves 4-6.

Overnight Bacon Casserole

1 pound sliced bacon
8 slices whole wheat bread
6 eggs

1 1/2 cups milk
1 cup shredded cheddar cheese
1/2 teaspoon dry mustard

Cut strips of bacon crosswise into 1/2 inch pieces. Cook in skillet over medium heat until crisp; remove to absorbent paper. Remove crusts from bread and cut bread slices into cubes; set aside. Beat eggs until foamy. Stir in milk, cheese, and mustard. Gently stir bacon and bread cubes into egg mixture; spoon into buttered 8 inch square baking dish. Cover tightly and refrigerate overnight. Remove from refrigerator and let stand at room temperature for 15 minutes. Bake, uncovered, at 325 for 45 minutes or until knife inserted in center comes out clean. Serves 6.

Breakfast Before

1 pound spicy pork sausage
6 eggs
2 cups milk
1 teaspoon salt

1 teaspoon dry mustard
2 slices white bread, cubed
1 cup sharp cheese, grated

Saute sausage; drain. Beat eggs, milk, salt, and mustard. Layer bread cubes, sausage, and cheese in a 9x13 baking dish. Pour egg mixture on top. Refrigerate overnight. Bake at 350 for 45 minutes or until center is set. Serves 6-8.

Crack of Dawn Casserole

3 slices white bread, quartered
2 cups small curd cottage cheese
6 eggs
¼ teaspoon salt
⅛ teaspoon pepper

1 cup cheddar cheese, shredded
4 slices Swiss cheese
   Parmesan cheese, grated
   Paprika

Line a lightly greased 12x8x2 baking dish with bread. Spread cottage cheese over bread. Combine eggs, salt, and pepper; beat well. Stir in cheddar cheese; pour over cottage cheese. Arrange Swiss cheese over mixture. Sprinkle with Parmesan cheese and paprika. Bake at 325 for 30 minutes. Serves 6.

Cheese Souffle

10 slices bread
 6 tablespoons butter, melted
 1 pound sharp cheese, grated

8 eggs
4 cups milk
½ teaspoon salt

Cut crusts off bread and slice each into 6 strips. Dip bread in melted butter. Line deep ungreased pan with bread. Sprinkle with cheese, then repeat layers. Beat eggs. Add milk and salt. Pour mixture over bread and cheese. Cover and refrigerate overnight. Bake at 325 for 1 hour. Serves 6.

Cheese Blintzes

12 slices white bread
8 ounces cream cheese
1 egg yolk
2 tablespoons sugar

1 teaspoon vanilla
1 cup sugar mixed with
   2 teaspoons cinnamon
1 stick butter, melted

Remove crusts from bread and flatten with a rolling pin. Mix together cream cheese, 2 tablespoons sugar, egg yolk, and vanilla. Spread mixture on slices of bread. Gently roll each slice, jelly roll style, and cut into half. Dip in melted butter, then roll in cinnamon sugar mixture. Place on cookie sheet and freeze 24 hours. Bake frozen in 350 oven for 15 minutes.

"This is great for early party preparation as it has to be frozen beforehand."

Ham Broccoli Brunch

6-8 slices bread
1/2-3/4 pound chipped ham*
1/4-1/2 pound Swiss cheese, sliced
2 packages chopped broccoli, thawed and drained

6 eggs, beaten
2 cups heavy cream
   Chives
   Salt and pepper

Butter 9x13 pan. Remove crusts from bread. Put in bottom of pan. Layer chipped ham, Swiss cheese, and broccoli over bread. Add eggs with cream and spices. Pour over dish. Refrigerate overnight. Bake at 375 for 40 minutes; check after 30 minutes.

*Recommend using Virginia baked ham. Buy at deli department and they will chip (shred) it for you.

Ham and Cheese Roll-Ups

2 cups Bisquick baking mix
1/2 cup water
1-2 tablespoons prepared mustard
6 ounces cooked smoked ham, thinly sliced

1 cup Swiss or cheddar cheese, shredded
1/4 cup green onions, sliced with tops
1 4 ounce can mushroom stems and pieces, drained

Mix baking mix and water until dough forms. Smooth into ball on cloth covered surface dusted with baking mix. Knead 15 times. Roll into rectangle, 15x9 inches; spread with mustard. Top with remaining ingredients. Roll up tightly, beginning at 15 inch side. Pinch edge into roll, moisten if necessary, wrap, and refrigerate at least 30 minutes but no longer than 24 hours. Heat oven to 400. Cut rolled dough into 12 slices. Place on greased and floured cookie sheet; replace filling if necessary. Bake until golden, 20 to 25 minutes. Serves 6-8.

Ham Roll-Ups

1 10 ounce package chopped frozen spinach
2 cups rice, cooked
1/2 cup onion, chopped
1/2 teaspoon dry mustard

2 eggs
25 slices of cooked, boiled ham
1 can cream of mushroom soup
1/2 cup sour cream
1/4 cup cheddar cheese, grated

Cook spinach according to package; drain and press dry. Combine spinach, rice, onion, mustard, and eggs, and mix well. Put 1 1/2 tablespoons of mixture on ham slice and roll up. Put seam down in 9x13 baking dish. Mix mushroom soup and 1/2 cup sour cream; pour over ham slices. Bake uncovered at 350 for 20 to 25 minutes. Serves 12-15.

Sausage Souffle Roll

4 tablespoons butter
¼ cup flour
½ teaspoon salt
¼ teaspoon pepper
1 cup milk
1½ cups cheddar cheese, shredded

4 eggs, separated
12 ounces bulk pork sausage
¼ cup onion, chopped
¼ cup green pepper, chopped
½ cup sour cream

Preheat oven to 350. Line 15x10 jelly-roll pan with foil and grease sides and bottom. In small saucepan, melt butter. Stir in flour, salt, and pepper. Whisk in milk, stirring constantly over medium heat until mixture thickens. Remove from heat and mix in cheese, stirring until cheese is melted. In large bowl, beat egg whites until stiff peaks form. In small bowl, whisk yolks until lemon-colored. Gradually stir cheese mixture into egg yolks. Gently fold yolk mixture into egg whites. Spread in pan and bake 25 minutes or until souffle is puffed and golden brown.

While souffle is cooking, combine sausage, onion, and green pepper in skillet. Cook until sausage is done and vegetables are tender; drain. Combine with sour cream. Turn souffle out of pan onto large piece of foil. Remove foil used for baking. Spread sausage filling on souffle. Lift foil at short end and gently roll souffle. Slice and serve immediately. Serves 6-8.

Creamy Ham and Cheese

1 5 ounce package noodles
⅔ cup milk
1 8 ounce package cream cheese, softened
½ teaspoon garlic salt

½ teaspoon salt
2 cups ham, diced
½ cup celery, diced
½ cup green pepper, chopped
½ cup Parmesan cheese

Prepare noodles according to directions and drain. Combine milk, cream cheese, garlic salt, and salt; mix well. Stir in noodles, ham, celery, and green pepper. Spoon half of ham mixture into lightly greased 1½ quart casserole. Sprinkle with ¼ cup Parmesan cheese. Repeat with other half of ham mixture and top with remaining Parmesan cheese. Bake at 350 for 30 minutes. Serves 4-5.

Torte Florentine

1 pound frozen puff pastry
1 tablespoon oil
1 tablespoon butter
1 pound fresh spinach,
   blanched and well drained
1/4 teaspoon garlic powder
1/4 teaspoon nutmeg
   Salt and pepper
1 small jar pimientos, well drained

5 eggs, reserve 1 tablespoon
   for egg brush
2 teaspoons chopped chives
2 teaspoons chopped parsley
1/2 teaspoon dried tarragon
2 tablespoons butter
8 ounces ham, thinly sliced
8 ounces Swiss cheese, thinly sliced

Lightly grease 8 inch springform pan. Roll both sheets into 14 inch squares. Drape one sheet inside pan to line sides and bottom. Keep second sheet refrigerated. Heat oil and butter in large skillet. Add spinach and garlic powder and saute 3 minutes. Add salt and pepper to taste. Drain. Lightly beat eggs, chives, parsley, and tarragon. Over medium heat, melt 1 tablespoon butter in 8 inch non-stick skillet. Pour in half of egg mixture. Cover and cook until eggs are completely set and top of omelet is no longer moist, about 3-4 minutes. Shake pan and slide omelet onto plate. Repeat with remaining butter and egg mixture. Position oven rack in lower third of oven and preheat to 350.

To assemble, layer ingredients in following order: 1 omelet, half spinach, half cheese, half ham and all pimientos. Repeat, layering in reverse order with remaining ingredients. Top with remaining pastry and crimp edges to seal. Decorate with scraps of pastry and brush with 1 tablespoon beaten egg. Place pan on baking sheet and bake until golden brown, or about 70 minutes. Slice with sharp, thin knife. Serves 6-8.

"Absolutely elegant meal."

Virginia Ham and Egg Bake

3 tablespoons butter or margarine
3 tablespoons flour
2½ cups milk
½ teaspoon salt
Dash of white pepper
1 cup cheddar or Monterey Jack cheese, shredded
2 tablespoons butter or margarine

2 cups Virginia country ham, chopped
½ cup green onion, chopped
½ pound mushrooms, sliced
12 eggs, beaten
¼ cup butter or margarine, melted
2 cups soft breadcrumbs

Melt butter in saucepan over low heat; blend in flour. Cook 1 minute. Gradually add milk; cook over medium heat until thickened, stirring constantly. Add salt, pepper, and cheese. Continue to cook and stir over low heat until cheese melts and mixture is thick and smooth. Set aside.

In large skillet over medium heat, melt 2 tablespoons butter. Add ham, green onion, and mushrooms; cook mixture until onions and mushrooms are just tender. Drain excess liquid; add eggs and cook over medium-high heat, stirring to form large soft curds. When eggs are just beginning to set, stir in cheese sauce. Spoon egg mixture into a buttered 13x9 baking dish. In a small bowl, combine ¼ cup melted butter and crumbs; mix well. Spread crumbs evenly over egg mixture. Cover and refrigerate overnight. When ready to bake, remove cover and let stand at room temperature about 30 minutes. Bake at 350 for 30 to 40 minutes or until heated through. Serves 12.

Broccoli Spaghetti

8 ounces spaghetti, cooked
1 head broccoli florets
4 ounces snow peas
1 cup celery

1 small onion
1 stick butter
3/4-1 cup Parmesan cheese
Toasted buttered almonds

Saute vegetables in butter. Add cooked spaghetti, Parmesan cheese, and toasted buttered almonds. Toss.

Spaghetti Coleslaw

½ pound spaghetti,
cooked and drained
1 medium onion, chopped
½ head raw cabbage, shredded
1 small green pepper, chopped
1 cup celery, chopped
1½ cups mayonnaise

1 teaspoon mustard
¼ cup vinegar
¼ cup salad oil
1 egg yolk
1 small can Eagle brand
condensed milk

Mix all together and refrigerate overnight.

Vegetable Fettuccini

4 eggs
¼ cup whipping cream
8 slices bacon, chopped
½ cup mushrooms, sliced
½ cup carrots, sliced
½ cup cauliflower, sliced
½ cup frozen peas, thawed
½ cup zucchini, sliced
½ red bell pepper, seeded and
cut in 1 inch strips

¼ cup green onion, sliced
1 garlic clove, chopped
1 pound fettuccini
¼ cup butter, cut in pieces
1 cup Parmesan cheese
Salt
Pepper

Beat eggs and cream and set aside. Cook bacon in large skillet until crisp. Remove, chop, and set aside. Add next 8 ingredients to skillet and saute until crisp-tender, about 5-7 minutes. Meanwhile, cook fettuccini in large amount of boiling water. Drain and put in large salad bowl. Add butter and toss. Add egg mixture and toss. Add vegetables, bacon, and cheese and toss. Season with salt and pepper. Serve hot.

"This dish reheats well!"

Antipasto Salad

1 pound box medium shell
  noodles, cooked
1 package sliced pepperoni,
  cut in half
1 package hard salami,
  cut in small pieces
1 can black olives
1 can green olives
1 green pepper, chopped

3 tomatoes, cut up
1 medium onion, chopped
3 stalks celery, chopped
  Sliced provolone cheese, cut up
3/4 cup oil
1/2 cup vinegar
1/2 teaspoon salt
1/2 teaspoon pepper
1/2 teaspoon oregano

Combine first 10 ingredients and stir. Mix oil, vinegar, and spices. Pour over noodle mixture. Stir well. Refrigerate before serving.

"Serves a large group!"

Veggie Vermicelli

1 pound vermicelli
1 cup green pepper, chopped
3 medium tomatoes, chopped
1 large red onion, chopped
3 cucumbers, chopped with
  peel left on

1 red pepper, chopped
1 jar McCormick Salad Supreme
1 16 ounce bottle
  Italian salad dressing

Cook and drain spaghetti. Run cool water over to cool down. Add remaining ingredients and put in refrigerator for several hours. Serve cold.

Broccoli and Zucchini over Spinach Noodles

2 cups fresh broccoli, chopped
2 cups zucchini, chopped
1/2 cup onion, chopped
1 clove garlic, minced
2 tablespoons butter or margarine
3 tablespoons all purpose flour
2 tablespoons fresh parsley, snipped
1/2 teaspoon salt

1/2 teaspoon dried oregano, crushed
3/4 cup milk
1 1/2 cups ricotta or cream style cottage cheese
8 ounces spinach noodles, cooked, drained, and buttered
Parmesan cheese

In medium saucepan in small amount of salted, boiling water, cook broccoli and zucchini together about 8-10 minutes; drain well. In large saucepan, cook onion, garlic, and butter until onions are transparent. Blend in flour, parsley, salt, and oregano. Add milk all at once. Cook and stir until thick and bubbly. Add ricotta cheese. Cook and stir until cheese is nearly melted. Stir in cooked vegetables and heat through. Serve over hot, cooked spinach noodles. Serve with Parmesan cheese.

Pasta Salad Carbonara

Spinach leaves
2 tomatoes, peeled, seeded, and chopped
1/2 cup green pepper, diced
1 cup ham, cut into strips

6 ounces pasta twists, cooked by package directions
1 3 ounce can sliced mushrooms
1 cup frozen green peas
1 1/4 cups ranch dressing

Wash and stem spinach leaves. Peel, seed, and chop tomatoes. Dice green pepper. Cut ham into strips. Cook pasta twists and drain. Bring mushrooms with broth to a boil in a 10 inch skillet. Add peas; cover and cook 3 minutes. Uncover and add ham. Heat and stir until broth is absorbed and peas are tender crisp. Toss cooked pasta twists, green pepper, and tomatoes with salad dressing. Stir in mushroom-pea-ham mixture. Chill. Serve in salad bowl or on platter lined with spinach leaves.

Greek Pasta Salad

2 tablespoons lemon juice
1/2 cup olive or vegetable oil
1/2 teaspoon salt
1/4 teaspoon pepper
1/4 teaspoon dried oregano
1 clove garlic, crushed
3 cups rotino pasta, cooked and cooled
2 tomatoes, cut into wedges

1 cucumber, peeled and thinly sliced
12 Greek olives
1 cup green pepper strips, thinly sliced
1 1/2 cups feta cheese, crumbled
8 radishes, thinly sliced
2 tablespoons chopped parsley
1/4 cup sliced green onion

Combine lemon juice, oil, salt, pepper, oregano, and garlic in blender (or jar). Blend well until thick and creamy. Chill. Combine cooled pasta with remaining ingredients. Pour dressing over and toss to coat pasta and vegetables evenly. Serve immediately. Serves 6-8.

Pasta Carbonara

1/2 pound fettuccini
1/2 cup skim milk
1/3 cup mayonnaise or salad dressing
1 garlic clove, minced
1 egg, beaten

5 bacon slices, crisply cooked and crumbled
1/3 cup Parmesan cheese, grated
1/4 cup chopped parsley
Basil leaves for garnish

Prepare fettuccini according to package directions; drain. Gradually add milk to combined salad dressing and garlic in small saucepan; heat thoroughly, stirring occasionally. Remove from heat; blend in egg. Toss with hot fettuccini until well-coated. Add remaining ingredients; toss lightly. Garnish with basil leaves.

Spaghetti with Bacon

1 pound bacon, diced	3 eggs, slightly beaten
1 onion, chopped	3/4 cup Parmesan cheese, grated
1/2 cup dry white wine	1/2 teaspoon salt
1 pound spaghetti	Dash black pepper

Cook bacon until crisp in heavy saucepot. Remove bacon; drain off drippings, returning 2 tablespoons to pot. Saute onion in drippings until transparent; add wine and cook until wine is reduced by half. Cook spaghetti according to package directions; drain well; return to pot. Add bacon, onion mixture, eggs, Parmesan cheese, salt, and pepper. Toss lightly, until spaghetti is well coated. Serves 4-6.

Upside Down Fettuccini Bake

1/2 pound Italian sausage, casing removed	8 ounces fettuccini noodles, cooked and hot
1/4 cup onion, chopped	1/4 cup Parmesan cheese, grated
1 16 ounce can tomatoes	3 eggs, beaten slightly
1 teaspoon oregano leaves	2 tablespoons butter
1/2 cup mozzarella cheese, shredded	2 tablespoons parsley, chopped
1/4 cup Parmesan cheese, grated	1/4 teaspoon garlic powder

Brown meat in 10 inch ovenproof skillet; drain. Add onion; cook until tender. Stir in tomatoes and oregano; bring to a boil. Simmer 20 minutes, stirring occasionally. Stir in mozzarella cheese. Sprinkle 1/4 cup Parmesan cheese over tomato mixture. Toss noodles with combined remaining ingredients. Spread noodle mixture over Parmesan cheese. Bake at 350 for 25 minutes. Invert on serving platter. Sprinkle with additional Parmesan cheese, if desired. Cut into wedges. Makes 6 servings.

"For a variation, 1/2 pound ground beef and 1/2 teaspoon salt may be substituted for Italian sausage."

Vegetable Marinade for Pasta

1 6 ounce can black or salad olives
1 14 ounce can artichokes
1 8 ounce can bamboo shoots
2 small zucchini, chopped
2-3 small tomatoes, chopped

1 small onion, chopped
1 envelope dry buttermilk
    dressing mix
1 16 ounce bottle
    Italian salad dressing

Drain and chop olives, artichokes, and bamboo shoots. In large container, mix together all vegetables. Sprinkle with dry buttermilk dressing mix and mix in Italian dressing. Cover and marinate in refrigerator 12 hours before using, stirring several times. This can be used as a topping over salad or pasta.
Makes 12 cups.

Wild Rice and Sausage Breakfast

2 pounds ground sausage
1 pound mushrooms, chopped
1/4 cup flour
1/2 cup cream or evaporated milk
2 1/2 cups chicken broth
1 teaspoon monosodium
    glutamate
    Generous pinch each of oregano,
    thyme, and marjoram

1 teaspoon salt
    Dash Tabasco
    Worcestershire sauce
1 tablespoon parsley
2 cups wild rice, cooked *or*
    1 cup wild rice and 1 cup white
    rice, cooked
1 cup slivered almonds, toasted

Saute sausage and drain well on towels. Saute mushrooms and onions for 5 minutes in sausage fat and drain. Mix flour with cream until smooth. Add broth to flour mixture and cook slowly until thickened. Add seasonings and mix well. Mix together well, rice, sausage, mushrooms, and onions and pour into a large greased casserole. Pour cream mixture over rice mixture and sprinkle with toasted almonds. Bake 25-30 minutes in 350 oven. Serves 12. This can be frozen. After it is defrosted, add a little more chicken broth and reheat in the oven.

Quiche Lorraine

1 9 inch pie crust
1 teaspoon butter
3 slices Canadian bacon, or
    8 slices bacon, cooked crisp
    and drained
1 medium onion, chopped
1/2 cup Swiss cheese, grated

4 eggs, slightly beaten
1/2 cup milk
1 cup whipping cream
    Pinch nutmeg
1/2 teaspoon salt
1/4 teaspoon pepper

In frying pan, saute Canadian bacon and onion; set aside. In bowl, fold 1/4 cup Swiss cheese, eggs, milk, cream, and seasonings; set aside. Layer pie shell with bacon and onion. Pour mixture into shell and top with remaining 1/4 cup Swiss cheese. Bake at 450 for 15 minutes. Lower temperature to 350 and bake for 30-45 minutes until set. Serves 6.

"For a completely different taste, use one package chopped spinach, cooked and drained, or omit bacon and add small can drained salmon, 1/2 cup fresh green peas, and 1 tablespoon sherry."

Three-Cheese Pie

1 cup milk
3/4 cup flour
1 egg
    Salt and pepper

1 cup combined grated
    Monterey Jack, Swiss, and/or
    cheddar cheese

Preheat oven to 400. Butter a 9 inch pie plate. Blend milk, flour, egg, salt, and pepper with electric mixer. Stir in 1/2 of cheese. Pour into pie plate and bake until puffy and golden, about 25 minutes. Sprinkle with remaining cheese and bake another 3-4 minutes. Cut into wedges and serve.

"Delicious served with a picante or taco sauce."

Asparagus Quiche

Pastry for 9 inch quiche pan
Dijon mustard
Fresh asparagus
1½ cup cream

3 eggs
Salt and pepper
Grated Parmesan cheese
Gruyere cheese

Line a 9 inch quiche pan with pastry and bake in 425 oven for 15 minutes. Remove from oven, brush bottom with Dijon mustard, and bake for an additional 2 minutes. Blanch and cool fresh asparagus and arrange in single layer on pastry. Combine cream, eggs, salt, and pepper; pour over asparagus. Thickly cover top with a mixture of grated Parmesan cheese and Gruyere cheese. Bake in 350 oven for 30 minutes.

Crab Meat Quiche

1 cup Swiss cheese, shredded
1 6 ounce package frozen Alaskan king crab meat, thawed
2 green onions with tops, sliced
3 eggs, beaten
1 cup light cream

1 teaspoon salt
1 teaspoon lemon peel, grated
¼ teaspoon dry mustard
½ cup toasted almonds, sliced
1 11 inch pie shell, unbaked

Sprinkle cheese in bottom of pie shell; top with crabmeat and onion. Combine remaining ingredients and pour over crabmeat. Bake at 350 for 45 minutes. Let stand 10 minutes before serving.

Crustless Spinach Quiche

1 large onion, chopped
1 tablespoon vegetable oil
1 10 ounce package frozen
   chopped spinach, thawed and
   pressed dry

5 eggs, beaten
3 cups (12 ounces) Muenster
   cheese, shredded
1/4 teaspoon salt
1/8 teaspoon pepper

In a large skillet, saute onion in oil until tender. Add spinach and cook until excess moisture evaporates; cool. Combine eggs, cheese, salt, and pepper; stir into spinach mixture. Pour into a greased 9 inch pie plate. Bake at 350 for 30 minutes or until set.

Puffed Apple Pancakes

2 eggs, separated
1/4 cup sugar
2/3 cup all purpose flour
1/2 teaspoon cinnamon
1/8 teaspoon salt

1 1/2 cups apples, peeled,
   cored, and grated
   Pinch of salt
   Cinnamon flavored sugar
   Maple syrup

Beat egg yolks with sugar until thick and light in color. Add flour, cinnamon, and salt; stir until well mixed. Fold in apples. Beat egg whites with a pinch of salt until stiff. Fold egg whites into apple mixture. Drop batter by heaping spoonfuls onto hot, buttered griddle and brown pancakes on both sides, turning them once. Sprinkle with cinnamon-flavored sugar and serve with maple syrup. Yields 16.

SURFSIDE SWEETS

Desserts

Banana-Coconut Cake

½ cup butter
1½ cups sugar
2 eggs, separated
2 bananas, mashed
1 cup sour milk

1 teaspoon baking soda
1 teaspoon vanilla
2 cups flour
Frosting

Mix butter, sugar, egg yolks, and bananas together in a bowl. Mix sour milk and baking soda; add to mixture with vanilla and flour. Beat egg whites until stiff and fold into batter. Place in 9 inch baking pans. Bake at 350 for 25 minutes.

Frosting for Banana-Coconut Cake

10 tablespoons brown sugar
6 tablespoons butter or margarine

4 tablespoons thick cream
1 cup coconut

To dissolve sugar, heat ingredients in non-stick or cast iron pan until sugar liquifies. Use immediately. This can also be done in microwave oven at high setting, approximately 2 minutes.

Banana Split Cake

2 cups graham cracker crumbs
1 stick margarine, melted
2 sticks margarine, softened
2 cups confectioners sugar
2 eggs
1 teaspoon vanilla
5 bananas, sliced lengthwise

1 no. 2 can crushed
  pineapple, drained
1 large container prepared
  whipped topping
½ cup chopped nuts
8 maraschino cherries, chopped

Combine crumbs and 1 stick margarine. Line a 13x9x2 pan with crust. Combine 2 sticks margarine, sugar, eggs, and vanilla. Beat at high speed not less than 15 minutes. Spread over crust. Slice bananas over top of this. Spread pineapple over bananas. Spread whipped topping over top. Sprinkle with nuts and cherries. Cover and refrigerate for 24 hours.

Island Pound Cake

1/2 cup shortening	1 teaspoon baking powder
1 cup butter or margarine	1/4 cup milk
2 3/4 cups sugar	1 teaspoon vanilla
6 large eggs	3/4 cup crushed pineapple, with juice
3 cups sifted flour	Glaze

Cream shortening, butter, and sugar. Add eggs one at a time, beating well after each addition. Sift flour and baking powder together and add alternately with milk. Add vanilla. Stir in crushed pineapple and blend well. Pour batter into well greased 10 inch tube pan. Place in cold oven at 325 for 1 1/2 hours. Let stand for about 10 minutes and remove from pan.

Glaze

1/4 cup butter	1 cup crushed pineapple, drained
1 1/2 cup powdered sugar	

Combine ingredients. Pour over cake while hot.

Mom's Pound Cake

1/2 pound butter	1/2 teaspoon salt
1/3 cup shortening	1/2 teaspoon baking powder
2 3/4 cups sugar	1 cup milk
5 eggs	1 teaspoon vanilla
3 cups flour, sifted	1 teaspoon almond extract

Cream butter, shortening, and sugar. Add eggs one at a time, beating after each addition. Alternately add sifted dry ingredients and milk, beginning and ending with dry ingredients. Add vanilla and almond extract. Bake in greased tube pan at 350 for 1 hour. Start in cold oven.

"Great texture and flavor—really a treat!"

Kiss-Me Chocolate Pound Cake

1 cup butter	1/2 teaspoon baking powder
1/2 cup shortening	1/2 teaspoon salt
3 cups sugar	1/2 cup milk
5 eggs	2 teaspoons vanilla
2 2/3 cups flour	Icing
1/2 cup cocoa	

Soften butter. In large bowl cream butter, shortening, and sugar until light and fluffy. Beat in eggs, one at a time. Sift together dry ingredients and blend into creamed mixture alternately with milk and vanilla. Turn into well greased, lightly floured bundt or tube pan. Bake 1 1/2 hours at 325.

Icing for Chocolate Pound Cake

1 cup sifted powdered sugar	1 1/2 tablespoons milk
1/2 teaspoon vanilla extract	

Combine powdered sugar, vanilla, and milk and spread over cake.

Almond Sour Cream Pound Cake

1 cup butter	1/2 teaspoon baking powder
1/2 cup Crisco	1 cup sour cream
3 cups sugar	1 teaspoon vanilla
6 eggs, separated	1 teaspoon almond extract
3 cups sifted cake flour	

Cream butter, Crisco, and sugar until light and fluffy. Add egg yolks, one at a time, beating well after each addition. Sift flour with baking powder; add alternately with sour cream to creamed mixture. Add vanilla and almond extract. Beat egg whites until stiff; fold into batter. Turn into greased and floured 10 inch tube or bundt pan. Bake at 300 for 1 hour and 50 minutes.

"This cake is better each day after it is baked!"

The Queen's Cake

1 cup boiling water	1 teaspoon vanilla
1 cup dates, chopped	1/2 teaspoon salt
1 teaspoon baking soda	1 1/2 cups flour, sifted
1 cup sugar	1/2 cup nuts, chopped
1/4 cup butter	Topping
1 egg, beaten	Whipped cream

Pour cup of boiling water over the chopped dates and 1 teaspoon soda. Let stand while mixing the cake. Cream together the sugar and butter. Add egg, vanilla, salt, flour, and nuts. Bake in a 9x12 pan at 350 for 35 minutes.

Topping

5 tablespoons brown sugar	2 tablespoons butter
5 tablespoons cream, half-half	

Boil together the brown sugar, cream, and butter for 3 minutes. Let cool. When ready to serve, cut cake in squares and pour warm topping over it. Add a dollop of whipped cream and a few chopped nuts sprinkled over it.

Dirt Cake

1 20 ounce package Oreo cookies, finely crushed	1 cup powdered sugar
1 8 ounce package cream cheese, softened	2 small packages vanilla instant pudding mix
1/2 cup margarine, softened	3 cups milk
1 large container Cool Whip (not jumbo)	

Sprinkle half of crushed Oreos in 9x13 casserole. Mix cream cheese, margarine, Cool Whip, and powdered sugar together. Beat pudding mix with milk in separate bowl and add to cream cheese mixture. Spread over cookie crumbs. Sprinkle remaining half of cookie crumbs on top. Chill at least 12 hours before serving.

Milky Way Cake

8 ounces of Milky Way bars
1 cup butter or margarine
1 cup pecans
2 cups sugar
1¼ cups buttermilk

½-1 teaspoon baking soda
4 eggs
2½ cups flour
2 teaspoons vanilla
Frosting

Melt Milky Way bars, margarine, and pecans over low heat; let cool. Mix sugar, buttermilk, soda, eggs, flour, and vanilla; beat for 2 minutes. Fold in candy mixture. Pour into greased and floured 10 inch pan and bake at 350 for 45 minutes, or until done.

Frosting

2½ cups sugar
1 cup evaporated milk
½ cup butter or margarine

1 6 ounce package semi-sweet chocolate chips
1 cup marshmallow creme

Cook sugar, margarine, and milk to softball stage. Add chocolate and marshmallow; beat. Spread over cake.

Turtle Cake

1 box German chocolate cake mix
1 14 ounce bag caramels
¾ cup butter

½ cup evaporated milk
1 cup semi-sweet chocolate chips
2 cups pecans, chopped

Mix cake by directions on the box. Bake half the batter in a greased and floured 13x9 pan at 350 for 15 minutes. In saucepan over low heat, melt butter, caramels, and milk. Remove cake from oven and pour caramel mixture over the cake. Top with chocolate chips and nuts. Pour remaining cake batter over top and return to oven. Bake another 20 minutes.

"Rich and delicious!"

Coca Cola Cake

2 cups flour
2 cups sugar
1 cup butter
3 tablespoons cocoa
1 cup Coca Cola
1/2 cup buttermilk
2 eggs, beaten

1 teaspoon baking soda
1 teaspoon vanilla extract
1 1/2 cups miniature marshmallows,
    white only
Coca Cola Icing or
Peanut Butter Icing

Grease and flour a 9x13 sheet cake pan or bundt pan. Combine flour and sugar in large bowl. Melt butter, add cocoa and Coca Cola. Pour over flour mixture and stir until well blended. Dissolve soda in with the buttermilk and add to flour mixture with eggs and vanilla. Mix well. Stir in marshmallows. Pour in prepared pan. Bake at 350 for 40 minutes. Remove cake from oven and frost while still warm with your choice of "Coca Cola Icing" or "Peanut Butter Icing."

Coca Cola Icing

1/2 cup butter
2 tablespoons cocoa
6 tablespoons Coca Cola

1 pound confectioners sugar, sifted
1 cup broken pecan pieces,
    toasted if desired

Bring butter, cocoa, and Coca Cola to a boil. Pour over sugar and beat. Stir in pecans and spread on cake.

Peanut Butter Icing

6 tablespoons butter
1 cup dark brown sugar,
    tightly packed

2/3 cup peanut butter
1/4 cup milk
2/3 cup chopped peanuts

Cream butter, sugar and peanut butter. Add milk and stir well. Add nuts. Spread over warm cake. Place frosted cake under broiler about 4 inches from heat source. Broil just a few seconds, until browned, watching carefully so that topping doesn't scorch. Let cool at least 30 minutes before serving.

Red Devil's Food Cake

2/3 cup shortening
2 cups sugar
2 eggs
4 tablespoons cocoa
1 teaspoon baking soda
1 cup buttermilk (or 2 tablespoons vinegar in 1 cup milk)

1 teaspoon salt
2¼ cups flour
1 teaspoon baking powder
2 teaspoons vanilla
1 cup boiling water
  Chocolate Sour Cream Frosting

Cream together shortening, sugar, eggs, and cocoa. Sift together salt, baking powder, and flour. Dissolve soda in the buttermilk, stirring constantly, and add alternately to the creamed mixture. Add the vanilla and the boiling water. Cook in a well greased and floured tube pan, or a 9x13 pan at 350 for 45 minutes, or until it springs back when you touch it.

Chocolate Sour Cream Frosting for Red Devil's Food Cake

1 6 ounce package semi-sweet chocolate chips
4 tablespoons butter
½ cup sour cream

1 teaspoon vanilla
¼ teaspoon salt
2½-3 cups powdered sugar

Melt chocolate chips and butter in a double boiler or in a glass bowl in the microwave. Remove and blend in sour cream. Add vanilla and salt and gradually add the sugar until it is of spreading consistency.

Secret Swirl Cupcakes

1   package chocolate cake mix
    and all ingredients called for
    on the box
1   8 ounce package of
    cream cheese

1/3 cup sugar
1   egg
1   6 ounce package semi-sweet
    chocolate pieces
    Paper baking cups

Mix cake mix and fill cups 2/3 full. Cream cheese with sugar and beat in egg and salt. Stir in chocolate pieces. Drop one rounded teaspoon of mixture into each cup. Bake as directed on package. Cheese and chocolate will sink to the bottom.

Note: This is good for kids' parties. There is no need for icing.

"Best cupcake—moist and flavorful!"

Chocolate Dream Cake

20 lady fingers
1/2 pound sweet cooking chocolate
3   eggs, separated

1   teaspoon vanilla
1   cup whipping cream

Line straight sided loaf pan, 11x4x21/2, with waxed paper, leaving an overhang. Separate lady fingers; place 8 halves in a row in the bottom of the pan. Melt chocolate over hot water; remove from heat; add egg yolks one at a time, beating vigorously after each addition. Beat egg whites until stiff; fold in. Add vanilla. Whip 1/2 cup cream, fold in. Spread 1/4 chocolate mixture on lady fingers in the pan. Add another row of lady finger halves. Repeat until there are 4 layers of chocolate. Top with remaining lady fingers. Chill several hours, or overnight. Lift cake from pan with waxed paper overhang. Remove waxed paper. Place on serving dish. Whip remaining cream and frost sides of the cake. Makes 8 servings and can be doubled.

Mississippi Mud Cake

1 cup margarine
2 cups sugar
2 tablespoons cocoa
4 eggs
1 teaspoon vanilla

1½ cups flour
1⅓ cups (4 ounces) coconut
1½ cups chopped pecans
1 large jar marshmallow cream
Frosting

Cream margarine, sugar, and cocoa. Add eggs and vanilla and mix well. Add flour, coconut, and nuts. Bake in greased and floured 9x13 pan at 350 for 30-40 minutes. When done, immediately spread marshmallow cream on top. Put pan on rack to cool.

Frosting for Mississippi Mud Cake

½ cup margarine
½ cup evaporated milk
⅓ cup cocoa

1 teaspoon vanilla
1 box powdered sugar, sifted

Mix all ingredients together, except powdered sugar, in a saucepan before putting on the stove to heat. Heat until the margarine melts. Add powdered sugar gradually to icing and beat until smooth. Drizzle frosting in lattice-like design over top of marshmallow cream. Refrigerate. Cut in squares. Can be frozen.

"A chocolate lover's delight!"

Mandarin Orange Cake

1 yellow cake mix
  (without pudding)
1 can mandarin
  oranges, undrained
3 large eggs
1/2 cup oil

1 15¼ ounce can crushed
  pineapple, undrained
1 9 ounce container Cool Whip
1 small package instant
  vanilla pudding

Combine cake mix, oranges, eggs, and oil and beat for 2 minutes on high speed. Reduce speed; beat 1 minute. Pour batter into 3 greased and floured 9 inch round cake pans. Bake at 350 for 20 minutes or until done. Cool and remove from pans. Combine last 3 ingredients and beat 2 minutes. Let stand for 5 minutes. Spread on layers and top of cake. Chill 2 hours before serving. Store in refrigerator.
    NOTE: You may use a tube pan and bake for 45 minutes. Slice in half and frost.

"Very moist and delicious!"

Pineapple Upside-Down Cake

1/2 cup brown sugar
  3 tablespoons butter
  1 1 pound can pineapple slices
    Maraschino cherries
  2 cups sifted cake flour
  3 teaspoons baking powder
1/4 teaspoon salt

1/4 cup shortening
  1 cup sugar
  1 egg, well beaten
  1 teaspoon vanilla
3/4 cup milk
    Whipping cream, optional

Set oven at 350. Sprinkle brown sugar in bottom of well greased 9x9x2 greased pan. Dot with butter. Melt mixture over low heat. Drain pineapple and place slices in pan with cherry in center of each. Sift together flour, baking powder, and salt. Cream shortening; add sugar gradually. Beat until fluffy; add egg and vanilla. Beat well; add flour mixture, a little at a time, alternately with milk. Pour batter over fruit. Bake 1 hour or until light brown. Turn upside down on serving plate at once. Serve with whipping cream, if desired. Yields 9 servings.

Pleasantly Plum Cake

2 cups sugar
3/4 cup oil
3 eggs
2 jars of plum baby food
1 tablespoon red food coloring
2 teaspoons vanilla
2 cups flour

1/2 teaspoon soda
1/2 teaspoon salt
1 teaspoon cinnamon
1 teaspoon ground cloves
1 cup nuts, chopped
    Glaze

Beat together first 6 ingredients. Sift together next five dry ingredients. Combine sifted ingredients with first ingredients. Add chopped nuts. Put in greased and floured bundt pan. Bake in oven at 350 for 1 hour. While cake is warm, drizzle glaze over it.

Glaze

Juice of 2 lemons

1 cup powdered sugar

With a whisk combine the juice and powdered sugar.

"So good! Allow cake to set in pan for ten minutes before removing for best results."

Mock Strudel

2 cups flour
3/4 cup butter
1/2 pint sour cream
1 16 ounce jar apricot preserves

1 cup chopped pecans
1 cup raisins
1/2 cup cinnamon sugar

Combine flour, butter, and sour cream to form a soft but workable dough. Chill 1 hour. Divide dough evenly into 3 sections. Roll out 1 section at a time on a floured board. Spread with preserves, nuts, raisins, and cinnamon sugar. Roll up, jelly roll fashion, and place on a well greased cookie sheet. Repeat with remaining 2 sections of dough. Bake at 350 for 1 hour. Slice while warm.
Yields 3 dozen pieces.

Cherry Berry Cake

2 20 ounce cans cherry pie filling
1 18½ ounce box white cake mix

1 cup butter or margarine, melted
1 cup chopped nuts (optional)

Pour pie filling into the bottom of a 13x9 greased pan. Sprinkle dry cake mix on top. Melt the butter or margarine and pour evenly over mixture. Sprinkle chopped nuts on top. Bake at 350 for 35 minutes. (You can use any canned fruit pie filling—apple, peach, blueberry, etc.)

Cherry Yum Yum

1 18½ box yellow cake mix
1 cup water
1 small jar maraschino cherries
3 eggs
1 3 ounce package walnuts

½ cup flaked coconut
½ cup maraschino cherry juice
    Red food coloring (optional)
    Vanilla Frosting

Grease and flour two 9 inch round cake pans. Preheat oven to 350. Drain cherries, reserving juice. Chop cherries and nuts in small pieces. Set aside. Combine cake mix, water, and ½ cup cherry juice. Add 3 eggs and mix well. Add the oil and vanilla and mix. Total mixing time with mixer is 4 minutes. Add cherries, nuts, and coconut. Blend well. Add food coloring if desired. Bake 30-35 minutes until lightly browned. Cool in pans 7 minutes. Remove from pans and cool. Frost with vanilla frosting when cool.

Vanilla Frosting for Cherry Cake

6 teaspoons butter or margarine
¼ cup shortening
1 pound confectioners sugar

   Evaporated milk
2 teaspoons vanilla

Cream butter with shortening until very smooth. Gradually add sugar, along with a few drops of milk until all sugar is added. Add vanilla. If frosting is too thick, add more milk. Beat several minutes until light and creamy.

Frosted Jam Cake

1 cup butter, softened
2 cups sugar
4 eggs
2 cups blackberry jam
3 cups flour
1 teaspoon baking powder
1 teaspoon baking soda

2 teaspoons ground allspice
2 teaspoons cinnamon
1 cup buttermilk
1 cup seedless raisins
2/3 cup nuts, chopped
Frosting
Pecan halves

Preheat oven to 300. Grease and flour 3 9-inch cake pans. Cream butter and sugar. Beat in eggs and jam. Sift dry ingredients together. Add to creamed mixture alternately with buttermilk, beating well after each addition. Stir in raisins and nuts. Pour batter into prepared cake pans. Bake 40 minutes, or until cakes test done. Cool cake on racks until room temperature and spread with warm frosting.

Frosting

1 cup cream
2 cups sugar

1 tablespoon butter

Combine cream and sugar in heavy saucepan. Bring to boil and cook 2-3 minutes. Candy thermometer will read 234 degrees. Cool slightly, then beat until it just begins to thicken. Beat in butter and immediately spread between layers and on top of cake. Leave sides unfrosted. Decorate with pecan halves.

Homemade Carrot Cake

2 cups flour
2½ cups sugar
2 teaspoons baking soda
½ teaspoon salt
2 teaspoons ground cinnamon
3 eggs
1 cup salad oil

1 teaspoon vanilla extract
1 cup dates, chopped
1 cup nuts, chopped
2 cups carrot, grated
1 cup crushed pineapple, drained
Frosting

Sift dry ingredients together. Make a well in center of ingredients and add eggs, oil, and vanilla. Mix and add dates, nuts, carrots, and pineapple. Mixture will be very stiff at this point. Pour into 13x9x2 greased and floured baking dish and bake for 1 hour at 350.

Frosting

1 8 ounce package cream cheese
½ cup butter, softened
2 teaspoons vanilla

1 pound box confectioners sugar, sifted

Combine all ingredients; mix well. Frost cooled cake.

Pina Colada Cheesecake

Crust

½ cup butter
¼ cup sugar

2 cups ground vanilla wafers

Melt butter over very low heat; combine with sugar and crumbs until well blended. Press mixture on bottom and sides of well greased 10 inch springform pan.

Filling

2 pounds (4 8-ounce packages)
  cream cheese
1½ cups sugar
2 teaspoons pineapple extract

2 round slices of pineapple
  soaked in 3 tablespoons dark
  rum for 1 hour—reserve
1 tablespoon rum
4 eggs
  Dash salt

Combine cream cheese with sugar and beat for 2 minutes until soft. Add pineapple extract, pineapple slices, and 1 tablespoon rum. Blend thoroughly. Add eggs one at a time until each has been incorporated. Add salt. Pour filling into crust and bake at 350 for 45 minutes. Let stand on a counter for 10 minutes. THIS IS ESSENTIAL.

Topping

2 cups sour cream
¼ cup sugar

1 teaspoon coconut extract

Combine sour cream, sugar, and coconut extract with rubber spatula. Spread evenly over baked filling. Bake at 350 for 25 minutes. Cool 1 hour and refrigerate. Yields 8-10 servings.

Heavenly Kahlua Cheesecake

1¼ cup graham cracker crumbs
¼ cup sugar
¼ cup cocoa
⅓ cup butter or margarine, melted
1 8 ounce package cream
   cheese, softened
¾ cup sugar
½ cup cocoa
2 eggs

¼ cup strong coffee
¼ cup Kahlua or other
   coffee flavored liqueur
1 teaspoon vanilla extract
1 8 ounce carton sour cream
2 tablespoons sugar
1 teaspoon vanilla extract
6-8 chocolate curls (optional)

Combine first 4 ingredients; mix well. Firmly press mixture into bottom of a 9 inch springform pan. Bake at 325 for 5 minutes; cool. Beat cream cheese with electric mixer until light and fluffy; gradually add ¾ cup sugar, mixing well. Beat in ½ cup cocoa. Add eggs, one at a time, beating well after each addition. Stir in next 3 ingredients. Pour into prepared pan. Bake at 375 for 25 minutes. (Filling will be soft but will firm up as the cake stands.) Combine sour cream, 2 tablespoons sugar, and 1 teaspoon vanilla; spread over hot cheesecake. Bake at 425 for 5-7 minutes. Let cool to room temperature on a wire rack; chill 8 hours or overnight. Remove sides of springform pan. To garnish place 3 chocolate curls in center of cheesecake; gently break remaining chocolate curls and sprinkle over cheesecake, if desired. Yields 8-10 servings.

Dream Cheesecake

4 tablespoons butter or margarine, melted
1 cup fine graham cracker crumbs
1 teaspoon cream of tartar
6 eggs, separated
19 ounces cream cheese

1½ cups plus 3 tablespoons sugar
3 tablespoons flour
½ teaspoon salt
1 pint sour cream
1 teaspoon vanilla

Butter generously a 9 inch springform pan. Mix butter and crumbs well. Reserve ¼ cup of crumbs and press remainder firmly on bottom of pan. Add cream of tartar to egg whites and beat until stiff. Set aside. Beat cheese until soft in a separate bowl. Mix sugar, flour, and salt and gradually beat into cheese. Add egg yolks one at a time, beating thoroughly after each. Add sour cream and vanilla. Mix well. Fold in egg whites thoroughly. Pour mixture into prepared pan. Sprinkle with reserved crumbs. Bake in moderate oven at 325 for 1 hour and 15 minutes or until firm. Turn off heat and open oven door. Let cake stand in oven for 15 minutes. Remove and place on cake rack away from drafts. Refrigerate after cake comes to room temperature. Yields 8-10 servings.

"Allow 1 hour minimum preparation. This cheesecake tastes best when made at least 1 day before serving."

Demi Cheesecake Melba

2 8 ounce packages cream cheese, softened
¾ cup sugar
½ teaspoon vanilla

3 eggs, room temperature, beaten
 Vanilla wafers
1 12 ounce can lemon pie filling

Blend together cream cheese, sugar, and vanilla. Beat in eggs. Line miniature muffin pans with paper cups. Arrange vanilla wafers in bottom, one per cup. Fill cups with cream cheese mixture. Bake 12 minutes at 350. Immediately top with pie filling. Let cool. Refrigerate until serving time. Yields 8-10 servings.

"This cheesecake is wonderfully delicious!"

Two-Tone Cheesecake

1½ cups crushed chocolate wafers, about 30 cookies
4 tablespoons butter or margarine, softened
5 8 ounce packages cream cheese, softened
1¾ cups sugar
5 eggs
¼ cup milk

3 tablespoons all purpose flour
2 squares semi-sweet chocolate
1 teaspoon grated lemon peel
1 teaspoon instant espresso coffee powder
½ cup sour cream
Lemon leaves or other non-toxic garnish

Mix chocolate wafers and butter or margarine by hand. Press into bottom and halfway up sides of 10x2½ springform pan, forming a scalloped edge. Set aside. In large bowl, with mixer at medium speed, beat cream cheese just until smooth; slowly beat in sugar. With mixer at low speed, beat in eggs, milk, and flour just until blended, occasionally scraping bowl.

Preheat oven to 300. In heavy, small saucepan over low heat, melt chocolate, stirring frequently. Pour 5½ cups cream cheese mixture into another large bowl; stir in lemon peel. Pour lemon cream cheese mixture into crust in pan. Into remaining cream cheese mixture with mixer at low speed, beat melted chocolate and espresso coffee powder until blended. Gently spoon chocolate cream cheese mixture on top of mixture in pan. Bake cheesecake for 55 minutes at 300. Turn off oven and let cheesecake remain in oven until cooled, for about 2 hours. Refrigerate cheesecake at least 4 hours or until well chilled. To serve, remove side of springform pan. Spoon sour cream centered on top of cake. Garnish with lemon leaves. Yields 8-10 servings.

Almond Cake with Raspberry Sauce

3/4 cup sugar
1/2 cup unsalted butter, softened
8 ounces almond paste
3 eggs
1 tablespoon Kirsch or Triple Sec

1/4 teaspoon almond extract
1/4 cup all purpose flour
1/3 teaspoon baking powder
Powdered sugar
Sauce

Butter and flour 8 inch round pan. Combine sugar, butter, and almond paste in medium mixing bowl and blend well. Beat in eggs, liqueur, and almond extract. Add flour and baking powder, beating until just mixed through; do not overbeat. Bake at 350 until tester comes out clean, about 40-50 minutes. Let cool. Invert onto serving dish and dust lightly with powdered sugar.

Sauce

1 pint fresh raspberries *or*
1 12-ounce package frozen, thawed

2 tablespoons sugar or to taste

Combine raspberries with sugar in processor or blender and puree. Gently press sauce through fine sieve to remove seeds. Serve cake on bed of sauce on individual dessert plates.

NOTE: Sugar can be omitted when using frozen raspberries.

"A favorite recipe."

Holiday Gift Cake

1 8 ounce package cream cheese, softened
1 cup butter or margarine
1½ cups sugar
1½ teaspoons vanilla
4 eggs
2¼ cups sifted flour
1½ teaspoons baking powder

1 8 ounce jar maraschino cherries, drained and quartered
½ cup chopped pecans
½ cup finely chopped pecans
Glaze
Candied cherries
Pecans

Thoroughly blend softened cream cheese, margarine, sugar, and vanilla. Add eggs one at a time, mixing well after each addition. Gradually add 2 cups of the flour sifted with the baking powder. Combine remaining ¼ cup flour with cherries and ½ cup chopped pecans and fold into batter. Grease and flour bundt pan or 2 loaf pans, and sprinkle with ½ cup finely chopped pecans. Pour in batter and bake at 325 for 1 hour and 20 minutes (about 1 hour for loaf pans). Cool 5 minutes before removing from pans. Glaze and decorate with candied cherries and pecans.

Glaze

1½ cups powdered sugar, sifted

2 tablespoons milk (may need more)

Mix powdered sugar and milk together until smooth. Drizzle on cake.

Harvest Pumpkin Cake

4 eggs
2 cups sugar
1 cup oil
2 cups flour
2 teaspoons baking soda

1 teaspoon baking powder
2 teaspoons cinnamon
1 scant teaspoon salt
2 cups pumpkin
Frosting

Mix together eggs, sugar, and oil until well blended. Add remaining ingredients and mix well. Grease and flour pan. Bake at 350 for 60 minutes.

Frosting

1/2 box confectioner's sugar
1/4 cup butter, softened
4 ounces cream cheese

1 teaspoon vanilla
1/2 cup pecans, chopped

Mix together and frost cooled cake.

Poppy Seed Cake

1 box deluxe white cake mix
   (no pudding)
1 6 ounce box vanilla
   instant pudding
4 eggs

3/4 cup sherry
3/4 cup oil
1 tablespoon poppy seeds
1 teaspoon vanilla
1 teaspoon almond extract

Beat all ingredients at least 4 minutes. Pour into well greased and floured tube pan. Bake at 350 for 50-60 minutes.

Optional Glaze for the Poppy Seed Cake

1 1/3 cups powdered sugar, sifted
1 tablespoon orange marmalade
1/3 cup fresh or frozen orange juice

1 teaspoon butter flavoring
1 teaspoon almond extract
1 teaspoon orange extract

Mix all ingredients until creamy. Spread on cake while warm.

Rum Cake

½ cup chopped pecans
1 package Duncan Hines golden yellow cake mix
1 3 ounce package vanilla instant pudding mix

½ cup vegetable oil
½ cup rum
½ cup water
4 eggs
  Sauce

Grease and flour bundt pan. Sprinkle pecans in bottom of pan. Combine cake mix, pudding mix, oil, rum, water, and eggs. Bake at 325 for 45-55 minutes. Put cake on plate and let cool 5 minutes. Prepare sauce and pour over cake. Let stand till sauce has soaked in.

Sauce

½ cup butter
1 cup sugar

¼ cup rum
¼ cup water

Combine all sauce ingredients and boil for 5 minutes.

Rum Bumble Cake

½ cup butter
  Brown sugar
8 cherries
  Nuts
1 box yellow cake mix

1 box vanilla instant pudding
4 eggs
¾ cup oil
⅓ cup rum
⅓ cup water

Melt butter and pour in bundt pan. Sprinkle brown sugar until absorbed. Press in cherries. Sprinkle nuts on top. Mix other ingredients together with beater. Pour on top. Bake at 325 for 45 minutes. Turn out immediately and put brown sugar back on top.

Miracle Prune Cake

1½ cups dates or raisins
1½ cups nuts
2½ cups flour
1 cup oil
1½ cups sugar
3 eggs

1 cup buttermilk
1 teaspoon soda, added to milk
1 teaspoon cinnamon
1 teaspoon allspice
1½ cups cooked prunes
Glaze

Dredge nuts and dates with some of flour. Mix oil and sugar; add eggs, milk, and soda, then flour to which spices have been added. Add prunes and then dates and nuts. Use tube pan and bake at 375 for about 50 minutes.

Glaze

1 cup sugar
¼ cup margarine
½ cup buttermilk

½ teaspoon vanilla
½ teaspoon soda
1 teaspoon Karo white syrup

Combine all ingredients. Cook to thin syrup or bring to good boil and pour over cake while it is still very warm. Use toothpick to punch holes in cake before putting on glaze.

Italian Cream Cake

½ cup butter
½ cup margarine
2 cups sugar
5 eggs, separated
2 cups flour
1 teaspoon soda (sift with flour)

1 cup buttermilk
1 teaspoon vanilla
1 small can coconut
(about 1⅓ cups)
1 cup chopped nuts
Icing

Cream butter, margarine, and sugar. Add yolks, flour, soda, buttermilk, vanilla, coconut, and nuts. Fold in well beaten egg whites. Bake at 350 for 40-50 minutes, until done. Makes 3 round 8 or 9 inch layers.

I bake at 325° for 25 min.

Icing

8 ounces cream cheese
¼ cup margarine
1 box powdered sugar

1 teaspoon vanilla
½-1 cup chopped nuts

Grease bottom of pan. Lay wax/parchment paper on top greased & floured not sides. paper — not sides.

Soften cream cheese and mix with margarine. Add sugar, vanilla, and nuts.

Banana Mandarin Pie

9 inch graham cracker crumb crust
1 8 ounce package cream cheese, softened
1 14 ounce can sweetened, condensed milk
⅓ cup lemon juice

1 teaspoon vanilla
3 bananas
1 can mandarin orange segments, well drained
2 tablespoons lemon juice

In large mixing bowl, beat cream cheese until fluffy. Gradually beat in sweetened condensed milk; stir in lemon juice and vanilla. Slice and arrange 2 bananas in the graham cracker crust with about ⅔ of the orange segments. Pour filling into crust. Slice third banana; dip in remaining lemon juice. Garnish top of pie with remaining bananas and remaining orange segments. Chill for 2 hours.

Apple Dapple Cake

3 eggs	Cinnamon (optional)
1¼ cups vegetable oil	Nutmeg (optional)
2 cups sugar	2 teaspoons vanilla
3 cups flour	3 cups chopped apples, peeled
1 teaspoon salt	1½ cups chopped pecans
1 teaspoon soda	1 cup raisins (optional)
2 teaspoons baking powder	Caramel Frosting

Cream eggs, oil, and sugar. Add flour, salt, soda, baking powder, cinnamon, and nutmeg. Add vanilla, apples, pecans, and raisins. Pour into greased and floured tube pan and cook at 350 for 1 hour and 25 minutes.

Caramel Frosting

½ cup butter	1½-2 cups powdered sugar
1 cup brown sugar	1 teaspoon vinegar
¼ cup milk	

Melt butter and add brown sugar. Boil; stir one minute, or until slightly thick. Cool slightly. Add milk and beat until smooth, add confectioners sugar and vinegar and beat until of spreading consistency.

Apple Blossom Pie

1 cup sugar	1 cup strained applesauce
Pinch of salt	1 pie shell
1 tablespoon cornstarch	Nutmeg
1 egg, beaten	Cinnamon
1 cup heavy cream	Whipped cream, optional

Blend sugar, salt, and cornstarch; add egg. Blend well; fold in cream and applesauce. Partially bake pie shell about 6 minutes at 425. Pour filling mixture into shell; sprinkle with nutmeg and cinnamon. Bake at 325 until center is firm. Chill; serve with whipped cream, if desired. Serves 6.

Lemon Chess Pie

1½ cups sugar
1 tablespoon flour
1 tablespoon yellow cornmeal
3-4 eggs, unbeaten

¼ cup milk
2 grated lemon rinds
¼ cup lemon juice
1 9 inch pie crust, unbaked

Combine sugar, flour, and meal; toss lightly with fork and add remaining ingredients. Beat well with rotary beater. Do not whip with mixer. Pour into pie crust. Bake at 375 until firm and brown on top, about 35 to 45 minutes. Do not overbake.

"When you're given lemons, make Lemon Chess Pie!"

Luscious Lemon Meringue Pie

1 3 ounce package
lemon pudding mix
⅔ cup sugar
¼ cup water
3 eggs, separated

2 cups water
2 tablespoons lemon juice
2 tablespoons butter
1 9 inch pie shell, baked
6 tablespoons sugar

Combine pudding mix, sugar, and ¼ cup water in saucepan. Mix in egg yolks. Add 2 cups water. Cook until mixture boils, about 5 minutes. Cool 5 minutes and blend in lemon juice and butter. Pour into pie shell. Beat egg whites until firm. Gradually add sugar. Spread on top and bake at 425 until golden.

Key Lime Pie

2 eggs, separated
1 can sweetened condensed milk
½ cup lime juice
1 tablespoon grated lime rind

¼ teaspoon vanilla
¼ cup sugar
1 9 inch pie shell, baked ·
  Meringue

Beat egg yolks until thick; combine with milk. Add lime juice, rind, and vanilla.
Beat egg whites until stiff; add sugar. Fold into lime mixture. Pour in pie shell.

Meringue

2 egg whites

4 tablespoons sugar

Beat egg whites until stiff; fold in sugar. Spread over pie. Brown under broiler. Serves 6.
  Note: One 6 ounce can limeade may be substituted for lime juice and rind.

"A cool and refreshing summer dessert."

Lucky Lime Pie

1 cup sugar
1 3 ounce package lime jello
1 cup boiling water
1 large can evaporated
  milk, chilled

Juice of 2 lemons
Green food coloring (optional)
2 chocolate or graham cracker
  crumb crusts

Combine sugar, jello, and boiling water and place in refrigerator until slightly
thickened. Chill evaporated milk overnight. Remove from refrigerator, add lemon
juice and beat until thick. Slightly beat jello mixture, add green coloring if desired,
and fold into whipped milk until well mixed. Pour into crust and put into
refrigerator to chill. Makes 2 9-inch pies.

"Lucky Lime Pie makes every day a lucky day!"

Cherry Blossom Treat

1/2 cup butter, softened
1 1/2 cups powdered sugar
1/4 teaspoon almond extract
2 eggs

3/4 pound vanilla wafers, crushed
1 20 ounce can cherry pie filling, ready prepared
1 cup heavy cream, whipped

Cream butter and sugar until light and fluffy. Add almond extract and egg, one at a time and continue creaming. Place half the crumbs in a 9 inch square pan and spread creamed mixture over crumbs. Top with cherry pie filling. Cover with whipped cream and sprinkle with remaining crumbs. Chill for several hours.

Crunchy Cherry Pie

1 graham cracker pie crust
1 egg yolk, beaten
1 tablespoon cornstarch
1 tablespoon water
1 20 ounce can cherry pie filling

3 tablespoons brown sugar
1/2 cup flour
1/2 cup quick-cooking oats
4 tablespoons butter, melted

Brush bottom and sides of pie crust with egg yolk and bake for 5 minutes on baking sheet. Mix cornstarch and water into a paste; combine with cherry pie filling. Add to pie crust. Mix remaining ingredients and sprinkle over top of pie. Bake at 375 about 30-35 minutes.

Cookie Peach Pie

2 cups peaches, sliced
3/4 cup sugar
1 1/2 tablespoons flour
Dash of salt

1/3 stick butter
1 package refrigerator sugar cookie dough

Fill 9 inch pan with peaches. Mix flour, sugar, and salt. Sprinkle over peaches. Dot with butter. Top with cookie dough sliced 1/4 inch thick. Bake at 350 for 45 minutes.

Easy Peach Cobbler

2 teaspoons lemon juice
1/4 teaspoon almond extract
1/2 cup brown sugar
1/8 teaspoon salt
2 tablespoons cornstarch

1/2 cup water
6 whole peaches, pared and sliced
1 large package refrigerated
  crescent rolls

Combine lemon juice, almond extract, sugar, salt, cornstarch, and water. Add peach slices and cook at medium heat until juice is clear and peaches tender, about ten minutes. Put in buttered casserole and top with crescent rolls, which have been cut in strips and arranged in criss-cross fashion over the top. Bake at 375 until rolls are brown. Serve hot for a treat!

Orange Chiffon Pie

1 cup sugar, divided
1/2 cup orange juice
1 tablespoon lemon juice
1/2 teaspoon salt
4 eggs, separated
1/4 cup cold water

1 envelope gelatin
1 tablespoon grated orange rind
1 8 or 9 inch pie shell,
  baked and cooled
  Whipped cream for topping

Combine 1/2 cup of the sugar, orange juice, lemon juice, and salt. Add to beaten egg yolks and cook over boiling water until the mixture is of custard consistency. Sprinkle gelatin over cold water, dissolve, and add to custard mixture. Stir until blended. Add grated orange rind and cool. When mixture begins to thicken, fold in stiffly beaten egg whites, to which the remaining 1/2 cup sugar has been added. Fill baked pie shell and chill. Serve with whipped cream.

Strawberry Bavarian Pie

½ cup walnuts
½ cup margarine
  at room temperature
2 tablespoons sugar
1 egg yolk
1 cup flour

1¼ cups fresh crushed strawberries
2 egg whites
1 cup sugar
½ teaspoon almond extract
¼ teaspoon salt
1 cup whipping cream

Preheat oven to 400. Put walnuts into blender or food processor and process until nuts are finely chopped. In small mixer bowl mix nuts, margarine, sugar, egg yolk, and flour at low, then medium low speed until mixed. Using spatula, spread mixture on bottom and sides of a 10 inch pie pan. Bake for 12 minutes and cool.

In large bowl, beat remaining ingredients, except whipping cream, at medium high until very thick and double in volume, about 10-15 minutes. Set aside. In small mixer bowl, whip cream first at low speed, then higher speed until stiff. Fold cream into strawberry mixture until blended. Pour into pie shell. Put uncovered pie into freezer and freeze until firm. About 1 hour before serving, put pie in refrigerator to soften.

Gourmet Strawberry Tart

1 10 inch pie shell, baked
1 3 ounce package vanilla
  pudding, not instant
2 cups half and half cream
2 tablespoons Cointreau liqueur

1 cup red currant jelly
4 tablespoons hot water
1 cup whipping cream, whipped
1 quart fresh strawberries, cleaned

Prepare pudding according to package instructions, substituting half and half for milk. Add Cointreau. Combine jelly and water in saucepan and heat until jelly melts. Combine whipped cream and cooled pudding mixture, stirring lightly with wire whisk. Pour into pie crust. Arrange berries on top and pour jelly mixture on top.

"Berry good!"

Blueberry Tarts au Cointreau

12 tart shells
1 3¼ ounce package instant vanilla pudding
1 cup milk
1 cup whipping cream

⅛ teaspoon salt
1 tablespoon Cointreau
3 cups blueberries, well drained and dusted with powdered sugar
Whipped cream

Prepare pudding mix according to package directions, using the milk and whipping cream for liquid. Add salt and then Cointreau. Fill tart shells with pudding mixture and heap with blueberries. Sprinkle blueberries with more powdered sugar. Serve with whipped cream.

Aloha Pineapple Pie

1 1 pound-4½ ounce can crushed pineapple
¾ cup sugar
¼ teaspoon salt
⅓ cup flour
2 egg yolks

½ cup flaked coconut
1 tablespoon butter
1 tablespoon lemon juice
1 9 inch pie shell, baked
Meringue

Combine undrained can of pineapple, sugar, salt, and flour. Cook over medium heat about 5 minutes, stirring constantly, until clear and thick. Remove from heat. Stir half of pineapple mixture into beaten egg yolks. Combine with remaining hot mixture. Add coconut. Cook a minute longer and then remove from heat. Stir in butter and lemon juice. Cool. Pour filling in baked pie shell and top with meringue.

Meringue

2 egg whites
½ cup sugar

¼ teaspoon salt
½ teaspoon vanilla

Beat egg whites until firm. Add sugar, salt, and vanilla. Pour over filling and brown under broiler until golden brown.

Rainbow Cream Pie

1 1/3 cups sweetened condensed milk
1/4 cup fresh lemon juice
1 cup sliced fresh fruit or drained
fruit cocktail

1/2 cup whipping cream
2 tablespoons confectioners sugar
1 8 or 9 inch pie shell,
baked and cooled

Blend condensed milk and lemon juice. Stir until mixture thickens. Fold in prepared fruit. Pour into baked pie shell. Whip cream and add sugar. Cover pie with whipped cream and chill.

"Brighten your day with a rainbow pie!"

Sinful Sundae Pie

Vanilla wafers
6 ounces chocolate chips
1 cup evaporated milk
1 cup miniature marshmallows
Dash of salt

2 pints vanilla ice cream,
somewhat softened
Salted peanuts or toasted
sliced almonds, optional

Grease 9 inch pie plate. Line with vanilla wafers. Make sauce by combining chips, milk, marshmallows, and salt in top of double boiler. Melt, stirring constantly, until thickened (thicker than chocolate syrup, but not quite as thick as hot fudge). Remove from heat and allow to cool. Put one pint of ice cream into shell. Drizzle with half the sauce and nuts. Top with second pint of ice cream. Drizzle with remaining sauce and nuts. Freeze for 4 hours. Serves 6-8.

"This is devilishly delicious! Always a hit!"

Chocolate Almond Chiffon Pie

Pie crust—either a chilled crumb
shell or a cooled baked pie crust
1/3 cup almonds, blanched,
shredded, toasted, and cooled
1 envelope gelatin
1/4 cup cold water
2 squares bitter chocolate
5-6 drops almond extract
2/3 cup sugar

1/4 teaspoon salt
1/2 cup hot milk
1 teaspoon vanilla
1 pint heavy cream
1/2 teaspoon salt
3 tablespoons almonds, ground
and blanched
Whipped cream

Spread the bottom of pie crust with almonds. Soak gelatin in cold water for
5 minutes, stirring occasionally. Melt 2 squares chocolate in the top of a double
boiler with almond extract. Stir in sugar, salt, and hot milk. Cook for 3-4 minutes,
stirring constantly, until thoroughly blended. Add the softened gelatin and stir until
dissolved. Cook until the custard begins to thicken and beat with a rotary beater
until very light, adding vanilla. Whip heavy cream with salt and fold into custard
along with blanched almonds. Turn this filling into the pie shell and chill. Decorate
with whipped cream forced through a pastry bag with a fancy tube.

"Elegant, creamy, and delicious."

Chocolate Chess Pie

1/4 cup margarine
1 1/2 cups sugar
3 1/3 tablespoons cocoa
Dash of salt
1 teaspoon vanilla

1 small can evaporated milk
2 eggs
1 9 inch pie shell, chocolate flake
or graham cracker

Melt margarine and cool. Mix sugar, cocoa, salt, vanilla, milk, and eggs together
well. Combine with margarine. Pour into pie shell and bake at 325-350 for
45 minutes.

Chocolate Silk Pie

1 cup butter, softened
1 1/2 cups sugar
 3 1 ounce squares unsweetened
   chocolate, melted and cooled

2 teaspoons vanilla
4 eggs
1 9 inch pie shell
  Whipped cream

Beat butter and sugar until smooth, fluffy, and pale. Blend in the chocolate and vanilla. Beat in eggs one at a time at medium speed, taking 5 minutes for each egg. Turn into shell and chill. Top with whipped cream. Yields 6 servings.

"Smooth as silk!"

Coconut Cream Pie

1/3 cup sifted flour, or
    1/4 cup cornstarch
2/3 cup plus 6 tablespoons sugar
1/4 teaspoon salt
 2 cups milk, scalded
 3 egg yolks, slightly beaten

2 tablespoons butter or margarine
1/2 teaspoon vanilla
1 9 inch pastry shell, baked
3 egg whites, stiffly beaten
1 cup shredded coconut

Mix flour, 2/3 cup sugar, and salt; gradually add milk. Cook over moderate heat, stirring constantly, until mixture thickens and boils; cook 2 minutes. Remove from heat; add small amount to egg yolks. Stir egg yolks into remaining hot mixture; cook 1 minute, stirring constantly. Add butter and vanilla; cool slightly. Pour into baked pastry shell; cool. Cover with meringue made of egg whites and remaining sugar; sprinkle meringue with coconut. Bake at 350 for 12-15 minutes.

For variety, slice 3 bananas in shell; add filling. Increase sugar to 1 cup; melt 2 1-ounce squares unsweetened chocolate in scalded milk. Add 1/2 cup thoroughly drained crushed pineapple. Serves 6.

"A creamy delight."

Millionaire's Pie

1 10 ounce package
   whipped topping
1 20 ounce can crushed
   pineapple, drained
1 can sweetened condensed milk

1 cup nuts, chopped
3 tablespoons lemon juice
2 8 or 9 inch graham cracker
   pie crusts

Mix all ingredients together. Pour mixture into pie shells. Refrigerate several hours until mixture is set. This can be made ahead and frozen.

"Feel rich? Enjoy a Millionaire's Pie."

Oatmeal Pie

2 eggs
3/4 cup sugar
1/2 cup butter, melted
3/4 cup oatmeal

3/4 cup waffle syrup
3/4 cup grated coconut
3/4 cup pecans, chopped
1 pie crust

Beat eggs; add sugar. Mix well; add melted butter. Add oatmeal, syrup, coconut, and pecans; pour into unbaked pie crust. Cook at 350 for 30-40 minutes. Serves 6.

Perfect Pecan Pie

3 eggs
1/4 pound butter, melted
3/4 cup brown sugar
3/4 cup dark Karo syrup

3/4 cup pecans, chopped
1 teaspoon vanilla
1 9 inch pie shell
   Pecan halves

Beat eggs thoroughly. Add melted butter, brown sugar, and dark Karo syrup. Beat mixture. Add chopped pecans and mix. Add vanilla and mix. Pour into unbaked pie shell. Cover top with pecan halves. Bake at 350 for about 40 minutes or until firm.

Little Shoofly Pies

1 cup margarine
6 ounces cream cheese
2 cups flour
2 eggs
1½ cups dark brown sugar

½ teaspoon vanilla
2 tablespoons milk
4 ounces margarine
1 cup sugar
1½ cups flour

Mix 1 cup margarine, cream cheese, and flour together and form into balls. Place in small, greased cupcake pans and press to sides (like small pie crusts). Combine eggs, brown sugar, vanilla, and milk. Put one teaspoon brown sugar mixture over each crust. Combine 4 ounces margarine, sugar, and flour. Spoon 2 teaspoons of this mixture on top of each pie. Bake at 375 for 15 minutes. Freezes well.

Crummy Pie

1 9 inch pie crust, partially baked
1 cup walnuts, chopped
    medium fine
1 cup granulated sugar
½ cup fine soda cracker crumbs
    (14-16 crackers)
¼ teaspoon soda

3 eggs, separated
¼ teaspoon salt
¼ cup lemon juice
1 teaspoon grated lemon rind
1 teaspoon vanilla
    Sweetened whipped cream

Roll and shape pie crust, making high fluted edge. Bake at 450 for about 7 minutes, or just until crust starts to brown. Remove from oven. Set temperature to 350. Mix walnuts and half of the sugar, cracker crumbs, and soda and set aside. Beat whites with salt until stiff, but not dry. Beat egg yolks until thick, then beat in remaining ½ cup of sugar. Stir in lemon juice, rind, and vanilla. Fold together whites, nut mixture, and yolks, just until well blended, and pour into crust. Bake at 350 about 30 minutes or until well browned. Top with whipped cream.

"This is often called 'Poor Man's Pie' as it does not have any fruit in it."

Buttermilk Pie

2 cups sugar
1/2 cup butter, melted
3 eggs
1 cup buttermilk

2 rounded tablespoons flour
1 tablespoon lemon extract
2 8 inch pastry shells

Mix all ingredients, except pastry shells, in a bowl. Pour into two pastry shells. Cook 30 minutes at 350 in preheated oven. Leave in oven overnight to cool.

"Very easy to make. The secret of success is leaving pies in oven overnight. No peeping!"

Kentucky Cream Pie

1/2 cup butter
2 cups sugar
5 eggs, separated
1 pint cream

1 1/2 teaspoons vanilla extract
   Pinch of salt
1 9 inch pie shell
6 tablespoons sugar

Melt butter; add sugar and beat well. Add egg yolks, beating well after each addition. Add cream, vanilla, and salt, blending well. Pour into 9 inch unbaked pie shell and bake at 350 until firm. Top with meringue made from 5 egg whites and remaining sugar.

"Bring home a little Bluegrass with a Kentucky Cream Pie."

Pumpkin-Pecan Pie

1/2 cup pecans, chopped
1 cup brown sugar
1/4 cup butter, melted
2 eggs
13/4 cups cooked pumpkin
1/2 teaspoon salt

1 teaspoon cinnamon
1/2 teaspoon nutmeg
1/2 teaspoon ginger
1 14 ounce can evaporated milk
1 9 inch pastry shell, unbaked

Combine pecans, 1/4 cup brown sugar, and melted butter in small bowl. Beat eggs slightly in large bowl; add remaining brown sugar, pumpkin, salt, and spices. Mix well. Stir in evaporated milk. Pour into pastry shell. Bake at 425 for 15 minutes. Reduce heat to 350 and bake for 20 minutes. Arrange pecan mixture around edge and in center of pie. Bake an additional 10 minutes. Serves 8.

Golden Pecan Fingers

3/4 cup shortening
3/4 cup confectioners sugar
1 1/2 cups flour
2 eggs
1 cup brown sugar

2 tablespoons flour
1/2 teaspoon baking powder
1/2 teaspoon salt
1/2 teaspoon vanilla
1 cup pecans, chopped

Preheat oven to 350. Cream shortening and confectioners sugar together. Blend in flour. Press evenly in bottom of ungreased 9x13 pan. Bake 12-15 minutes. Mix eggs, remaining 2 tablespoons of flour, baking powder, salt, vanilla, and pecans. Spread over hot baked layer and bake another 20 minutes. Cool and cut into bars. Yields 2-3 dozen.

Creamy Cheesecake Bars

Crust

1/3 cup brown sugar
1 cup flour

1/2 cup chopped walnuts
1/3 cup butter, melted

Mix together brown sugar, flour, walnuts, and butter in a bowl. Set aside 1/2 cup of the mixture. Press into an 8 inch ungreased pan. Bake crust at 350 for 12-13 minutes and cool.

Topping

8 ounces cream cheese
1/4 cup sugar
1 egg

1 tablespoon lemon juice
2 tablespoons milk or cream
1 teaspoon vanilla

Beat together cream cheese and sugar and add egg, lemon juice, milk and vanilla. Pour over crust and sprinkle reserved crumbs on top. Bake at 350 for 20-25 minutes. Watch carefully so it does not burn. Cut into 12-16 bars.
    Note: Double the recipe for a 9x13 pan.

German Chocolate Caramel Bars

1 14 ounce package Kraft
    caramels, light
1/3 cup evaporated milk
1 12 ounce bag chocolate chips
1/3 cup evaporated milk

1/2 cup butter, softened
1 cup chopped nuts
    (walnuts or pecans)
1 box German chocolate cake mix

Melt caramels in microwave with 1/3 cup milk. Combine cake mix, milk, nuts, and butter to form dough. With buttered fingers, press only 2/3 of batter in a 9x12 pan, sprayed with Pam. Bake for 15 minutes at 325. Remove and sprinkle chocolate chips on top and spread melted caramels over top. Crumble remaining 1/3 of batter dough on top. Bake at 350 for 23 minutes. Cool 20 minutes, refrigerate for 20 minutes only, and cut into small bars. Makes approximately 60 bars per pan.

Black Forest Bars

2 cups flour
1/2 cup sugar
1/2 cup brown sugar, packed
1 1/2 teaspoons baking powder
1/2 teaspoon salt
3/4 cup milk
1/2 cup soft margarine or butter

1 teaspoon vanilla
2 eggs
1 cup (10 ounce jar) maraschino
  cherries, drained and halved
6 ounces chocolate chips
1 cup walnuts
  Frosting

Combine first 9 ingredients; blend until moistened at low speed. Stir in cherries, chocolate chips, and walnuts. Spread in either jelly roll pan or cookie sheet with sides ungreased. Bake at 325 for 25-30 minutes until golden brown. Cool.

Frosting

1/2 cup butter or margarine
4 cups powdered sugar

4 tablespoons milk
1 teaspoon vanilla

Melt butter over low heat in medium saucepan. Add next ingredients and blend until smooth. Spread frosting while still warm over cooled bars. Yields 3-4 dozen bars.

Chocolate Mystery Bars

1/2 box club crackers
1/2 cup butter
1 cup brown sugar
1 cup coconut, shredded

1 cup graham cracker crumbs
1/3 cup milk
6-8 Hershey bars
1 cup nuts, chopped (optional)

Line a 9x13 pan with crackers, salt side down. Melt butter, sugar, coconut, graham cracker crumbs, and milk in a saucepan. Bring to a boil. Continue boiling for 7 minutes, watch closely, stirring occasionally. Pour filling over crackers and top with another layer of crackers, salt side down. Top with Hershey bars and then chopped nuts. Put in warm oven to melt chocolate slightly. Remove. Chill. Cut into bars. Yields 5 dozen.

Luscious Lime Squares

2 cups flour
1 cup butter

1/2 cup confectioners sugar

Sift flour and sugar into bowl. Using pastry knife, blend in butter until well mixed. Using hands, gather mixture together to form a ball. Pat dough evenly into bottom of 9x13 baking pan. Bake at 350 for 20 minutes.

Topping

4 eggs
1 teaspoon baking powder
5 tablespoons lime juice

Dash of salt
2 cups granulated sugar

Beat all ingredients together well. Pour over hot baked crust and return to oven. Bake at 350 for 20-25 minutes. Cool on rack. Sprinkle with powdered sugar and cut into squares. Yields approximately 30 squares.

Neiman-Marcus Bars

1 box yellow cake mix
4 eggs
1/2 cup butter, melted

8 ounces softened cream cheese
1 pound confectioners sugar

Mix cake mix, 1 egg, and melted butter. Spread in greased 9x13 pan. Beat softened cream cheese with confectioners sugar. Add 3 eggs. Beat and pour over cake mixture. Bake 1 hour at 350. Cool and slice into squares. Yields approximately 16 bars.

"Gooey, but so good!"

Nova Scotia Shortbread

2 cups rice flour
1 cup sugar

2 cups all purpose flour
1 pound butter, softened

Mix all ingredients together with hands. Mixture will be extremely crumbly until well blended. Form a small piece of dough into a ball about the size of a walnut and place on an ungreased cookie sheet. Press gently with the bottom of a drinking glass to flatten. Bake at 325 for 20 minutes. Do not brown! Makes approximately 15 dozen.

"Rice flour is the secret ingredient to these delicate cookies and may be purchased at oriental food markets."

Nut Horns

4 cups flour, sifted
1 pound butter or margarine
3 eggs
12 ounces cream cheese
   Powdered sugar

1 pound walnuts, finely chopped
1 cup sugar
3 egg whites, beaten
1 teaspoon cinnamon

Combine flour and butter as for pie crust. Combine eggs and cream cheese and add to flour mixture. Roll into walnut sized balls and refrigerate overnight or approximately 12 hours. Roll out on powdered sugar. Combine walnuts, sugar, egg whites, and cinnamon well. Fill each flattened cookie with nut filling. Put on ungreased baking sheet and bake at 350 for 15-20 minutes. Yields approximately 3-4 dozen.

Tempting Butter Cookies

1 pound box confectioners sugar
1 cup granulated sugar
1 pound butter
½ cup shortening
3 eggs
1 tablespoon water

1 teaspoon soda
1 teaspoon salt
2 teaspoons vanilla
6 cups unsifted flour
  Icing

Sift both sugars together. Cream butter and shortening together. Add the rest of the ingredients, except flour. Then add flour. Roll and cut the cookies on a floured surface. Bake on ungreased cookie sheet for 7-10 minutes at 350. You may decorate.

"This is a wonderful recipe for Christmas."

Cookie Icing

2 egg whites
¼ teaspoon cream of tartar
  Dash salt
2 teaspoons vanilla

3 cups confectioners sugar
  Food coloring (optional)
  Sprinkles (optional)

Beat egg whites, cream of tartar, and salt until stiff. Add vanilla and sugar. Beat until peaks form. Add food coloring if desired. Spread with a knife on the cookies when they are cool.

You can ice the cookies and then add the sprinkles or decorations. The icing becomes firm so they can be frozen or stored easily. Children enjoy helping to create beautiful cookies.

Microwave Peanut Brittle

1 cup sugar
1 cup raw peanuts
¼ teaspoon salt
½ cup light corn syrup

1 teaspoon vanilla
1 tablespoon butter
1 teaspoon soda

Combine sugar, peanuts, corn syrup, and salt in a 2 quart casserole pan. Stir well. Microwave on high for 7-8 minutes, stirring after 4 minutes. Mixture will look light brown. Add butter and vanilla. Blend well. Microwave on high for 1-2 minutes. Be careful as it will burn. Stir in soda quickly until light and foamy. Pour onto greased cookie sheet. Let cool 1 hour. Break and store in airtight container.

"Easy and delicious! This makes a quick and easy gift item."

Texas Size Pralines

3 cups sugar
1 cup buttermilk
1 teaspoon soda

1 teaspoon vanilla extract
1 tablespoon butter
2-2½ cups pecan halves

Combine sugar, buttermilk, soda, and vanilla in heavy dutch oven; cook over medium heat to 234 (soft ball stage), stirring constantly. Remove from heat, stir in butter. Beat 2-3 minutes, just until mixture begins to thicken. Stir in pecans. Working rapidly, drop mixture by tablespoons onto lightly buttered waxed paper. Let cool. Yields 2 dozen 3 inch pralines.

"Tastes like they're fresh from the French Quarter of New Orleans."

Toll House Kookie Brittle

1 cup margarine	1 6 ounce package semi-sweet
1½ teaspoons vanilla	chocolate morsels
1 teaspoon salt	1 cup walnuts or pecans,
1 cup sugar	finely chopped
2 cups sifted flour	

Combine margarine, vanilla, and salt in bowl and blend well. Gradually beat in sugar. Add flour, chocolate morsels, and ¾ cup nuts and mix well. Press evenly into greased 15x10x1 pan. Sprinkle remaining nuts over top and pat in lightly. Bake at 375 for 25 minutes or until golden brown. Cool. Break into irregular pieces. Makes about 1⅓ pounds.

"A wonderful variation of chocolate chip cookies."

Beacon Hill Cookies

1 cup semi-sweet chocolate chips	½ teaspoon vanilla
2 egg whites	½ teaspoon vinegar
Dash of salt	¾ cup walnuts, chopped
½ cup sugar	

Melt semi-sweet chocolate chips over hot water, then cool. Beat egg whites with salt until foamy. Gradually add sugar, beating well until peaks form. Beat in vanilla and vinegar. Fold in melted chocolate and chopped walnuts. Drop by teaspoonfuls on greased cookie sheet. Bake at 350 for 10 minutes. Remove immediately. Yields 2-3 dozen.

Chocolate Bittersweets

Cookie

½ cup butter
½ cup confectioners sugar
¼ teaspoon salt

1 teaspoon vanilla
1¼ cup flour

Cream butter, add sugar, salt, and vanilla. Mix well. Add flour. Shape into small balls. Place on lightly greased cookie sheet and flatten with thumb. Bake at 350 for about 10 minutes. Cool.

Filling

3 ounces cream cheese
1 cup confectioners sugar
2 teaspoons flour

1 teaspoon vanilla
½ cup pecans, finely chopped

Cream the cheese, add sugar, flour, and vanilla. Mix well and add nuts. Place a small spoonful on each cooled cookie.

Frosting

3 ounces semi-sweet
  chocolate pieces
2 teaspoons water

2 tablespoons butter
½ cup sifted confectioners sugar
1 teaspoon vanilla

Melt chocolate pieces with water and butter over low heat. Add sugar and beat until smooth. Add vanilla. Frost cookies and refrigerate. Makes 36 cookies.

"Delicious and so festive!"

Coconut Macaroons

2/3 cup sweetened condensed milk
  8 ounces shredded coconut
  1 teaspoon vanilla

3/4 teaspoon almond flavoring
  1 6 ounce package semi-sweet or
    milk chocolate pieces

Mix all ingredients and drop by teaspoonfuls onto well greased cookie sheet. Bake for 8-10 minutes at 350. Remove from cookie sheet immediately. Yields 2-3 dozen.

Date Pinwheel Cookies

  1 pound pitted dates
1/2 cup sugar
1/2 cup water
  1 cup shortening
  1 cup sugar
  1 cup brown sugar

   3 eggs, beaten
   1 teaspoon vanilla
4 1/2 cups flour
 1/2 teaspoon salt
   1 teaspoon baking soda
 1/2 cup nuts, chopped

Cut dates into pieces, add sugar and water. Cook over low heat until thick. Set aside to cool. Beat shortening. Add both sugars and beat thoroughly. Add eggs and vanilla. Blend in dry ingredients and mix well. Cool in refrigerator 30 minutes. Divide dough into three equal parts. Roll 1/2 inch thick. Spread with date mixture. Sprinkle with nuts and roll as a jelly roll. Slice 1/4 inch thick. Bake cookies at 375 for about 7 minutes. Yields 4 dozen.

"Our favorite!"

Honeybunch Munchies

1¼ cups rolled oats
1 cup coconut
½ cup all purpose flour
½ teaspoon baking powder
½ teaspoon ground cinnamon
¼ teaspoon salt
¼ teaspoon ground nutmeg

½ cup margarine or butter
¾ cup packed brown sugar
3 tablespoons honey
½ cup semi-sweet chocolate pieces
   Pecan halves (optional)
   Whole, dried apricots (optional)

In a large mixing bowl stir together oats, coconut, flour, baking powder, cinnamon, salt, and nutmeg. In a small saucepan cook and stir margarine or butter, sugar, and honey over medium heat until sugar dissolves. Remove from heat; pour over oat mixture. Mix well.

Grease 1¾ inch muffin pans. Place 1 tablespoon of the oat mixture into each prepared muffin cup. Bake in a 350 oven for 12-14 minutes or until golden brown. Cool in pan for 10 minutes. Using a knife or small metal spatula, loosen edges and remove munchies from pans. Cool completely on wire racks.

Meanwhile, in a small heavy saucepan, melt chocolate over low heat, stirring until smooth. Dip the narrow end of each munchy into chocolate; let stand, dipped side up, on waxed paper. Top with a pecan or apricot cut into a heart shape. Makes 32 munchies.

Mom's Oatmeal Cookies

2 cups oatmeal
2 cups flour
1 cup sugar
1 heaping teaspoon cinnamon
   Pinch of salt
1 cup butter, melted

1 cup raisins
1 cup nuts
½ teaspoon vanilla
2 eggs
4 tablespoons milk
1 scant teaspoon baking soda

Mix dry ingredients. Add melted butter, raisins, and nuts. Beat eggs with vanilla, milk, and baking soda and add to flour mixture. Drop by teaspoonfuls on greased baking dish. Bake until golden brown at 350.

"A family recipe."

Lacy Oatmeal Cookies

2 sticks margarine or butter	¼ teaspoon baking powder
2 cups sugar	½ teaspoon salt
2 cups quick-cooking oatmeal	2 eggs
¼ cup flour	1 teaspoon vanilla

Melt margarine in saucepan. Remove from heat and add dry ingredients. Add eggs and vanilla. Drop by scant teaspoon on aluminum foil. Bake at 350 about 5 minutes or until golden. Let cool completely before removing from foil. Yield: 6-7 dozen. Note: The secret is in the aluminum foil. If not used, cookies will never come off pan!

Fruit Pizza

1 18 ounce package refrigerator sugar cookie dough, sliced	Assorted fruits, fresh, canned, or frozen
1 8 ounce package cream cheese	½ cup orange marmalade
⅓ cup sugar	2 tablespoons water
½ teaspoon vanilla	

Preheat oven to 375. Cut cookie dough ⅛ inch thick, line ungreased 14 inch pizza pan with cookies, overlapping slightly. Bake 12 minutes. Cool. Combine softened cream cheese, sugar, and vanilla. Mix well until blended. Spread on cookie crust. Arrange fruit over cream cheese. Glaze with combined marmalade and water. Chill until served. Cut into pizza wedges. Serves 10-12.

"So good and it really looks like pizza."

Peanut Butter Blossoms

1¾ cups flour
½ cup sugar
½ cup brown sugar, firmly packed
1 teaspoon soda
½ teaspoon salt
½ cup shortening

½ cup peanut butter
2 tablespoons milk
1 teaspoon vanilla
1 egg
40 chocolate kisses

Combine ingredients, reserving kisses, and mix at low speed. Shape into balls with hands. Bake at 375 for 10-12 minutes. After baking, put a chocolate kiss in center of each cookie and push down (do this while cookie is still soft). Yields 40 cookies.

Prize Pecan Cookies

¼ pound butter
3 tablespoons sugar
1 teaspoon vanilla
1 cup pecans, finely chopped

Food coloring (optional)
1-1¼ cups flour, sifted
1 egg
Confectioners sugar

Mix ingredients. Roll into pecan size balls. Bake for 20 minutes. While still warm, roll in confectioners sugar. Note: Red or green food coloring may be added. Yields 3-4 dozen.

Pecan Kisses

2 egg whites
⅛ teaspoon salt
2 cups powdered sugar, sifted

1 teaspoon vinegar
1 teaspoon vanilla
1½ cups pecans

Beat egg whites with salt until soft peaks form. Gradually beat in sugar, vinegar, and vanilla; continue beating until very stiff. Fold in pecans. Drop by teaspoonfuls onto greased cookie sheet. Bake at 300 for 15-20 minutes or until firm. Cool on rack. Yields 3 dozen.

Sugar and Honey Pecans

1½ cups sugar
½ cup water
¼ cup honey

¼ teaspoon salt
½ teaspoon vanilla extract
3 cups pecan halves

Combine first 4 ingredients in a saucepan, mix well. Cook mixture over medium heat, stirring constantly, until sugar dissolves. Continue cooking, without stirring, until mixture reaches 240 (soft ball stage). Remove from heat, stir in vanilla. Beat with a wooden spoon until mixture begins to thicken. Stir in pecan halves. Working rapidly, pour mixture onto waxed paper and separate pecans with a fork. Let cool. Yields 4 cups.

"Great for Christmas sharing."

Spanish Gold Bricks

1 package graham crackers
½ cup pecans, finely chopped
½ cup butter

½ cup margarine
½ cup sugar

Separate sections of graham crackers and line on ungreased jelly roll pan so that the sides of the graham crackers are touching. Finely chop pecans in the food processor, and sprinkle evenly over graham crackers. In a saucepan, melt together butter, margarine, and sugar. Boil and stir for 2 minutes. Pour slowly and evenly over the top of the graham crackers and nuts until all are covered. Bake at 325 for 8-10 minutes. Cool in the pan for about 10 minutes. Separate with a knife. Store in an airtight container. These can be frozen.

"So easy and just delicious!"

Frosted Pumpkin Cookies

2 cups sugar
2 cups shortening
1 16 ounce can pumpkin
2 eggs
2 teaspoons vanilla
4 cups sifted flour
2 teaspoons baking powder
1 teaspoon baking soda

1 teaspoon salt
2 teaspoons ground cinnamon
1 teaspoon ground nutmeg
1/2 teaspoon ground allspice
2 cups raisins
1 cup chopped nuts
  Cream Cheese Frosting

In mixing bowl, thoroughly cream together sugar and shortening. Add pumpkin, eggs, and vanilla and beat well. Sift together flour, baking powder, soda, salt, and spices. Add to creamed mixture and mix well. Stir in raisins and nuts. Drop dough from rounded teaspoon onto greased cookie sheet, about 2 inches apart. Bake in 350 oven for 12-15 minutes. Remove from baking sheet to cool. Frost with Cream Cheese Frosting. Makes 7 dozen.

Cream Cheese Frosting

3 ounces cream cheese
1 teaspoon vanilla

1 1/2 cups confectioners sugar, sifted

Cream all ingredients together until fluffy. Spread on cooled cookies.

"Great for Halloween parties!"

Chocolate Coconut Marlo

1 6 ounce package of semi-sweet
   chocolate chips
1 13 ounce can evaporated milk
1 10½ ounce package
   miniature marshmallows
1½ cups coconut
6 tablespoons margarine
2 cups Rice Krispies, crushed
1 cup chopped walnuts
½ gallon vanilla ice cream

In a saucepan, melt chocolate in milk. Bring to a boil; boil gently, uncovered for 4 minutes or until thick. Stir constantly. Add marshmallows, heat, and stir until melted. Chill. In skillet, cook and stir coconut in margarine until lightly toasted. Stir in cereal and nuts. Spread 3 cups of the cereal mixture in bottom of a 13x9 pan. Cut ice cream in half lengthwise, and then horizontally into 12 slices making a total of 24 pieces. Arrange half of the ice cream over the cereal. Spread with half of the chocolate mixture. Repeat layers. Top with remaining cereal. Cover and freeze until firm. Let stand at room temperature 5-10 minutes before serving. 16-20 servings.

Chocolate Creme Gateau

1 6 ounce package semi-sweet
   chocolate pieces
4 eggs, separated
¼ cup sugar
1 cup heavy cream
1 10 inch angel food cake
1 cup nuts, chopped

Melt chocolate in saucepan over low heat, then cool. Beat egg yolks until light and stir into chocolate. Beat egg whites until stiff, adding 2 tablespoons sugar gradually, and fold into chocolate mixture. Whip the cream until stiff and add remaining sugar. Fold into chocolate mixture, reserving small amount for topping. Place alternate layers of cake, chocolate mixture, and nuts in a glass baking dish. Chill 12 hours. Cut into squares and top with reserved whipped cream. Yields 10-12 servings.

"Serve in parfait glasses or other pretty stemware. Instead of slicing cake and layering in large dish, break up cake and layer in stemware."

Chocolate Delight

1 cup flour
1/2 cup butter
1/2 cup nuts, chopped
12 ounces Cool Whip
8 ounces cream cheese
1 cup powdered sugar

2 small boxes instant
  chocolate pudding
3 cups milk
1/4 cup nuts, chopped for garnish
1/4 cup grated chocolate, for garnish

Preheat oven to 375. Combine flour and butter and work together like a pie crust. Then mix in chopped nuts. Press into a 9x13 pan. Bake at 375 for 15 minutes.

Combine 1 cup of the Cool Whip, cream cheese, and powdered sugar. Beat together and spread over crust while still warm. Combine chocolate pudding mix with milk and whip until thick and spread on second layer. Spread remaining Cool Whip on top. Sprinkle with nuts and grated chocolate. Refrigerate. Note: If desired, change flavor of pudding or nuts. Approximately 12 servings.

Mocha Ice Cream Torte

1 1/2 packages lady fingers
2 quarts vanilla ice cream
4 teaspoons instant coffee
2 tablespoons boiling water
10 Heath bars, crushed,
   or 1 10 ounce package crushed
   butter brickle

1 cup whipping cream
4 tablespoons Creme de Cacao

Line sides and bottom of springform pan with lady finger halves. Mix coffee and the water together until the coffee is dissolved. Mix ice cream, Heath bars, and coffee and pour into the pan. Place this mixture into the freezer until frozen. Whip the whipping cream, stir in the Creme de Cacao, and spread on top of the dessert. Sprinkle a few reserved pieces of brickle to decorate top. Keep in freezer until ready to serve. Serves 8.

An extra delicious option is to spread a layer of fudge topping before the whipped cream is spread on top.

Viennese Torte

1/4 pound butter	1/8 cup warm water
1 tablespoon powdered sugar	1 teaspoon vanilla
4 egg yolks	1 6 ounce frozen Sara Lee
1 6 ounce package semi-sweet	pound cake
chocolate chips	Whipped cream (optional)
1½ tablespoons Kahlua	Strawberries (optional)

Put butter, powdered sugar, egg yolks, chocolate chips, Kahlua, warm water, and vanilla into the blender. Blend until mixture reaches spreading consistency. Add a little more warm water if necessary. Using an electric knife, separate the pound cake into 5 layers; each should be approximately 1/4-1/2 inch thick. Spread the blender mixture on top of each layer, ending with the top of the uppermost layer of cake. Do not "frost" the sides. Place this into the freezer. Serve in 1 inch slices. A serving suggestion is to serve with a spoonful of whipped cream and several strawberries. Serves 6-8.

"Very elegant and delicious."

Arctic Snow

1/2 gallon vanilla ice cream	6 large coconut macaroons,
3/4 cup sherry	crushed
	1/2 cup chopped pecans

Toast crushed macaroons and nuts on a cookie sheet in oven at 350 until lightly brown.

Beat ice cream and sherry with mixer. Spoon half the ice cream into glass. Layer with half the macaroons, half the nuts, and top with remaining ice cream, macaroons, and nuts. Cover and freeze. Yields 6 servings.

"So easy and good."

Lemon Bisque

Vanilla Wafer Crust

1½ cups vanilla wafer
crumbs, crushed

¼ cup butter, melted

Mix and press into a 9x13 pan.

Filling

1   3 ounce package lemon jello
1¼ cups boiling water
¾ cup sugar
1   cup evaporated milk,
chilled and whipped

1   lemon, grated rind and juiced
Pinch of salt

Combine jello, water, and sugar and place in refrigerator until slightly thickened.
Chill evaporated milk overnight. Remove from refrigerator, add lemon juice, rind,
and salt and beat until thick. Slightly beat jello mixture and fold into whipped
mixture until well mixed. Pour into crust and put into refrigerator to chill.

"This is a lovely light summer dessert."

Lemon Raspberry Torte

Lemon Thins
4   eggs, separated
1   cup sugar
1½ tablespoons lemon peel

½ cup lemon juice
1½ cup whipping cream
1   package frozen raspberries,
thawed (optional)

Line springform pan with Lemon Thins, curved side out. Beat egg whites until very
stiff. Gradually beat in ¾ cup sugar, one tablespoon at a time until mixture is glossy
and forms stiff peaks. Don't wash beaters. Beat yolks, ¼ cup sugar, lemon peel,

Continued on next page

and lemon juice until blended. Wash beaters. Whip cream until mixture holds its shape. Fold all three mixtures together into egg white mixture. Spoon into pan, smooth top and freeze. Let thaw briefly before serving. Top with thawed raspberries if desired. Serves 8.

"This recipe is somewhat tedious to make, but well worth the effort."

Peppermint Dessert

1 box chocolate wafer cookies	1/2 cup crushed peppermint candy
1 pound marshmallows	Red food coloring (optional)
1 cup milk	1 pint whipping cream, whipped

Crush cookies and put 1/2 in bottom of 8x12 cake pan. Melt marshmallows in milk in double boiler and cool. Add crushed candy and enough food coloring for deeper color candy. Fold in whipped cream and pour over cookie crumbs. Sprinkle rest of the cookie crumbs over top. Refrigerate at least 8 hours. This makes 12 servings.

"So refreshing."

Strawberries in Cream

2 cups whole fresh strawberries	2 cups softened vanilla ice cream
1 cup heavy cream, whipped	2 tablespoons rum

Carefully wash strawberries, leaving the hulls on them. Beat the ice cream until it is smooth; add the whipped cream, and stir in the rum. Serve the berries and the cream in separate bowls so that the berries can be dipped in the cream.

Snowballs

½ cup butter
1 cup granulated or
  confectioners sugar
2 egg yolks, well beaten
1 cup crushed pineapple, drained
1 cup chopped nuts

2 egg whites
2 boxes vanilla wafers
½ pint whipping cream
1 teaspoon vanilla
1 package coconut

Cream butter and sugar together. Add egg yolks, crushed pineapple, and chopped nuts. Beat egg whites until stiff, and fold into pineapple mixture. Stack 3 or 4 wafers with filling in between. Chill for 24 hours. Cover with whipped cream sweetened with additional teaspoon sugar and vanilla. Sprinkle with coconut. This may be prepared 1 hour before serving, if necessary. Yields 12-15 balls.

"A special treat!"

Frosted Raspberry Zing

1¼ cups flour
1¾ cups sugar
¼ teaspoon salt
1 cup butter
4½ tablespoons cornstarch
3 10 ounce packages frozen
  raspberries, thawed

45 large marshmallows, melted
  and cooled
1 cup milk
1 cup heavy cream, whipped

Preheat oven to 350. Combine flour, ¼ cup of the sugar, and salt. Cut in butter. Pat into 13x9 pan. Bake at 350 for 15-18 minutes. Cool. Combine cornstarch, 1½ cups sugar, and raspberries and cook until thick and clear. Cool slightly and pour over crust. Combine cooled marshmallows, milk, and whipped cream and pour on top of cooled raspberry mixture. Chill several hours or overnight before serving. Yields 12-16 servings.

Strawberry Dream

2 7 ounce packages Nabisco
   sugar wafers, crushed
3/4 cup butter
1 cup sifted powdered sugar
1/2 teaspoon vanilla extract
1/4 teaspoon almond extract

2 large or 3 small eggs, separated
5 10 ounce packages frozen
   strawberries, thawed and drained
1/2 cup coarsely chopped nuts
2 cups heavy cream, whipped

Spread half of the Nabisco wafer crumbs into 12x8x2 baking dish. Mix butter, sugar, and extracts. Add yolks, one at a time, beating after each one. Beat whites until stiff, but not dry. Fold into butter mixture. Spread thin layer on crumbs. Spoon on berries. Sprinkle with nuts, cover with the whipped cream, and top with remaining crumbs. Refrigerate a minimum of 12 hours and longer if possible. Yields 12-16 servings.

Strawberry Heaven

1 quart strawberries, hulled
2 ripe bananas
2 ounces cream liqueur flavor of
   your choice

1/4 cup milk
2 teaspoons sugar
1 tablespoon lemon juice
   Whipped cream

Wash and slice strawberries. Spoon into individual serving dishes. Place remaining ingredients in blender or food processor and whip until smooth. Pour over strawberries, cover, and chill 1 hour. Serve with whipped cream. Serves 6.

"This is also good in individual graham cracker shells."

Drunk Bread Pudding

1 loaf French bread
1 quart milk
3 eggs, beaten
2 cups sugar
2 tablespoons vanilla extract

2 teaspoons cinnamon
1 cup raisins
3 tablespoons unsalted butter
  Sauce

In bowl, break bread with crust into bite size pieces. Cover with milk and soak for one hour. Mix well. Beat eggs with sugar, vanilla, and cinnamon. Add to bread mixture along with raisins. Melt butter in 13x9x2 baking dish (coating dish). Pour in pudding and bake for 1 hour at 375. Serve warm or cold with sauce.

Sauce

½ cup butter
1 cup sugar

1 egg, beaten
¼ cup bourbon

Melt butter with sugar over low heat. Using a wire whisk, beat until sugar is dissolved. Remove from heat; cool slightly. Add bourbon. Pour warm sauce on pudding and serve. If not serving immediately, save sauce until ready to serve. Delicious! Yields 10-12 servings.

"Everyone loves this one!"

Maple Bread Pudding

7 slices bread
3 cups milk, scalded
⅔ cup maple syrup
2 eggs, beaten

1 teaspoon salt
1 teaspoon cinnamon
½ cup raisins
  Cream

Break bread in buttered baking dish and pour scalded milk over bread. Mix in syrup, eggs, salt, cinnamon, and raisins. Bake 1 hour at 350. Serve hot with thin cream or whipped cream. This yields 8 servings.

Delicate Banana Pudding

3¾ cups milk
2 3¼ ounce packages vanilla
   pudding and pie mix
3 eggs, separated
3 teaspoons vanilla, divided

1 cup whipping cream, whipped
1 3 ounce package lady fingers
4 bananas, sliced thinly, crosswise
¼ teaspoon ground nutmeg
⅓ cup sugar

In saucepan, blend milk and pudding mix. Add egg yolks and 1 teaspoon vanilla, beating with mixer until smooth. Cook, stirring constantly, until boiling. Cover with plastic wrap and cool about 20-30 minutes. Fold in whipped cream to which remaining vanilla has been added. Arrange half the lady fingers in bottom of 2½ quart baking dish. Spoon half of pudding over cake and arrange half of bananas over pudding. Sprinkle layer with half of nutmeg. Repeat layers. Beat egg whites and add sugar until stiff. Spoon meringue over cooled pudding and bake at 350 for 7-8 minutes until lightly browned. Serves 8.

Tutti-Fruitti Lemon Pudding

1 8¾ ounce can pineapple tidbits
1 11 ounce can mandarin
   orange sections
1 17 ounce can fruit cocktail
½ cup flaked coconut

2 tablespoons lemon juice
1 3¾-3⅝ ounce package instant
   lemon pudding mix
2 bananas
   Cool Whip for topping

In large bowl, combine undrained pineapple tidbits, undrained mandarin orange sections, and undrained fruit cocktail with the flaked coconut and lemon juice. Sprinkle the instant lemon pudding mix over fruits and toss lightly to combine; chill. Just before serving, peel and slice bananas to make 1½ cups. Fold bananas into lemon-fruit mixture. Serve in dessert dishes or sherbets; top with the thawed whipped dessert topping, if desired. Makes 10 servings.

"Serve these with Lorna Doone Cookies."

Lady Manchester Trifle

Boiled Custard

1 pint milk
1/2 cup sugar
1/2 teaspoon flour

1 egg, beaten
1/2 teaspoon vanilla

In top of double boiler bring milk just to a boil. Blend sugar and flour, and add to egg. Slowly add hot milk and vanilla to egg mixture and then return custard to top of double boiler. Cook over hot water until custard thickens slightly.

Trifle

1 8 ounce sponge cake
1 10 ounce jar strawberry or raspberry jam
1 17 ounce jar fruits for salad, drained

2 ounces Irish whiskey
1 cup whipping cream, whipped
Fresh fruit in season

Split sponge cake in half and spread each half with jam. Put halves together again and cut into small squares. Place cake squares in crystal bowl. Cut large pieces of fruits for salad in half and add fruit to bowl. Sprinkle with Irish whiskey and pour boiled custard over all. Chill. Garnish with whipped cream and fresh fruit. Serves 8.

Honey Rice Pudding

1/2 cup uncooked rice
4 cups milk
1/4 cup honey
1/2 teaspoon salt

1/2 cup seeded raisins
1/4 teaspoon ground nutmeg
1 teaspoon grated lemon peel

Combine rice, milk, honey, salt, raisins, nutmeg, and lemon peel in a greased 1 1/2 quart baking dish. Bake at 300 for 2 hours or until pudding is of creamy consistency. Serve with honey or cream. Serves 6.

Creme Caramel

1/2 cup sugar, divided
4 eggs
2 cups milk
1 teaspoon vanilla extract

1/4 teaspoon salt
6 lemon peel twists for garnish
6 small nontoxic leaves for garnish

This should be prepared about 2 1/2 hours before serving or early in the day. Preheat oven to 325. Grease six 6 ounce custard cups. In small saucepan over medium heat, heat 1/4 cup sugar until it melts and turns a light caramel color, stirring constantly. Immediately pour into prepared custard cups. In a large bowl beat eggs and 1/4 cup sugar with a wire wisk or fork until well blended. Beat in milk, vanilla, and salt until well mixed; pour mixture into custard cups. Place custard cups in 13x9 baking pan; fill pan with hot water to come halfway up sides of custard cups. Bake 50 to 55 minutes until knife inserted in center of custard comes out clean. Remove cups from water in baking pan; cover and refrigerate until chilled, about 1 1/2 hours.

To serve: Unmold each custard onto a chilled dessert plate, allowing caramel topping to drip from cup onto custard. Garnish each custard with a lemon peel twist and a leaf. Makes 6 servings.

Pots de Creme

1 cup whipping cream
1 6 ounce package
   semi-sweet morsels
2 egg yolks

2 (or less) teaspoons brandy
   or Amaretto
3 tablespoons Cool Whip

Bring whipping cream to foaming point (just before boiling) over medium high heat. Combine chocolate pieces, egg yolks, and liqueur in blender and pour hot whipping cream over mixture. Turn blender on "liquefy" for two minutes. Pour into small custard cups. Refrigerate and top with a spoonful of Cool Whip. Serves 4-6.

"Rich and delicious."

Raspberry Mousse

1 10 ounce package frozen
   raspberries, thawed
¾ cup sugar
1 cup water, divided

1 envelope unflavored gelatin
1 cup whipping cream, whipped
3 tablespoons Kirsch

Blend raspberries in blender or food processor and strain (if desired) to remove seeds. In saucepan, stir sugar and ¾ cup water together. Boil without stirring until syrup registers 240 on a candy thermometer. Cool slightly. Soften gelatin in ¼ cup water and add to hot syrup. Stir until dissolved. Add syrup to raspberry puree and chill until syrupy, stirring occasionally. When mixture begins to thicken, fold in whipped cream that has been flavored with Kirsch. Spoon into cups and chill. Top with whipped cream. Yields 6 to 8 servings.

Fantasy Island Chocolate Sauce

⅔ cup cocoa
6 tablespoons margarine
½ cup boiling water

1 cup superfine granulated sugar
2 tablespoons light corn syrup
2 teaspoons vanilla

In a saucepan, combine cocoa, margarine, and boiling water. Cook over moderate heat, stirring occasionally for 3 minutes or until well combined. Add sugar and corn syrup and simmer for 3-4 minutes until thickened. Let cool and add vanilla. Serve over ice cream. Yields approximately 1½ cups.

Cream Puff Magnifique

1 cup water
1/2 cup butter or margarine
1/4 teaspoon salt
1 cup sifted flour
4 eggs
2 3 ounce packages
  vanilla pudding mix

3 cups milk
1 cup heavy cream, whipped
1/4 cup light rum
  Confectioners sugar

In medium saucepan, over low heat, bring one cup of water, butter, and salt to boiling. Remove from heat. With wooden spoon, beat in flour all at once. Return to low heat and continue beating until mixture forms ball and leaves side of pan. Remove from heat. Beat in eggs by hand, one at a time, beating hard after each addition until mixture is smooth. Continue beating until dough is shiny and satiny and breaks into strand.

Turn mixture onto ungreased cookie sheet. Spread to make 1 inch (donut shaped) circle, about 1 inch thick. Bake at 375 until puffed and deep brown. Leave in oven with heat off for 30 minutes. Remove and cool at least one hour before filling.

While cream puff bakes, prepare pudding mix according to package directions, using 3 cups milk. Pour immediately into bowl, covering with waxed paper on surface. Refrigerate several hours until chilled.

Beat cream until whipped, and fold whipped cream and rum into chilled pudding. Split cream puff horizontally in half. Fill bottom half with pudding mixture. Replace top half. Sprinkle with confectioners sugar. To serve, cut in wedges at table.

"So elegant!"

Almond Puff Pastry

Step one:
1/2 cup butter, no substitute
1 cup flour
2 tablespoons water

Step two:
1/2 cup butter
1 cup water
1 teaspoon almond extract
1 cup flour
3 eggs

Step three:
1 1/2 cups confectioners sugar
2 tablespoons butter or margarine, softened
1 1/2 teaspoons almond extract
1-2 tablespoons warm water

Step one: Cut butter into flour. Sprinkle with water and mix well. Round into ball and divide in half. On ungreased baking sheet, pat each half into a 12x3 strip. Strips should be 3 inches apart.

Step two: In medium saucepan, heat butter and water to a rolling boil. Remove from heat and quickly stir in almond extract and flour. Stir over low heat until mixture forms a ball, about 1 minute. Remove from heat. Beat in eggs all at once, until smooth. Divide in half, spreading each half evenly over strips, covering completely. Bake at 350 for 1 hour.

Step three: Mix ingredients and ice cooled pastry. Cut in 1 inch strips and serve.

"Wonderful as a dessert or for brunch."

NATIVE
TREASURES

Local Restaurants

Scallops Florentine

Tandom's Pine Tree Inn—Virginia Beach, Va.

1 12 ounce package chopped spinach	1 tablespoon pepper
1 quart mushrooms, sliced	1 tablespoon salt
1 tablespoon garlic	2 pounds scallops
	2 cups Hollandaise sauce

Saute mushrooms in butter and add to drained spinach. In large bowl, combine spinach, garlic, pepper, and salt, and mix well. Saute scallops in butter until half cooked. Place spinach in bottom of casserole dish and cover with scallops. Cover scallops with Hollandaise sauce and bake for 10-12 minutes.

Mussels Mariner

Gus' Restaurant—Virginia Beach, Va.
Chef Tom Evaldi

5 pounds mussels	1 cup dry white wine
Pinch thyme	1/2 teaspoon fresh, coarse
Few bay leaves	ground pepper
1 teaspoon garlic, minced	1/2 stick of whole butter
1/4 cup shallots, chopped	Parsley, chopped

Clean mussels thoroughly to remove any seaweed and the ''beard'' that holds the mussels in clusters. In a large pot or Dutch oven with cover, place the garlic, shallots, white wine, and spices and bring to a boil. Add the cleaned mussels; cover and cook briskly on a strong fire until mussels are all opened. Melt butter in a large skillet. Pour all the juice of the steamed mussels on top of the butter and reduce until half of its original amount. Add a little fresh chopped parsley. Pour the sauce back over the mussels. Reheat if necessary and serve with garlic bread on the side.

Shrimp Scampi

Crusoe's Cellar—Norfolk, Va.

4 dozen medium shrimp	Feta cheese
Butter	Marinara Sauce
Garlic	Scampi Sauce

Prepare marinara and scampi sauces. Blanch shrimp with butter and garlic in a saucepan until shrimp are half cooked. Divide shrimp into 4 ovenproof au gratin dishes and cover generously with scampi sauce. Garnish each dish generously with crumbled feta cheese. Bake uncovered at 450 for about 20 minutes or until sauce starts to bubble. Finish quickly under broiler until the feta cheese browns. Garnish with chopped scallions.

Marinara Sauce

1½ tablespoons oil	1 teaspoon basil
2 cloves garlic, finely chopped	1 tablespoon oregano
½ cup onion	1 teaspoon sugar
1 14½ ounce can peeled tomatoes in sauce	1 teaspoon salt
	1 teaspoon fennel
4 ounces tomato paste	½ teaspoon crushed red pepper

Saute oil, garlic, and onion until onions are translucent. Pour sauce from peeled tomatoes into pan with garlic and onion, then finely dice tomatoes and add to onion mixture. Add all other ingredients and simmer for 2 hours. Reserve leftovers for other pasta recipes.

Scampi Sauce

⅓ cup butter	¾ cup Marinara Sauce
½ ounce fresh garlic, chopped	1 ounce grated Parmesan cheese
2 tablespoons Madeira	2 egg yolks
½ teaspoon leaf oregano	½ tablespoon roux (flour and water thickener)
½ teaspoon leaf basil	
1 tablespoon tarragon vinegar	

In at least a 3 quart saucepan, slowly simmer butter, garlic, wine, oregano and basil over low heat until hot but not scalding. (Do not let butter separate.) Add vinegar and marinara sauce and bring back to a slight simmer. Again, do not overheat. Add egg yolks and Parmesan; stir with a wire whisk. Add roux and stir until sauce barely peaks.

Shrimp Marinara

Seawall Restaurant—Portsmouth, Va.
Chef Steve Maiorana

1 pound medium shrimp, 36 to 40 count	3 cups marinara sauce, hot
2 tablespoons olive oil	1 pound pasta (linguine or spaghetti), cooked al dente

Saute shrimp lightly in olive oil. Add hot marinara sauce and simmer for 1 minute. Serve over pasta and garnish with fresh chopped parsley.

Marinara Sauce

8 ounces onion, medium dice	1/4 cup sugar
2 tablespoons garlic, minced fine	1/2 teaspoon crushed red pepper
1/4 cup olive oil	3 tablespoons oregano
1 cup Chablis wine	1 teaspoon basil
2 large cans Italian plum tomatoes	1 teaspoon salt
1 large can crushed tomatoes	

Saute onions in olive oil until transparent. Add garlic and continue to saute over low heat for 1 minute. Add wine and simmer until reduced 50 percent. Add tomatoes and sugar and blend well. Simmer for 20 minutes. Add seasonings and simmer for 10 minutes. Serves 4.

Steamed Shrimp

The Lighthouse—Virginia Beach, Va.
Chef Clint Stephenson

2 pounds shrimp	1 teaspoon seafood seasoning
1 can beer	Juice and rind of 1 lemon
Bay leaves	

Bring all ingredients (except shrimp) to a boil. Add shrimp and cook 3 minutes. Do not overcook as shrimp will become tough. Remove from heat and sprinkle extra seasoning on top.

Langoustines aux Pates Fraiches (Jumbo Shrimp with Fresh Pasta)

La Yaca—Williamsburg, Va.

¾ stick butter
2 large tomatoes, peeled, seeded, and crushed
1 onion, minced
2 carrots, peeled and cut into rounds
1 leek or 2 spring onions, washed and minced
1 bouquet garni
2 tablespoons Jack Daniels
2 cups dry white wine
2 cups fish fumet (or reduction of Court Bouillon)

Cayenne to taste
Salt to taste
Pepper to taste
1½ cups heavy cream
1 pound fresh pasta, fettuccini or tagliatelle type (you can mix spinach pasta and regular for color)
20 jumbo shrimp, peeled and deveined
4 large basil leaves (or parsley if basil is not available)

Heat ¾ stick of butter in a large saucepan. Add tomatoes, onions, carrots, leek, and bouquet garni. Saute 3-4 minutes, stirring occasionally. Sprinkle with Jack Daniels and flambe. Add the wine and the fish fumet, cayenne, salt, and pepper. Cook uncovered over medium to low heat (depending on your stove) for approximately 30 minutes. Strain the liquid and vegetables through a fine mesh strainer, pressing with the back of a spoon to extract all the juices. Discard the vegetables and bouquet garni and return the pan to heat—at least 5 minutes to reduce the liquid. Cook the pasta in boiling salted water until "al dente." Drain well. Put the pasta in deep dish plate and keep warm while reheating the shrimp and finishing the sauce. Add cream and remaining butter to the reduced liquid. Whisk well together and let simmer for 5 more minutes. Add the shrimp during the last minute. Divide equally the shrimp onto 4 plates. Spoon the sauce on top. Sprinkle with basil or parsley. Serves 4.

NOTE: You may sprinkle a little diced raw tomato if you are serving a fancy dinner.

Shrimp Ajillo
La Broche—Virginia Beach, Va.

10 shrimp, peeled and deveined
1 garlic clove
 Crushed red peppers
 Old Bay Seafood Seasoning

1/2 cup olive oil
 Parsley
1 fireproof casserole dish

Place casserole dish on medium flame. Add olive oil, crushed red pepper, and garlic. Heat until garlic floats on top of oil. Sprinkle Old Bay over shrimp and add to boiling oil. Cook shrimp until oil boils again, or they are pink in color. Remove from fire, sprinkle with parsley, and serve immediately in casserole dish. Yields 1 serving.
 NOTE: When cooking with open flame and oil, extreme caution must be taken.

"LaBroche Restaurant proudly presents our own recipe for the most exquisite tasting shrimp this side of Louisiana."

Batter Fried Shrimp
Blue Pete's Seafood Restaurant—Virginia Beach, Va.

1/2 pound or 7 jumbo shrimp
 per person
3 cups milk

2 eggs, beaten
1 teaspoon Old Bay seasoning
1 cup self-rising flour

Preheat a high-quality liquid shortening to 350 degrees. Peel shrimp, leaving tail attached. Devein shrimp by cutting down the back of each and removing the black streak. Wash shrimp and set aside. Whip together milk, eggs, and seasoning until well mixed. Roll shrimp in flour. Dip in egg mixture. Roll in flour again. Place tail of shrimp between fingers and shake. With shrimp still between fingers, slowly drop in heated shortening. Fry until golden brown.

Grilled Sea Scallops with Red Pepper Pesto

Town Point Club—Norfolk, Va.
Chef John Stephen Milleson

Pesto

1 red pepper, roasted and cleaned	1 teaspoon Parmesan cheese
1/2 teaspoon garlic	2 tablespoons olive oil
1/2 teaspoon shallots	1 teaspoon lemon juice
4 leaves fresh basil	

Puree all ingredients in food processor or chop fine and blend in oil.

Pasta

Pasta, cooked	Brandy
Oyster mushrooms	Benedictine
Peanut oil	Chicken stock

Toss pasta and oyster mushrooms in peanut oil and flame with brandy and Benedictine and moisten with a little chicken stock.

Scallops

7 ounces scallops, trimmed of muscle	Peanut oil, to coat
	Black pepper, fresh ground

Skewer scallops, coat with oil and fresh ground pepper. Place on grill or under broiler until firm and slightly browned. Makes 1 portion.

Tortellini Pescatore

Omni Virginia Beach Hotel—Virginia Beach, Va.
Chef Tom Flynn

Cheese filled pasta served in a marinara sauce with seafood and topped with Parmesan cheese.

Serves one person:
- 7 ounces tortellini
- 3-4 ounces seafood, like sealegs
- 5 ounces marinara sauce
- 1 ounce Parmesan cheese

Marinara sauce: serves 8
- 1 garlic clove, minced
- 2 tablespoons olive oil
  Liquid from anchovies
- 4 cups Italian tomatoes
- 4 finely chopped anchovies
- 1/2 teaspoon oregano
- 1 tablespoon parsley, chopped

Marinara sauce: Lightly saute garlic clove in olive oil and oil from anchovies. Add Italian tomatoes slowly. Stir in anchovies, oregano and parsley. Mix with already cooked tortellini and sealegs. Garnish with sprinkled Parmesan cheese. Serves 7.

Seafood Pasta

Holiday Inn—Northampton Boulevard—Norfolk, Va.
Chef Bob Mitchell

- 8 ounces rotini macaroni
- 2 ounces popcorn shrimp
- 2 ounces sealegs
- 2 ounces Italian dressing
- 1 tablespoon Chablis wine

- 1/4 teaspoon Old Bay Seasoning
  Salt to taste
  Pepper to taste
- 8 ounces broccoli florets, divided

Cook macaroni. Drain. Mix all ingredients in plastic bowl. Serve mixture with 1 1/2-2 ounces broccoli florets on top. 4 servings.

Fettucini with Fresh Roe

Sheraton Beach Inn—Virginia Beach, Va.
Chef Michael Rosen, C.W.C.

4 tablespoons olive oil	Black pepper, freshly
1/2 pound ripe tomatoes, peeled, seeded and chopped	ground to taste
	3/4 pound fettucini
2 garlic cloves, finely chopped	2 tablespoons heavy cream
1/2 pound fresh flounder or shad roe	2 tablespoons finely
Salt to taste	chopped parsley

Heat the 4 tablespoons olive oil in a large skillet. Add the tomatoes and garlic and saute over moderate heat until the tomatoes are softened, about 8 to 10 minutes. Add the roe to the skillet and cook over low heat until the roe begins to get firm, about 10 minutes. Gently break up the roe with a wooden spoon. Season with salt and pepper.

Cook the fettucini in a large pot of boiling salted water until it is al dente. Drain well. Transfer the fettucini to a serving dish and toss with olive oil.

Add the cream to the skillet with the roe. Stir in the parsley. Pour the sauce over the fettucini. Toss gently but well and serve at once. Serves 4.

Pasta Primavera

Cavalier Golf and Country Club—Virginia Beach, Va.

1 tablespoon oil	1/2 cup crushed tomatoes
4 slices zucchini	1/2 cup chicken stock
5 flowerettes broccoli	Salt to taste
1 tablespoon minced onions	Pepper to taste
3 sliced snowpeas	Pasta (angel hair)
3 tablespoons grated Parmesan cheese	

Heat oil in a pan. Saute onions until translucent. Add remaining vegetables and saute. Add salt and pepper to taste. To this mixture add chicken stock, tomatoes, and grated cheese. Cook down by half. Serve over angel hair pasta.

Fisherman's Bowl

Duck-In Restaurant—Virginia Beach, Va.

1 4 ounce can sliced
   mushrooms, drained
2/3 cup celery, thinly sliced
2 cloves garlic, minced
4 tablespoons butter
2 cans cream of potato soup

2 soup cans milk
2 cups backfin crabmeat
2 cups small shrimp, cooked
1/4 teaspoon dill weed
1/4 teaspoon Tabasco

Saute celery with garlic and mushrooms in butter until tender. Add remaining
ingredients. Heat. Stir now and then, being careful not to scorch. Serves 6.

Crab Cakes

Pasta & Company—Virginia Beach, Va.

2 pounds fresh or frozen crabmeat,
   well picked
1 cup celery, finely chopped
1 cup onion, finely chopped
4 cups bread crumbs
3 eggs
1 1/2 cups mayonnaise
1/8 cup Dijon mustard
2 tablespoons Seafood Seasoning
1 teaspoon Texas Pete Hot Sauce
1 tablespoon fresh lemon juice

4 tablespoons Worcestershire sauce
2 tablespoons fresh parsley,
   chopped (optional)
2 cups vegetable oil for frying
   Salt and pepper to taste
For Dredging:
1 cup flour
4 eggs, lightly beaten with
   1/2 cup cream
2 cups finely ground bread crumbs

Mix all ingredients together gently and form into patties of desired size. Roll in flour,
then dip in egg batter mixed with a little cream and then dip into finely ground
bread crumbs. Fry in hot vegetable oil until browned on one side, turn and brown
on the other side. Drain and serve hot with tartar or cocktail sauce.

Baked Bluefish Fillets

Shoreline Seafood—Virginia Beach, Va.
Chef Tracy Anderson

Bluefish fillets	1/2 pound fresh mushrooms
6-8 whole small boiling potatoes	Marinara Sauce
1 whole small onion, peeled	

Place bluefish fillets in a deep glass baking dish or pan. Surround the fillets with whole boiling potatoes, whole small onions and fresh mushrooms. Pour Marinara Sauce over fillets and vegetables. Bake uncovered for one hour or until vegetables are tender.

Marinara Sauce

2 cans whole tomatoes, cored and crushed	1 teaspoon parsley
	1 teaspoon oregano
1 4 ounce can tomato sauce	1 teaspoon sugar
4 cloves garlic, chopped	Salt to taste
4 tablespoons olive oil	Pepper to taste

Fry garlic, parsley, and oregano in olive oil until garlic turns light brown. Add remaining ingredients and simmer, uncovered, for about 30 minutes.

Warm Quail Salad

Broad Bay Country Club—Virginia Beach, Va.
Chef Denny Fulmer

2 quail, partially boned and split
  Blueberry Vinaigrette
  Mixed greens:
1/4 head radicchio
1/2 head romaine lettuce
1 head bibb lettuce

1/3 bag spinach, stems removed
1 large tomato, wedged
1 cucumber, peeled and sliced
3-4 radishes, sliced
1/2 red pepper, julienne cut
  Mesquite chips

Marinate quail in vinaigrette for 1 hour. Light charcoal fire. Soak mesquite chips for 5 minutes, then drain. Wait for charcoal to turn white; add mesquite chips. Remove quail from marinade; set aside remaining marinade. Pat quail dry with paper towel; this will avoid flare-up. Grill quail 3-4 minutes on each side or until done; do not overcook. Place mixed greens on chilled plate in a decorative manner. Place quail in the center of the greens. Place tomato, cucumber, radishes, and red pepper around quail. Spoon remaining vinaigrette over salad. Grind fresh pepper over salad. Serves 2.

Blueberry Vinaigrette

1/4 cup blueberry vinegar
3/4 cup salad oil
1/2 teaspoon garlic, chopped
1/2 teaspoon salt
1 teaspoon sugar
2 tablespoons Vidalia
  onions, chopped

1/4 teaspoon fresh parsley
1/4 teaspoon fresh rosemary
1/4 teaspoon fresh thyme
1/4 teaspoon fresh tarragon

Mix ingredients well.

"Great with a Chardonnay wine and French bread."

Roast Duck with Stuffing

Wesley's—Virginia Beach, Va.

Duck Stuffing

1 tablespoon salt
1 teaspoon celery salt
1 teaspoon granulated garlic
2 teaspoons lemon juice
1/3 cup orange juice
1 tablespoon Worcestershire sauce

2 oranges, cut into 1/4 to
    1/2 inch cubes with rind
2/3 stalk celery, cut into 1/4 inch slices,
    including leaves
2 large onions, cut into 1/4 to
    1/2 inch cubes

Preheat oven to 500. Mix all ingredients together by hand in a bowl. Open the neck cavity, pack the duck tightly with the stuffing and put the remaining juice into the cavity. Pin the cavity closed as tightly as possible. Sprinkle with white pepper lightly over the top skin and massage in. Place on a rack in a roasting pan. Place in oven for 1 1/2 hours. After 30 minutes, pierce the duck with a sharp fork all over the top, especially in the areas with a high fat concentration (around the thighs). After 15 minutes, and every 15 minutes thereafter, thoroughly baste duck with the hot drippings. After the initial 1 1/2 hours at 500 is up, depending on the color of the skin, lower the temperature to between 350 and 450. If the skin is light or fairly light, lower it to 400 or 450. If the skin is brown, lower the temperature to 350. Bake at that temperature for another hour. Continue to baste every 15 minutes. After the 2 1/2 hours roasting time is up, remove the duck from the oven and remove the duck from the pan, place on a plate or platter with the chest cavity down so that any remaining juice in the stuffing can be absorbed by the breast meat. When you are ready to serve with your favorite topping, cut the duck in half straight down the breast bone, remove and discard the stuffing. Remove the major bones in the chest cavity. To bring it back up to temperature, place it in an oven at 450 for 15 minutes. If you use a topping, heat it separately on the stove and pour over the duck after it has been brought up to temperature. If you intend to roast the duck in advance, do not remove the stuffing. After the duck has cooled, wrap thoroughly in plastic wrap. Do not cut the duck or remove the bones or stuffing until ready to serve.

Chicken Szechwan

Omni International Hotel—Norfolk, Va.
Chef Daniel Murphy

2 cups soy sauce
2 cups sherry, dry
1 teaspoon fresh ginger
4 garlic cloves
1 teaspoon thyme leaf

1 teaspoon red pepper, crushed
2½ pounds whole chicken
2 cups peanut oil
2 cups currant jelly

Peel and mince ginger. Peel and mince garlic. In mixing bowl add sherry, soy sauce, prepared ginger, garlic, thyme leaf and crushed red pepper. Wash and cut chicken into 8 pieces. Marinate in sauce for 30 minutes. In skillet heat peanut oil. Add chicken and cook over medium heat until done. In saucepan, add currant jelly and ¼ cup of marinade. Bring to a boil. Remove from heat. Use as a sauce for chicken.

Steak au Poivre (Pepper Steak)

La Caravelle Restaurant—Virginia Beach, Va.
Chef Tam Nguyen

4 10 ounce New York strips or
    tenderloins, well trimmed
½ teaspoon salt
3 tablespoons crushed
    black peppercorns

4 tablespoons (½ stick) sweet butter
3 shallots, peeled and minced
2 tablespoons good Cognac
½ cup heavy cream
    Cup beef consomme

Sprinkle both sides of steak with salt, then coat with crushed peppercorns. This is done by spreading the crushed pepper on the table and pressing both sides of the steak onto it. Heat 2 tablespoons of the butter in a large heavy iron skillet. When the butter is a rich hazelnut color, saute the steaks for 3-4 minutes on each side, until medium rare. Lift the steaks from the pan to a warm platter and keep warm in 200 oven. Add shallots to the pan and saute for 1 minute. Add the Cognac and flambe. When flames die out, add heavy cream and consomme and bring to boil for a few minutes. This will reduce the sauce and bring it to the right consistency. Add the remaining butter and taste for seasoning. Pour sauce over steaks and serve.

Beef with Broccoli

Bamboo Hut—Virginia Beach, Va.
Chef Stan Tseng

5 ounces flank steak or beef	1/8 teaspoon salt
3 ounces broccoli	1/2 teaspoon rice wine
1 ounce bamboo shoots	1/2 egg
3 cups cooking oil	1 teaspoon cornstarch
Sesame oil	Bamboo Hut Sauce

Prepare beef by cutting into narrow 2 inch strips. Cut broccoli into small bite-size pieces. Coat the beef with salt, wine, egg, and cornstarch. Deep fry all the meat and vegetables over high heat until color changes. Remove all but 1 tablespoon of oil from the pan. Put Bamboo Hut Sauce in pan and warm. Add all the meat and vegetables. Stir fry until heated evenly. Add sesame oil. Serve.

Bamboo Hut Sauce

1 teaspoon sugar	Green onion
1 1/2 teaspoons soy sauce	Garlic
1 teaspoon white wine	Ginger
1 teaspoon cornstarch	Pepper
4 ounces water	Five Spice Powder

Rum Buns

Flagship Restaurant—Washington, D.C.

1   cup milk
1/2 cup sugar (divided)
1/4 cup solid vegetable shortening
1   teaspoon salt
1   package active dry yeast
1   egg, lightly beaten
2 1/2 teaspoons rum extract

3 1/2 cups sifted all-purpose flour
2   tablespoons unsalted
    butter, melted
2   tablespoons hot water
1/2 cup raisins, chopped
1   cup confectioners sugar

Scald milk in small heavy saucepan over low heat; remove from heat. Pour hot milk over 1/4 cup sugar, shortening, and salt in large bowl; stir to blend; cool mixture until lukewarm. Crumble yeast into cooled milk mixture; whisk until smooth. Add beaten egg, 1 1/2 teaspoons rum extract, and half the flour. Whisk again until smooth. Add remaining flour and milk until smooth; dough should be soft but not sticky. Cover bowl with kitchen towel; let rise in warm place until double in bulk, about 1 1/2 hours.

Grease 36 3-inch muffin tins. Punch dough down; divide in half. Keeping one half covered, roll out remaining piece of dough on lightly floured surface in a 12x4 rectangle. Dough should be about 1/2 inch thick. Brush with half the melted butter. Sprinkle with half the remaining sugar and half the raisins. Roll dough up, pulling out at edges to a uniform log shape; pinch long edge to seal. Log will be about 15 inches long. Repeat procedure with second half of dough, using remaining butter, sugar, and raisins. Cut each dough roll into 18 slices; place slices in prepared muffin tins. Cover with kitchen towel; set rolls to rise in warm draft-free place until doubled in bulk, about 30 minutes.

Preheat oven to 400. Bake rolls 15-20 minutes. While rolls are baking, combine confectioners sugar, 2 tablespoons hot water, and remaining teaspoon rum extract in small bowl; stir until smooth. When rolls are golden brown, remove from tins to wire rack. Brush tops with glaze. Serve warm.

Boulettes de Crevettes (Cajun Shrimp Balls)

Chef Instructor Susan Yelliott—Norfolk, Va.

2 pounds shrimp, peeled	1 clove garlic, crushed
1 medium onion, quartered	1 teaspoon salt
2 eggs	1 teaspoon pepper
1/2 cup parsley, chopped	1/2 teaspoon cayenne pepper,
1/2 cup green onion, chopped	or to taste
1/2 teaspoon white pepper	Juice of 1 lemon or lime
1/2 teaspoon cumin powder	Vegetable oil for frying
1/8 teaspoon leaf thyme	

In a food processor with a steel blade, grind shrimp with onion, using an on-off motion. Add the green onions, parsley, eggs, and seasonings. Heat oil to 375 and drop shrimp mixture in one tablespoon at a time. Cook until golden brown; turn and brown on the other side. Drain well and serve hot. Makes approximately 24 shrimp balls. Seasonings may be adjusted to taste. These can be made ahead of time and refrigerated. Crisp in a hot oven to serve. They are best made fresh.

Hot Spinach Dip

La Primavera Cafe—Virginia Beach, Va.
Phyllis Moy

2 10 ounce packages chopped spinach	1/2 teaspoon pepper
1/4 cup butter, melted	3/4 teaspoon celery salt
2 tablespoons onion, chopped	3/4 teaspoon garlic salt
3 tablespoons flour	1 teaspoon Worcestershire sauce
1/4 cup evaporated milk	6 ounces jalapeno pepper cheese

Cook spinach and drain well, reserving 1/2 cup liquid. Combine butter, onion, flour, and cook 1 minute. Add spinach liquid and evaporated milk; cook until thickened. Add seasonings and cheese, heating until cheese is melted. Stir in spinach and heat through. Serve warm with crackers.

Vegetable Latkes

Princess Anne Country Club—Virginia Beach, Va.
Chef Vince Bogan

1 cup rutabagas, peeled
1 cup potatoes, peeled
1 cup parsnips, peeled
1 tablespoon fresh parsley, chopped
1 tablespoon green and red
   pepper combined, diced
1 tablespoon carrot, peeled and
   grated

2 tablespoons onion, diced
3 eggs
1 teaspoon salt
1/2 teaspoon white pepper
3/4 cup flour
1/2 cup Smithfield ham, julienned
2 tablespoons flour
   Peanut oil

Combine rutabagas, potatoes, and parsnips using the shredding blade in the food processor. Blend this mixture in a bowl with parsley, peppers, carrot, onion, eggs, salt, pepper, flour, and ham. Mix ingredients together with spoon and let stand for 1/2 hour. Stir in additional flour to absorb any excess moisture. Cover bottom of large skillet with peanut oil to 1/4 inch depth and heat. Form mixture into portions by scooping a heaping amount with a large spoon or ice cream scoop. Drop into hot oil and brown on one side, then gently turn with a spatula to brown other side. Drain on a paper towel. Serve hot as a side dish to a meal or use a melon scoop to create mini pancakes and serve as an appetizer.

Chocolate Crepes with Hazelnut Sauce

Julian's Gourmet Desserts—Virginia Beach, Va.
Chef David Robins

1 pint milk
4 ounces butter
3 ounces cake flour
3 ounces bread flour
2 ounces cocoa powder

4 ounces sugar
4 whole eggs
4 egg yolks
Vanilla extract
Sauce

Mix dry ingredients in a bowl. In a pan, warm milk, butter and sugar. Add whole eggs and egg yolks to dry ingredients. Add liquid. Add vanilla extract. Put through strainer. Cook in a small, greased, heated skillet. Add 1/2 ounce of mixture. Cook for 1/2 minute, flip, cook additional 1/2 minute.

Sauce

1 cup milk
1 cup heavy cream
4 ounces sugar
5 egg yolks

Vanilla extract
Frangelico to taste
Hazelnuts, chopped

Bring liquids to a boil. In a bowl mix egg yolks, sugar, and vanilla extract. Add 2 ounces of hot mixture to the bowl. Mix and add to the pan. Stir, using a whisk, on low heat; cook for 2 minutes or until it coats the spoon. Take off stove, put through strainer. Add Frangelico and chopped hazelnuts. Yields 20 crepes.

Apricot Almond Bread

The Trellis Cafe, Restaurant and Grill—Williamsburg, Va.
Chefs Desaulniers, Delaplane, and Zearfoss

3/4 cup unsalted butter	1 1/4 teaspoon salt
1 1/2 cups sugar	1 cup toasted sliced almonds
3 large eggs	2 teaspoons almond extract
2 teaspoons baking powder	2 cups chopped apricots
1 1/2 teaspoons baking soda	1 1/2 cups all-purpose flour
1/2 teaspoon cinnamon	1/2 cup sour cream

Butter and flour two 9x5x3 inch loaf pans. In mixing bowl, cream butter and sugar until smooth. Gradually add eggs and beat until smooth. Add baking powder, soda, almonds, salt, cinnamon, almond extract, and chopped apricots. Mix until smooth. Add flour and mix until smooth. Add sour cream and mix until smooth. Place mixture into buttered and floured baking pans. Bake at 325 for about 1 hour and 10 minutes. Allow bread to cool in pan before removing.

Cherries Jubilee for Two

Harbor Club—Norfolk, Va.
Chef Ruedi Weber

12 patties butter	6 dark cherries per serving
1 tablespoon sugar	(approximately)
1/2 teaspoon cinnamon	Juice from cherries
Lemon juice, squeeze	1 ounce Kirschwasser
of fresh lemon	1 ounce brandy
Orange juice, squeeze	2 portions vanilla ice cream
of fresh orange	

Melt butter in a pan; add sugar and cinnamon. Heat until sugar begins to caramelize, adding lemon and orange juice. Add cherries and juice, heating cherries through. Add Kirsch and brandy and flame. Pour liqueur first into sauce boat, then into pan. Serve over vanilla ice cream.

   NOTE: Never add alcoholic beverages directly from the bottle. This presents a very serious fire hazard.

Key Lime Pie

Island Republic Restaurant—Virginia Beach, Va.

Crust

2 cups graham cracker crumbs
1/2 cup powdered sugar

Just under 1/2 stick butter or
margarine, melted

Combine all ingredients and press into bottom of 2 9-inch pie pans. Bake for
15 minutes at 300. Cool completely.

Filling

5 egg yolks
5 cans of Borden's sweetened
condensed milk

3/4 bottle Nellie & Joe's Key West
Lime Juice (or other bottled
Key lime juice)

Whip all ingredients together with a wire whisk. Pour filling into cooled pie crust.
Bake at 350 for 18 minutes.

Peanut Pie

Tale of the Whale Restaurant—Nags Head, NC

4 ounces cream cheese, softened
1 cup confectioners 10X sugar
1/2 cup creamy peanut butter
1/2 cup milk
9 ounce Cool Whip topping

1 9 inch graham cracker crust,
baked and cooled
1/4 cup finely chopped
salted peanuts

Whip cheese until soft and fluffy. Beat in sugar and peanut butter. Slowly add milk,
blending into mixture. Fold topping into mixture. Pour into baked pie shell. Sprinkle
with chopped peanuts. Freeze until firm and serve.

Rice Pudding

The Mall Restaurant—Norfolk, Va.

2 quarts milk
2/3 cup small grain rice
3 tablespoons butter
1/2 cup sugar

2 egg whites, lightly beaten
1 teaspoon vanilla extract
   Cinnamon (optional)

Cook rice in water according to package directions until tender. Add remaining ingredients, except cinnamon. Simmer until reduced to creamy consistency. Sprinkle on cinnamon.

$250.00 Cookie

2 cups butter
2 cups sugar
2 cups brown sugar
4 eggs
2 teaspoons vanilla
4 cups flour
5 cups oatmeal (measure, then
   blend in blender until fine)

1 teaspoon salt
2 teaspoons baking powder
2 teaspoons baking soda
16 ounces mini chocolate chips
1 8 ounce grated Hershey bar
3 cups chopped nuts

Cream butter and both sugars. Add eggs and vanilla. Mix together with flour, oatmeal, salt, baking powder, and soda. Add chips, Hershey bar, and nuts. Roll into balls and place 2 inches apart on cookie sheet. Bake 6-8 minutes at 375. Makes 112 cookies. Recipe can be halved.

For the best cookies, do not omit any ingredients, and bake until cookies are still light in color (not browned).

"After tasting this delicious dessert, the recipe was purchased from the dining room of a prestigious department store."

French Baked Alaska

Le Charlieu—Norfolk, Va.
Chef Richard Tranchard

Sponge cake
Grand Marnier
2 1 pound cans of pears or peaches
2 cups fresh strawberries
   or raspberries

Strawberry ice cream
Vanilla ice cream
10 egg whites
¼ cup sugar
    Pinch of salt

Cut the excess brown crust off the sponge cake. Cut sponge cake into ¼-½ inch slices and line the bottom of a pan (like a pie pan). Use 4 ounces Grand Marnier to pour over sponge cake. Drain liquid from pears. Slice pears and lay flat on the sponge cake. May not use all of the pears. Add a little Grand Marnier on top of pears to absorb liqueur. Add one cup of berries on top of pears. Slice strawberry ice cream and put on top of fruit to cover ice cream. Put in freezer. Put the rest of the fruits on top of the ice cream, first the pears, then the berries. Put back in the freezer. Beat 10 egg whites (egg whites separate better when cold). When firm, add ¼ cup of sugar and continue beating. Add meringue to top of fruit. Never put meringue in the refrigerator—it will melt. Keep in freezer to the last minute. Turn on broiler and leave the oven door open. Put in broiler as close as you can to the heat for about 2 minutes until golden brown. Heat Grand Marnier, flame it, and pour over Baked Alaska. To serve elegantly, pour flaming Grand Marnier into an egg shell which has been placed in the center of the Baked Alaska.

Contributors

Our Thanks To...

Sarah Abernathie
Arlene Aquino
Trudie Arrington
Donna Beale
Jackie Beamer
Pam Behrens
Kathy Bell
Imelda Bisser
Betsy Bixler
Pattie Bonney
Rita Bowers
Terri Boyce
Kim Bram
Kay Breseman
Ruth Bridges
Lynda Briggs
Janet Brittingham
Mary Brown
Jerry Lou Brown
Jeanne Browney
Oscar Bryan
Allison Buckler
Clara Capps
Susan Carden
Jean Carlston
Sue Carpenter
Arlene Case
Dorothy Cassada
Jane Cheek
Faye Clark
Linda Clukey
Judy Coleman
Connie Collins
Harriett Condrey
Anneke Cools
Lynette Crain
Pat Creech
Carolyn Croshaw
Vesta Cruser
Vernelle Curtis
Amy Curtis
Marian Curtis
Daphne Curtis
Martha Daniels
Dorothey Davis
Lisa Deford
Karen Dickinson
Virginia Dickinson
Edna Dickson

Jessie Doornbos
Cheri Downing
Grace Dragas
Lee Duberstein
Janet Dunn
Barbara Elks
Joyce Fain
Susan Faust
Alice Fentress
Nelda Fink
Susan Fisher
Susan Flavin
Susan Freeman
Dorothy Friend
Sue Frost
Vici Genesevich
Mary Gibbs
Yvonne Gooch
Suzanne Gravitt
Sandy Greenway
Kathryn Grigg
Kay Gross
Susan Hall
Suzanne Hanley
Muriel Hanwit
Sharon Hardison
Judith Harris
Alyce Heckler
Linda Hedrick
Diane Heidt
Jo Ann Hinchee
Helen Hoffman
Mae Holliday
Lynn Hudgins
Theresa Hudgins
Grace Jaffee
Cheryl Jenkins
Karen Jenkins
Amanda Jensen
Kathy Jensen
Trudy Jewell
Helen Johnson
Marja Kamencik
Jeanne Kaye
Peggy Keane
Alice Kellam
Connie Kellam
Helen Kellam

Margaret Kerr
Bettye Kight
Phyllis Kinney
Marie Laboon
Sue Landon
Kathy Lazzarotti
Bill Leigh
Sue Leonard
Ann Lindsey
Candace Logan
Joy Lucht
Polly Lumsden
Barbara Lux
Ramona Maloney
Lauren Manson
Evelyn Mason
Minnie Mathias
Ellen McCoy
Robin McDonald
Kathie McGrattan
Suzanne Meade
Tom Meade
Judi Mezzullo
Diane Miller
Ellen Miller
Virginia Mills
Sue Mills
Bonnie Molloy
Jackie Moore
Marlene Morley
Carolyn Nisbet
Nancy Nisbet
Julianna Nisbet
Angie Noe
Virginia O'Donnell
Margaret Odell
Emma Olds
Anne Oliver
Linda Overstreet
Jo Ann Peterson
Nancy Polatty
Brenda Portlock
Bob Pridge
Margaret Quarberg
Wendi Raiken
Olivia Redford
Beth Renfro
Brenda Rhoads

Carolyn Rivamonte
Dee Roberts
Sally Rogers
Kathy Rula
Frances Sadler
Mary Ann Shults
Mona Sherwood
Sara Shield
David Shirk
Kit Shoup
Shirley Shuman
Millie Simpson
Miriam Simpson
Ellen Sinclair
Linda Smith
Betty Anne Smolka
Joan Speisser
Becky Standing
Sandy Standing
Pam Steele
Ann Stephens
Betty Stephenson
Anna Stewart
Virginia Stewart
Nann Swertfeger
Gwynne Taylor
Bettye Teague
Mona Teague
Mary Thompson
Elizabeth Thomson
Judy Tralla
Maria Vandenheiligenberg
Christine Vrooman
Lou Watson
Sandy Weaver
Marisa Weiss
Terry Weller
Caroline Williams
Cathy Williams
Margaret Williams
Sybil Williams
Titi Williams
Kyle Williams
Evelyn Williamson
Anne Wilson
Peggy Winquist
Linda Winslow
Jane Wool

Index

B

GOURMET BY•THE•BAY

Dolphin Circle of The King's Daughters and Sons
P.O. Box 8335
Virginia Beach, VA 23450

Please send _____ copies of   GOURMET BY•THE•BAY   at ...... $18.95 each
Virginia residents add 4.5% sales tax .... $ .85 each
Postage and handling .... $ 3.00 each

Enclosed is check or money order for the amount of $ _____
made payable to Gourmet By The Bay.
Name _____
Address _____
City _____ State _____ Zip _____
☐ Please send as gift to
Name _____
Address _____
City _____ State _____ Zip _____
Card enclosure to read _____

GOURMET BY•THE•BAY

Dolphin Circle of The King's Daughters and Sons
P.O. Box 8335
Virginia Beach, VA 23450

Please send _____ copies of   GOURMET BY•THE•BAY   at ...... $18.95 each
Virginia residents add 4.5% sales tax .... $ .85 each
Postage and handling .... $ 3.00 each

Enclosed is check or money order for the amount of $ _____
made payable to Gourmet By The Bay.
Name _____
Address _____
City _____ State _____ Zip _____
☐ Please send as gift to
Name _____
Address _____
City _____ State _____ Zip _____
Card enclosure to read _____

Notes

Gourmet By The Bay
Founding Members

Lois Marie Baker

Donna McIntyre Beale

Nida Beath Beech

Imelda Rodriguez Bisset

Lynda Haynie Briggs

Janet Oliver Brittingham

Clara Elks Capps

Susan Gilliam Carden

Connie Kinney Collins

Lynette Kelly Crain

Carolyn Croshaw

Daphne Clark Curtis

Martha Smith Daniels

Karen Jensen Dickinson

Cheri O'Donnell Downing

Janet Gail Dunn

Joyce Humphreys Fain

Susan Faust

Susan Friend Fisher

Sue Loudon Frost

Susan Chamberlin Hall

Sharon Stewart Hardison

Linda Poston Hedrick

Jo Ann Howard Hinchee

Theresa Napolitano Hudgins

Grace Estes Jaffee

Bettye Teague Kight

Sue Todd Landon

Candace Jones Logan

Robin Goldblatt McDonald

Susan Nye Mills

Bonnie Browney Molloy

Diane Quarberg Newbern

Julianna Teague Nisbet

Jo Ann Melchor Peterson

Carol Page Preston

Roberta Cadow Rutherford

Sara Pearson Shield

Kit Allen Shoup

Betty Anne Stephenson
    Smolka

Elizabeth Guy Thomson

Maria Vandenheiligenberg

Lou Watson

Terry Bittner Weller

Kyle Gooch Williams

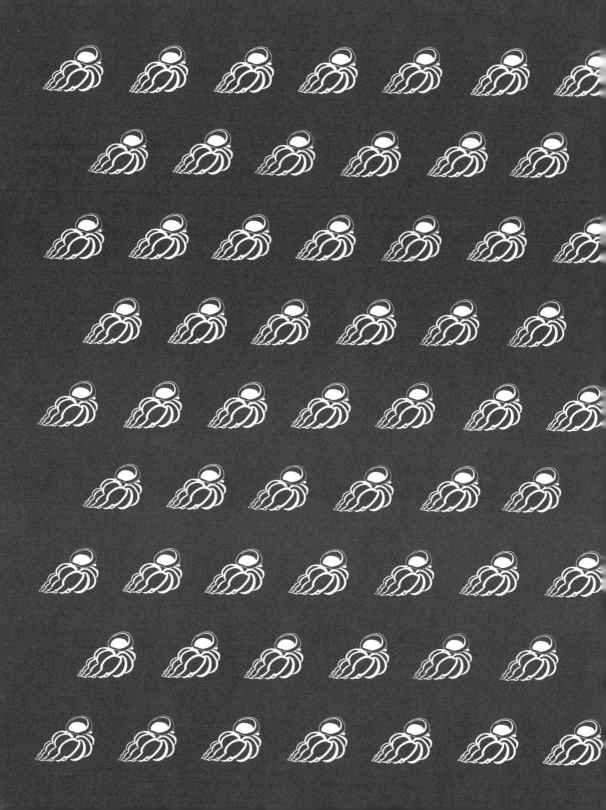